Online Intercultural Excha

LANGUAGES FOR INTERCULTURAL COMMUNICATION AND EDUCATION

Editors: Michael Byram, *University of Durham, UK*
Alison Phipps, *University of Glasgow, UK*

The overall aim of this series is to publish books which will ultimately inform learning and teaching, but whose primary focus is on the analysis of intercultural relationships, whether in textual form or in people's experience. There will also be books which deal directly with pedagogy, with the relationships between language learning and cultural learning, between processes inside the classroom and beyond. They will all have in common a concern with the relationship between language and culture, and the development of intercultural communicative competence.

For more details of these or any other of our publications, please contact:
Multilingual Matters, Frankfurt Lodge, Clevedon Hall,
Victoria Road, Clevedon, BS21 7HH, England
http://www.multilingual-matters.com

LANGUAGES FOR INTERCULTURAL
COMMUNICATION AND EDUCATION 15
Series Editors: Michael Byram and Alison Phipps

Online Intercultural Exchange
An Introduction for Foreign Language Teachers

Edited by
Robert O'Dowd

MULTILINGUAL MATTERS LTD
Clevedon • Buffalo • Toronto

Library of Congress Cataloging in Publication Data
Online Intercultural Exchange: An Introduction for Foreign Language Teachers.
Edited by Robert O'Dowd.
Languages for Intercultural Communication and Education: 15
Includes bibliographical references and index.
1. Language and languages–Study and teaching. 2. Multicultural education.
3. Language and languages–Computer-assisted instruction. I. O'Dowd, Robert
P53.45.O55 2007
418.00285–dc22   2007020107

British Library Cataloguing in Publication Data
A catalogue entry for this book is available from the British Library.

ISBN-13: 978-1-84769-009-8 (hbk)
ISBN-13: 978-1-84769-008-1 (pbk)

Multilingual Matters Ltd
UK: Frankfurt Lodge, Clevedon Hall, Victoria Road, Clevedon BS21 7HH.
USA: UTP, 2250 Military Road, Tonawanda, NY 14150, USA.
Canada: UTP, 5201 Dufferin Street, North York, Ontario M3H 5T8, Canada.

The policy of Multilingual Matters/Channel View Publications is to use papers that are natural, renewable and recyclable products, made from wood grown in sustainable forests. In the manufacturing process of our books, and to further support our policy, preference is given to printers that have FSC and PEFC Chain of Custody certification. The FSC and/or PEFC logos will appear on those books where full certification has been granted to the printer concerned.

Typeset by Datapage International Ltd.
Printed and bound in Great Britain by the Cromwell Press Ltd.

Contents

Part 4: Practical Accounts and Experiences of Online Exchange

Notes on Contributors

Paul Alexander received his Master of Educational Technology degree in 2006 from the University of British Columbia (UBC), Vancouver, Canada. Having taught EFL and multimedia-enhanced courses at Myongji University, Seoul, Korea from 2004 to 2007, Paul is now currently teaching within the Graduate School of Digital Media at Sangmyung University, Seoul. Paul has also coordinated and/or conducted government-sponsored EFL teacher-training programs at UBC and Yonsei University. His professional interests involve how the use of communicative applications such as wikis, video logs, learning management systems and videoconferencing can be appropriately used to enhance intercultural interactions.

Julie A. Belz (Ph.D., University of California at Berkeley) is Associate Professor of English and World Languages and Cultures at Indiana University/Purdue University and Scholar-in-Residence at the Indiana Center for Intercultural Communication. She specializes in Internet-mediated language learning, intercultural communication, pragmatics, learner corpus research, discourse analysis, learner identity, multilingual writing and German applied linguistics. Julie has taught linguistics, applied linguistics, discourse analysis, ESL, EAP and German language and literature in both the U.S. and Europe. She is the co-editor of *Internet-mediated Intercultural Foreign Language Education* (Heinle & Heinle, 2006) and guest editor of a special issue of *Language Learning & Technology* on telecollaboration. Her 2002 *LL&T* article on the social dimensions of networked foreign language study received the Finalist Award for 'Best Article in an Electronic Journal' given by the American Educational Research Association (AERA). Julie has published extensively in refereed outlets and serves on the editorial boards of *Applied Linguistics* and The American Association for University Supervisors and Coordinators of Foreign Language Programs (AAUSC).

María Luisa Pérez Cañado is a lecturer at the Department of English Philology of the University of Jáen, Spain, where she is also Vicedean of the Faculty of Humanities and Education. Her research interests are in Applied Linguistics, English for Specific Purposes, and the intercultural component in language teaching. Her work has appeared in scholarly journals such as *The Reading Teacher*, *Language Awareness*, *Language and Intercultural Communication*, *English Teaching professional*, *Scripta Manent*, *The Grove, or English for Specific Purposes*, and as book chapters in a notable number of edited volumes. She is also author of three books on the interface of second language acquisition and second language teaching, co-author of an instructional method for the teaching of Spanish orthography and written composition in Spain and Mexico, and co-editor of two books and one ELT journal. Dr. Pérez Cañado has been serving as reviewer for *ELIA*, *The Grove*, and *Reading and Writing: An Interdisciplinary Journal*, and has taught and lectured in Belgium, Poland, Germany, Ireland, England, The United States, and all over Spain.

Christopher Chase is an Associate Professor of English Language Education, currently teaching at Seinan Gakuin University, in Fukuoka, Japan. His research interests include learner-centered education, systems theory, learner autonomy, second language acquisition and computer-mediated communications. Christopher is a co-author and illustrator of *The Accelerated Schools Resource Guide* (Jossey Bass, 1993) and *Natural Speaking* (Intercom Press, 1994). He graduated from Stanford University's School of Education, in 1993, with a Ph.D. in Psychological Studies in Education.

James Crapotta is Language Coordinator and Senior Lecturer in the Department of Spanish and Latin American Cultures at Barnard College (New York). He received his Ph.D in Romance Languages and Literatures from Harvard University in 1979 and has taught at Barnard since 1975. Among his publications are the books *Kingship and Tyranny in the Theater of Guillén de Castro* (London: Tamesis, 1984), *Facetas: Conversación y redacción* (Boston: Heinle & Heinle, 1995) and an annotated edition of *Las mocedades del Cid* (Newark: Cervantes & Co., 2002) . He has also written articles on Golden Age theater and language pedagogy and is the author of seven video activities manuals for textbooks published by Prentice Hall. He has written monthly video-viewing materials for *Spanish TV-Magazine* and was the video/film review editor for the *Northeast Conference Newsletter*. He served as Director of the Northeast Conference on the Teaching of Foreign Languages from 1992 to 1995. He has given many workshops at conferences on topics such as teaching with video, theater in the language classroom, creating internet tasks and teaching culture and critical thinking through film.

Christine Develotte is a senior lecturer of Applied Linguistics at the Ecole Normale Supérieure – Lettres et Sciences Humaines de Lyon and a member of the ICAR research lab. For the last ten years her main research interests have been linked to computer-mediated communication (CMC). Her research includes two aspects: the semio-linguistic aspect (understanding the features of the computer screen through 'multimedia discourse analysis', which she created), and the social aspect, (focusing on the analysis of human behavior). Since 2002, the data has been taken from fieldwork conducted in classrooms where distance learning and teaching interactions have been emphasised, particularly through the project *Le français en (première) ligne*.

Melinda Dooly received her Ph.D. in Didactics of Language and Literature from the Universitat Autònoma de Barcelona, Spain, where she works as a teacher trainer. Melinda has been involved in International Relations at the Education Faculty for many years and this has led to her interest in telecollaboration in the area of education. Melinda's other area of research interest is plurlingualism through interactionalist analysis. Melinda divides her teaching between the Universitat Autònoma de Barcelona and Lee University (Tennessee, USA) where she serves as guest lecturer in the Post-graduate courses in Education.

Mirjam Hauck is a Senior Lecturer and Head of German in the Department of Languages at the UK's Open University (OU) where she has been involved in investigations of virtual learning spaces such as audio-graphic conferencing for the learning of languages and culture online for almost a decade. In 2005, while working as a research scholar in the Modern Languages Department at Carnegie Mellon University in Pittsburgh/US she set up and ran the TRIDEM project together with her OU colleague Tim Lewis. Her current research and publications focus on the interdependence between multimodal communicative competence and intercultural interaction in telecollaboration.

Lina Lee is Associate Professor of Spanish at the University of New Hampshire where she teaches courses in second language acquisition and teaching language methodology, trains teaching assistants, and supervises foreign language interns. She has published articles on language pedagogy and Internet technologies for foreign language instruction in *Foreign Language Annals*, *Hispania*, *CALICO*, *Language Learning & Technology*, *ReCALL*, *System* and *NECTFL Review*. She is the author of web sites for the Spanish textbooks *Mosaicos* (2nd edn) and *Puentes*, as well as the e-book for *Avenidas*.

Tim Lewis is currently a Lecturer in French at the Open University. From 1993 to 2001 he was Director of the Modern Languages Teaching Centre of the University of Sheffield. The MLTC was the UK partner in the International Email Tandem Network, which means that Tim has been telecollaborating for longer than he cares to remember. He is currently co-editing a volume on *Language Learning Strategies in Independent Settings*, and is trying to learn Polish as part of the Grundtvig-funded Literalia project, co-ordinated by friends and colleagues from the Volkshochschule Hannover Ost-Kreis.

François Mangenot is Chair Professor of Applied Linguistics at Stendhal–Grenoble 3 University (France), member of the research lab Linguistique et Didactique des Langues Etrangères et Maternelle– Lidilem (where he coordinates the branch 'Foreign Language Education and ICT'). He currently leads a Master Degree in French as a Foreign Language, also taught as an e-learning program. He has previously worked in Besançon, Lyon, Turin, Belgrade and Vienna. He has been researching in CALL for now more than 20 years (Ph.D., habilitation). He has published several pieces of software, two books (*Les aides logicielles à l'écriture*, 1996, *Internet et la classe de langue*, 2006, with E. Louveau), coordinated several journal issues (e.g. *Le Français dans le monde, Recherches et applications* 40, *Les échanges en ligne dans l'apprentissage et la formation*, 2006) and written a number of papers about Internet and e-learning in Foreign Language Education (e.g. in *Recall* and *Calico Journal*).

Alfred Markey currently teaches English language and twentieth century British and Irish literature at the University of León, Spain. Born in Ireland, he has lived in Spain for more than a decade, teaching previously at the Universities of Vigo and A Coruña. His principal field of research has been that of Irish Studies and Comparative Literature, and recently, arising out of the practical use of new technologies in the language classroom, he has begun engaging in research in the field of CALL. A member of the research project 'Telecollaboration in the Teaching of Foreign Languages' at the University of León, he is particularly interested in the application of Moodle to online exchanges.

Antonia Domínguez Miguela teaches English in secondary education and she is also an assistant professor in the department of English at the University of Huelva. She earned her Ph.D. in English in 2002. She has published two books on US Latino/a literature and has recently co-authored a book on integrating Information and Communication Technologies in the language classroom *Guía para la integración de las TIC en el aula de idiomas* (University of Huelva, 2007). Her work has appeared in different volumes, journals and conference proceedings. Her current research interests are CLIL (Content Integrated Language Learning) and the use of ICT in the foreign language classroom.

Andreas Müller-Hartmann is Professor of Teaching English as a Foreign Language (TEFL) in the Department of English at the University of Education, Heidelberg, Germany. He has worked as a secondary school teacher of English, French and German in various schools in Germany, France, and the USA. He holds an MA in Southern Studies from the University of Mississippi, USA, and a Ph.D. in American Studies from the University of Osnabrueck, Germany. His research and teaching interests are located in the following areas: the teaching of literary texts, cultural studies, intercultural learning, the new media in the English language classroom and teacher education.

Robert O'Dowd teaches EFL and Foreign Language Methodology at the University of León in Spain and has a Ph.D. on the development of intercultural competence through the use of networked technologies in the foreign language classroom. He is currently on the executive committees of both Eurocall and the International Association for Language and Intercultural Communication and is also involved in various international research projects related to online intercultural exchange. He has published widely on the themes of online foreign language education and on the role of culture in foreign language learning in journals such as *ReCALL*, *The Calico Journal* and *ELT Journal*.

Breffni O'Rourke is Lecturer in Applied Linguistics and Manager of Language Learning Technologies and Resources in the School of Linguistic, Speech and Communication Sciences, Trinity College Dublin. He teaches courses in language pedagogy and acquisition, including technologies in language learning and teaching, as well as in other areas of language studies such as discourse analysis and aspects of written language. His research interests include computer-mediated communication in foreign-language learning, cognitive and sociocultural perspectives in L2 studies, and experimental approaches to language processing.

Jesús Suárez-García has worked as a teacher of Spanish as a foreign language at the University of León in Spain, at the Moscow State University in Russia, at the University of Wales–Swansea in the United Kingdom, and at Duke University in the USA. He currently works as a language lecturer at Barnard College–Columbia University in the City of New York. His research focuses on vocabulary acquisition in foreign languages, language teaching methodology and the use of the new technologies in the teaching/learning of languages.

Isabel Pérez Torres is currently the coordinator of the international e-learning networks in the Virtual Learning Centre of the University of Granada (CEVUG). She holds a Ph.D. from the University of Granada. In the last twelve years, she combined her work as a secondary teacher and her research in the field of new technologies and education in all educational levels. She has worked as a teacher trainer specialized in the topic of ICT and e-learning and participated in regional, national and European e-learning projects, She received 'The European Label for innovative projects in language teaching and learning' in 2003 and 2005.

Margarita Vinagre holds an M.Phil in Applied Linguistics from Trinity College Dublin and a Ph.D. in English from Seville University. She currently lectures in English Language and Linguistics on the following degree programmes at Antonio de Nebrija University in Madrid: Applied Languages and Marketing, Applied Languages and Tourism, and Translation and Interpreting Studies. She also lectures and coordinates the areas of Sociolinguistics and Sociopragmatics on the Master's and Doctorate Programmes in Teaching Spanish as a Foreign Language at the same university. Her main research interests are the use of new technologies in language learning and the development of intercultural communication in the foreign language classroom. She has published numerous articles within these fields and is currently directing two research projects with the Open University UK and Dublin City University on the use of wikis and e-tandem in language learning, respectively.

Paige D. Ware earned her doctorate from the Education, Language, Literacy and Culture program at the University of California at Berkeley in 2003. Her research interests include technology and language learning;

writing and second language development; and multimedia technologies and literacy. Her research has examined the use of web-based writing for promoting cultural understanding; the literacy practices of elementary and middle school children composing multimedia stories; and the use of teacher research in technology-integrated classroom teaching and learning. She is currently Assistant Professor in the School of Education at Southern Methodist University.

Eva Wilden is a graduate research assistant and doctoral student at the University of Kassel, Germany, where she also teaches Foreign Language Methodology. Furthermore, she has conducted various in-service language teacher trainings. She holds a degree in teaching History and English as a Foreign Language from the University of Duisburg-Essen, Germany. Eva Wilden has been involved in various projects using computers and the internet for learning and teaching. Her current research interests include intercultural learning, computer-assisted language learning, learning strategies and qualitative methodology and her Ph.D. thesis focuses on the Self and the Other in intercultural online communication.

Katerina Zourou, Ph.D., is a researcher in the field of computer-supported collaborative language learning at the University of Grenoble III (France). Her research topics involve effects of computer mediation in foreign language education and telecollaborative practices online. Working in multicultural teams abroad in the last years, she currently provides consultation on educational issues to the European Commission in Brussels.

Foreword

PROFESSOR JOHN CORBETT

In May 1960, around the time he was working on *The Gutenberg Galaxy*, the pioneering media commentator, Marshall McLuhan, was interviewed by Alan Millar for an episode of the Canadian Broadcasting Corporation's television series, *Explorations*[1]. In the programme, McLuhan coined the expression 'the global village', arguing that electronic technology (principally television) was responsible for a youth-led revolution in communications and consciousness. Put simply, McLuhan claimed that the pre-electronic, book-loving adolescent was being replaced by the tribalised teenager, whose individuality was at risk of being submerged in one of many rival, electronically-mediated subcultures. In 1995, with the advent of the Internet, McLuhan's prophecy of world connectivity was finally realised. Today, as the children born at the dawn of the Internet revolution become the first 'digital natives' (Prensky, 2001) to reach young adulthood, their teachers are faced with something like the challenges McLuhan predicted half a century ago. How can we support learners in their explorations of cultures and languages, so many aspects of which are instantly available at the touch of a button? What happens to the individual's relationship with the collective when that collective is suddenly expanded to global proportions by instant messaging, virtual chatrooms, and teleconferencing? As tools for connecting learners proliferate, how can teachers, who may or may not be 'with it' (in McLuhan's now quaint phrase from the 1960s), begin to exploit the enormous potential the electronic media now afford? And how can we deal with the inevitable problems that accompany each innovation in learning technology?

Online Intercultural Exchange brings together a wealth of inspirational case studies, hard-won wisdom and sound, practical advice for teachers embarking on the adventure of using communications technology to explore language and culture. As someone who has dipped his toe in virtual learning environments and had it painfully stubbed several times, I wish this book had been available to me some time ago. It gives an admirable survey of the procedures followed by early experiments such as the *Cultura* project and the *Tandem* scheme, and a rich sample of more recent successors, offshoots and variants – from telecollaboration on a shoestring, to Rolls Royce ventures at institutions awash with the most up-to-date equipment. All the chapters tap into the excitement of connecting learners across languages and cultures, while acknowledging that the availability of the newest and most expensive gadgets does not necessarily guarantee successful collaborative learning. Some chapters give a clear-eyed assessment of the different means of communicating at a distance that are currently available, and the joys and frustrations of, say, speaking and listening in real-time, versus reading, writing and reflecting over a longer period. Other chapters in the book treat with a refreshing frankness the illusory glamour of technological innovations, and the difficulties faced when digital natives from different zones just don't get on.

Out of this rich stew of experience, recurrent themes emerge. One is that human beings need time and space – real or virtual – and common ground rules to establish and sustain relationships. Online collaboration requires the definition and development of shared expectations, e-literacy skills and netiquette for successful connections to occur. The 'with it' teacher needs to acquire skills not only in using a myriad of technological tools, but also in managing the kind of misunderstandings, disappointments and confusions that occur when people engage in interactions in an environment that is fraught with the potential for miscommunication. If the teacher mishandles the collaboration, the kind of negative tribalism that McLuhan envisaged might all too easily be the unfortunate result. On the other hand, the potential power of online collaboration is undeniable, and on the evidence of the case studies in this book, much of that power resides in giving students a genuine audience for the outcomes of their communicative tasks. Whether participants are presenting aspects of their own lives to groups elsewhere, or whether individuals are working with distant partners on a project to present to their home group, there is an authenticity and urgency to the task that drives cultural and linguistic learning.

This important volume shares a treasury of good practice, as well as insights from collaborative projects gone wrong, and in doing so it affords teachers of language and culture with an essential *vade mecum* for digital learning. It also stimulates us to think of ways in which telecollaboration could be extended. The chapters in this volume tend to treat other cultures as other *national* configurations. Telecollaboration between cultural groupings based not so much on nationality as on, say, gender, age or religious affiliation might be worth pursuing. In the meantime, however, the editor and contributors to this volume have done the educational community a service by illuminating an important and fast-developing area that will increasingly shape our professional practices.

Note

1. If you are reading this book within reach of a computer with Internet connection, then you can view archive clips of this interview at <http:// archives.cbc.ca/IDC-1-69-342-1814/life_society/mcluhan/clip2>.

References

McLuhan, Marshall (1962) *The Gutenberg Galaxy.* Toronto: University of Toronto Press.
Prensky, Marc (2001) Digital natives, digital immigrants. *On the Horizon* 9 (5), 1–2. NCB University Press.

Part 1

Introduction to this Volume and its Theme

Chapter 1

Introduction

ROBERT O'DOWD

New Challenges in Foreign Language Education

The first decade of the 21st century has been a time of significant development and change for foreign language education. Issues such as globalisation, the rise of the internet as a tool of communication and self-expression, the controversial role of English as a global language and the recent developments in the so-called 'clash of civilisations' have all had effects (both positive and negative) on the importance attributed to foreign language learning and how languages should be learned (Block & Cameron, 2002; Crystal, 2001). The overall aims of foreign language education have also been subject to change. The Common European Framework of Reference for Languages (Council of Europe, 2001), for example, has been widely taken up as a common basis for language syllabuses, textbooks and examinations in many European countries. This framework emphasises the importance of 'plurilingualism and pluricultural competence' (Council of Europe, 2001: 168) and calls on educators to develop their learners' ability to apply their linguistic and communicative skills across various languages and communicative situations. Recent years have also seen an important shift from the previously common goal of 'communicative competence' to that of 'intercultural communicative competence' (Byram, 1997), which underlines the need for language learning to develop learners' cultural sensitivity and their ability to mediate between different cultural perspectives in communicative situations.

In the light of these new objectives, many foreign language educators have looked to the potential of networked technologies to enhance and supplement the traditional activities of the communicative classroom, which are often seen as limited and over-focussed on the exchange of information (Block, 2001; Greenfell, 2000). In particular, the opportunities offered by engaging learners in online collaborative project work with members of other cultures has been identified as being an authentic and effective way of preparing learners for the complex yet enriching experience of foreign language and culture learning. Through online

3

interaction, it is argued that learners can become aware that communicating in a foreign language involves not only the exchange of information, but also the expression of speaker identity and the development of relationships in situations of intercultural contact. With this in mind, this volume aims to examine what one of the most popular online activities, online intercultural exchange, involves on a pedagogical level and also to explore the promises and the challenges that it can bring to the foreign language classroom.

The term 'online intercultural exchange' refers to the activity of engaging language learners in interaction and collaborative project work with partners from other cultures through the use of online communication tools such as e-mail, videoconferencing and discussion forums. The aims of such online interaction can be to develop students' communicative ability in the target language, to increase intercultural sensitivity and to encourage learner independence (Belz, 2003). In the past, the activity has been referred to in many different ways including 'e-pals', 'keypals', 'e-tandem', 'telecollaboration' or, more recently, as 'internet-mediated intercultural foreign language education' (Belz & Thorne, 2006). However, there has also been some debate in the literature as to the appropriateness of this terminology. For example, authors have questioned whether terms such as 'keypals' in some way trivialise this learning endeavour (Müller-Hartmann, 2000), while others have suggested that the phrase 'telecollaboration' fails to capture all the activity's facets (Thorne, 2006). Nevertheless, in this volume many of these terms will be used interchangeably as it will become clear that the quality of the activity far outweighs the significance of the particular terminology. For this reason, practitioners are encouraged to choose for their own work the terms of reference with which they are most comfortable.

The Origins of Online Exchange

For the unsuspecting reader encountering this area of online foreign language education for the first time, the history of telecollaboration may seem surprisingly rich and complex. The first reports of online collaborative project work between language learners in different locations only began to appear in the early 1990s when foreign language teachers and learners gained access to the internet on a relatively regular basis. However, the principle of engaging students in collaborative tasks with partners in geographically distant locations has been traced back much further in history to the pioneering work of French educationalist Célestin Freinet in the 1920s (Cummins & Sayers, 1995; Müller-Hartmann, this volume). Freinet encouraged his students to carry out project work on issues that were of personal interest to them and then to publish their findings in a newspaper, which they produced with the help of a printing press. The finished newspapers were then exchanged with classes located in other parts of France who had also created their own publications.

The work of social psychologist G.W. Allport (1979) is also said to have contributed to the rationale for online intercultural exchange. Allport, studying intercultural relations in North American society, looked at a technique used in progressive schools in the USA at the time called 'social travelling', which involved bringing groups that held negative stereotypes of each other into contact together. He mentions an example that involved bringing white middle-class students to spend time with African–American families in Harlem. He concluded that contact in itself was no guarantee of improving attitudes to other groups and that understanding and tolerance would only come about by getting members of the different cultures actually working together:

> The nub of the matter seems to be that contact must reach below the surface in order to be effective in altering prejudice. Only the type of contact that leads people to do things together is likely to result in changed attitudes. (Allport, 1979: 276)

In the 1990s the first publications began to make the world of foreign language education aware of the potential of online exchange for language teaching purposes. Cummins and Sayers (1995) reported on the Orillas Network, a clearinghouse for online exchange projects between distant partner classes in the American continents and in Europe. These projects covered foreign language learning as well as other subjects and included activities such as dual community surveys, science investigations, contrastive geography projects and comparative oral history and folklore studies. The Learning Circles project (Riel, 1997), sponsored by the American telephone company AT&T, was one of the first to bring together primary and secondary school foreign language learners from countries all over the world in collaborative project work. In this period the first reports of the use of online technology for tandem learning also began to appear (see O'Rourke, this volume for an in-depth exploration of e-tandem and its historical background) and Mark Warschauer, one of the earliest and most prolific writers on online language learning, published 'Virtual Connections' (1995), a vast collection of practitioners' reports on how the internet and the networked communication tools of the time were being used to engage learners in communicative language learning. Over a decade later, although many of the references in this volume to the common communication tools of the time may sound dated (i.e. principally mailing lists and e-mail), issues which many of these educators deal with in their reports in relation to good online pedagogy and task design continue to be of relevance and are returned to here again in these pages.

While these publications were appearing in print, the number of web pages dedicated to organising and supporting online exchange also began to increase significantly. The Intercultural E-mail Classroom Connections (IECC) website (see list of online references at the end of this chapter) gave teachers the opportunity to post announcements looking for partner classes, while the e-tandem website allowed language learners to be paired individually with speakers of their target language and also provided a huge source of activities upon which learners could base their online interaction. Well known practitioners such as Reinhard Donath in Germany and Ruth Vilmi in Finland also published many reports and descriptions of their students' online projects and in the process helped to make the activity better known among the growing number of foreign language teachers who were beginning to look for ways to use the internet as a language teaching tool.

Current Areas of Research and Debate

In terms of substantive research in the area, the period from 1998 to 2006 has seen important advances. Many of the earlier publications on telecollaborative exchange were inevitably anecdotal in nature and very often the fact that students reported having enjoyed their virtual contact was deemed as sufficient justification of the activity's value (Richter, 1998). However, since the turn of this decade the growing number of journals dedicated to technology-enhanced language learning (e.g. the *CALICO Journal*, *Language Learning and Technology* and *ReCALL*) and the publication of various collections of articles in the area (Belz & Thorne, 2006; Ducate & Arnold, 2006; Warschauer & Kern, 2000) has allowed for a significant increase in the number of qualitative studies into online student interaction and exchange. These pieces of research have looked at certain issues and questions that inevitably arise repeatedly when two or more sets of learners in different locations interact and collaborate together in their respective foreign languages. These issues include the following:

- To what extent can telecollaboration achieve the aims of modern foreign language education including the development of inter-cultural awareness, learner autonomy and grammatical competence

(Belz, 2003; Brammerts, 2005; O'Dowd, 2003; O'Dowd & Ware, in press; O'Rourke, 2005)?

- How should online tasks be structured in order to encourage and support interaction and language learning (Meskill & Ranglova, 2000; Müller-Hartmann, 2000)?
- What factors lead to communication breakdown and the failure of online exchanges (O'Dowd & Ritter, 2006; Schneider & von der Emde, 2006; Ware, 2005)?
- How do the students' socioinstitutional contexts influence the outcome of exchanges (Belz, 2001; Belz & Müller-Hartmann, 2003; O'Dowd, 2005)?

The text-based nature of online interaction has meant that telecollaboration has also become a prime source of data for researchers from both interactionist and sociocultural approaches who are investigating second language acquisition. Studies of online learning from the interactionist perspective explore the application of Long and Robinson's (1998) Interaction Hypothesis to online environments (Blake, 2000; Pellettieri, 2000; Tudini, 2003). This theory proposes that when learners have to negotiate meaning in interaction, they are exposed to foreign language input that is both linguistically and interactionally modified. Such input draws learners' attention towards grammatical form, pushes them to modify their own output, and consequently helps them to develop their interlanguage. In an interactionist approach, negotiation of meaning and peer correction are seen as processes that occur naturally and automatically as interlocutors seek to understand and clarify each others' utterances. Such negotiation of meaning appears to occur most often in online environments when learners are writing in real-time (i.e. synchronously). Consequently, research into second language acquisition online has typically focused on synchronous communication tools (e.g. chats, MOOs) and has concentrated on calculating and examining the episodes of negotiation of meaning that occur in the online interaction.

Researchers coming from a sociocultural perspective have criticised interactionism for its overly cognitive orientation, which depicts learning as taking place solely in the learner's mind. A sociocultural approach puts much greater emphasis on the social aspects of *language use* and its interrelatedness with the cognitive processes of *language learning* (Zuengler & Miller, 2006). In the context of online intercultural exchange, various sociocultural studies of online interaction have looked at themes such as how the requirements and affordances of particular learning contexts influence student participation in online exchange (Belz & Müller-Hartmann, 2003), the intercultural aspects of online learning partnerships (O'Dowd, 2003) or the development of learners' pragmatic competence in the target language through their experience of online language socialisation (Belz & Kinginger, 2002).

Issues Facing Telecollaborative Teachers

Any educators considering engaging their learners in online exchange with a partner class in another culture will inevitably have to make various methodological decisions as to how the exchange should be organised and implemented. Although this book aims to make the reader aware of the questions that need to be asked before and during an exchange, there is no attempt to impose one appropriate approach on running such a project. It is our belief that educators need to be aware of the technological and methodological options available to them and should then be able to make principled choices based on their and their teaching partners' students, learning contexts and pedagogical aims. Some of the most important questions, which will be dealt with in the following chapters, include the following.

What should be the role of the teacher in the exchange?

Teachers are often unsure to what extent they should get involved in an exchange of written or spoken correspondence between two or more individuals. Should teachers check and correct messages before they are sent? Should they make sure that students are writing before the established deadlines? To what extent should teachers decide what the content of the correspondence involves? The answers to these questions may depend, to a certain extent, on the particular model or structure of online exchange that is chosen (see Chapters 3–5). Some models of online exchange are quite strict about what students write about, while others (such as tandem) see the content of messages as a matter for the students. However, the role of the teacher in an exchange may also reflect their own philosophical beliefs about education and pedagogy. Many teachers believe, for example, that integrating the exchanges into their classes allows the teacher to guide and motivate the learners in their online activities. In the words of one practitioner:

> Online exchanges should be integrated into the regular classes in the way which the teacher finds most effective. When students are left to themselves they lose interest in the process fairly soon. As any other teaching/learning process, this should be well-planned, organized

and controlled – then it brings results. (Private correspondence with author, 07.05.2001)

However other educators can see things very differently and argue for giving the learners a more independent role in the exchanges. One teacher of Spanish as a foreign language in the USA recently wrote the following when her partner teacher complained that his students were not receiving any messages from their American counterparts:

They [her students] know how telecollaboration functions and what impact it has on their grade. If they don't intend to take it seriously on their own, their grade will suffer. Although they might not learn a lot of Spanish from that, it'll be a valuable lesson in other senses: namely, I always tell my students that part of their academic experience is not only to learn about the subject matter, but also to learn responsibility, (self)discipline, time-management, collective awareness as well as many other concepts and principles on which the adult world operates. So, if my students don't grasp the subjunctive fully, but I manage to teach them some of the afore-mentioned principles – that satisfies me as a teacher as well. Ideally, I'd want to have them grasp both aspects, but that's not always possible. (Private correspondence with author, 13.10.2006)

Should students write in the L1 or L2?

A second inevitable question is how to organise language use in an exchange. In a project involving students from various countries the use of a lingua franca such as English or French may be the obvious course of action (see the description of the eTwinning model by Domínguez Miguela in this volume). However, if both sets of students are learning each other's languages (Irish learners of French and French learners of English, for example), then the question arises as to how both languages should be used. Probably the most common approach is that adapted by the Tandem Network (see O'Rourke, this volume), which involves each student writing half of their message in the foreign language and half in their native tongue. The principle is justified as it allows both learners the opportunity to speak and write in the target language and to listen to and read messages written by their native speaking partners.

However, other practitioners have argued that requiring students to interact in the foreign language may mean that they inevitably simplify the content of their messages or neglect content altogether due to the need to focus on linguistic accuracy in the target language. The original developers of the Cultura model, for example, propose asking learners to always write in their first language and justify this choice in the following way:

> We wanted to make sure that students were able to express their thoughts in all their complexity as fully and as naturally as possible ... what students may 'lose', by not writing in the target language, is largely offset by the gains they make by getting access to a rich, dynamic and totally authentic language. (Cultura Website, 2001)

Various chapters in this volume will return to this question and will look at the consequences for language choice in online telecollaboration.

Should students correct their partners' linguistic errors?

Online exchange can be seen as an opportunity for learners to improve their communicative competence in the target language in various ways. They have the chance to interact with native speakers of the target culture, they are exposed to authentic input in the target language from their partners and they are free to express themselves away from the watchful gaze of their classroom teacher. There is also the possibility that their partners can correct their errors in the target language. However, the issue of peer correction can be more complicated than first imagined. Questions arise as to whether the fact that someone is a native speaker makes them qualified and capable of correcting and explaining errors in their own mother tongue. Also, as Ware and O'Dowd (in press) found out in their research on a Spanish–American exchange, students may feel uncomfortable about the effects which correcting their partners' work may have on their relationship. An American student explained:

> I wasn't so sure [about providing feedback], because I don't know what kind of people they are, and I don't want like the second time I talked to them, to be like, 'Oh wow, this is what was wrong with your paper.' ... I was like I'm going to do my best to not make it seem like I'm a teacher ... I don't want to appear like I'm trying to teach them English. (Interview data taken from Ware & O'Dowd, in press)

Another related question is whether students expect to receive feedback from their partners. While many students often prefer to focus on the content of their interaction, others may expect to receive feedback on grammatical and linguistic issues in order to feel that they are truly benefiting from the activity. More student feedback, this time from a Spanish student, helps to illustrate this point:

> No, she's too polite [to comment on grammar]. But I prefer it if she does because if they don't correct you, you can't improve. It [participating in an exchange] is useful because you see how language works but it's not enough because you can't improve your writing because they don't say to you what you are doing wrong. (Interview data taken from Ware & O'Dowd, in press)

What types of tasks are most effective?

Once a partner class has been found, the teachers in both locations have to agree on the type of tasks that their students have to carry out together. These tasks can range from the conversational (e.g. 'discuss with your partner what you did last weekend') to more formal activities that require high levels of interaction, cultural analysis and collaboration (e.g. 'compare the American and Spanish films *Vanilla Sky* and *Abre Los Ojos* with your partner and together create a powerpoint presentation which presents your findings').

Unsurprisingly, there are many views as to what a successful task should involve. One experienced practitioner and researcher reports the following:

> Many of the studies of network-based interaction report on activities in which large groups of students discuss their opinions about current affairs, world politics, or even upcoming class assignments – in short, conversation type activities ... However research has proven that ... the negotiation of meaning and the resultant learner modifications are much more prevalent in goal-oriented, task-based interaction than in usual conversation. (Pellettieri, 2000: 64)

This particular author is coming from an interactivist background and appears to equate successful language learning with regular episodes of negotiation of meaning. However, other writers who put emphasis on the social and cultural nature of language learning would probably argue that so-called 'conversation type activities' about current affairs or other activities such as interviews can also carry great language learning potential as they allow learners to learn about other cultural perspectives and also provide opportunities for the development of learners' social identity in the second language.

What communication tools to use?

Online intercultural exchanges have come a long way since the early days when e-mail was usually the only communication tool available to teachers and learners. Users can now choose between using text-based synchronous tools (i.e. tools which allow communication in real time) such as chats, Microsoft Messenger and MOOs, or asynchronous tools such as discussion forums, blogs and wikis. Better internet connections mean that audio and videoconferencing communication is also a realistic possibility with tools such as Netmeeting and Horizon Wimba becoming increasingly popular in language classrooms. The question of course is how to choose the appropriate tool (or combination of tools) for your particular online exchange. As the following chapters clearly show, many factors should influence how this particular decision is made. Factors include learners' and teachers' familiarity with the different tools available, the levels of access to the technology that exist in each local context and how the interaction is to be organised. Inevitably, teachers will need to engage in a considerable amount of action research and consultation with their students and their partner classes in order to identify the right tool for their particular exchange context.

A short anecdotal example may serve to illustrate the complexity of choosing the right communicative tools for an exchange. Recently, this author and a partner teacher introduced a combination of written and oral discussion forums in an online exchange between American and Spanish learners. The oral discussion forums allowed the students to record messages using a microphone and leave them for their partners to listen to at a later date. Both teachers expected that the oral forums would prove to be far more popular with their students than the text-based communication as they allowed students to hear their partners' voices and would therefore lead to a much more personal and realistic form of interaction. However, end-of-exchange feedback revealed that students felt much more comfortable with the written forums for various reasons. Some of their comments included the following:

> I prefer the written one because it's easier to write than speaking. It would be easier to speak if we could see them but talking to a computer screen is not very personal.

> It's easier to understand them in the written forum because on the spoken forum we have to listen to the recordings at least twice to catch the idea.

Obviously factors related to ease of communication and the psychological aspects of speaking into a computer microphone greatly influenced the students' preferences for communication.

About this Volume

In the following chapter of this volume we carry out an overview of how online technologies are being used in foreign language education and look at what current research has to say about some of the widely held beliefs about what online interaction can contribute to the foreign language classroom. The chapter proposes that teachers adopt a 'social realist' approach which involves, firstly, an awareness of how the impact of new technologies is often determined by the socioinstitutional contexts in which they are used and, secondly, an understanding that the innovative potential of technologies depends on the approach and skills of the teacher involved. The three chapters of the second part of the volume present three different 'models' of telecollaboration. While teachers use many different configurations to structure the type of tasks and to establish to what extent students should use their target language and their first language, several distinct models of telecollaboration have emerged in recent years that offer practitioners a relatively defined structure within which to organise their students' online interaction. This first section looks at three of the best known models of online exchange: Breffni O'Rourke presents *e-tandem* learning, Jesús Suarez and Jim Crapotta look at the *Cultura* model and, finally, Antonia Domínguez Miguela writes about the *eTwinning* system which has become popular among primary and secondary school educators in Europe in recent years. In each case, the authors present the key principles of their chosen model, the rationale that underlies its structure and then they go on to present some practical research findings to demonstrate the models' strengths and weaknesses.

The third section of the publication deals with questions and issues that regularly emerge from the research literature and from the practical reports on online projects. The chapters by Paige Ware and Marisa Pérez and by Julie Belz underline that improvements in either grammatical competence or in intercultural awareness should not be taken for granted in these activities and that careful structuring of tasks combined with student preparation and training and a proactive role on behalf of the teacher are necessary to ensure the maximum benefit from exchanges. Specific examples of tasks and authentic extracts from previous online exchanges are used to illustrate the authors' arguments. Following these discussions on the potential benefits of online exchange, the next three authors in this section provide a practical overview of aspects of telecollaboration which are often overlooked in the literature: Andreas Müller-Hartmann outlines the role of the teachers in online exchange and discusses issues such as how they can set up exchanges, design tasks and solve emerging problems and misunderstandings in various educational contexts including primary, secondary and university education. Melinda Dooly examines the different facets of online communication tools currently available to teachers (e.g. discussion boards, instant messaging, videoconferencing) and explains how the choice of communication tool should depend on factors such as the type of task the students have to carry out, the intended outcome of the exchange and the particular socioinstitutional contexts in which they are studying. Finally, Isabel Pérez and Margarita Vinagre will look at how online exchanges can be adapted for use in classes of younger learners in primary and lower-secondary education and will highlight the activities, outcomes and problems that are particular to this group of learners.

The fourth section of the publication presents a number of short reports by practitioners at secondary and university level institutions who report on their own personal experiences of online exchange. These reports illustrate how the models and principles outlined in the previous sections are being adapted and put into practice on a day-to-day basis in classrooms around Europe and the rest of the world.

References

Allport, G.W. (1979) *The Nature of Prejudice*. Reading: Addison-Wesley.

Belz, J. (2001) Institutional and individual dimensions of transatlantic group work in network-based language teaching. *ReCALL* 13 (2), 213–231.

Belz, J. (2003) Linguistic perspectives on the development of intercultural competence in telecollaboration. *Language Learning and Technology* 7 (2), 68. On WWW at http://llt.msu.edu/vol7num2/belz/.

Belz, J. and Kinginger, C. (2002) The cross-linguistic development of address form use in telecollaborative language learning: Two case studies. *Canadian Modern Language Review/Revue canadienne des langues vivantes* 59 (2), 189–214.

Belz, J. and Müller-Hartmann, A. (2003) Teachers negotiating German–American telecollaboration: Between a rock and an institutional hard place. *Modern Language Journal* 87 (1), 71–89.

Belz, J.A. and Thorne, S.L. (eds) (2006) *Internet-Mediated Intercultural Foreign Language Education*. Boston, MA: Heinle & Heinle.

Blake, R. (2000) Computer mediated communication: A window on L2 Spanish interlanguage. *Language Learning & Technology* 4 (1), 120–136. On WWW at http://llt.msu.edu/vol4num1/blake/.

Block, D. (2001) 'McCommunication': A problem in the frame for SLA. In D. Block and D. Cameron (eds) *Language Learning and Teaching in the Age of Globalization* (pp. 83–100). London: Routledge.

Block, D. and Cameron, D. (eds) *Language Learning and Teaching in the Age of Globalization*. London: Routledge.

Brammerts, H. (1995) Tandem learning and the Internet. Using new technology to acquire intercultural competence. In A. Jensen, A. Kirsten and L. Annette (eds) *Intercultural Competence. A New Challenge for Language Teachers and Trainers in Europe. Vol. II. The Adult Learner* (pp. 209–222). Aalborg: Aalborg University Press.

Byram, M. (1997) *Teaching and Assessing Intercultural Communicative Competence*. Clevedon: Multilingual Matters.

Council of Europe (2001) *Common European Framework of Reference for Languages: Learning, Teaching, Assessment*. Strasbourg: Cambridge University Press.

Crystal D. (2001) *Language and the Internet*. Cambridge: Cambridge University Press.

Cummins, J. and Sayers, D. (1995) *Brave New Schools. Challenging Cultural Literacy through Global Learning Networks*. New York: St. Martin's Press.

Ducate, L. and Arnold, N. (eds) (2006) *Calling on CALL: From Theory and Research to New Directions in Foreign Language Teaching*. Texas: CALICO.

Furstenberg, G., Levet, S., English, K. and Maillet, K. (2001) Giving a virtual voice to the silent language of culture: The CULTURA project. *Language Learning & Technology* 5 (1), 55–102. On WWW at http://llt.msu.edu/vol5num1/furstenberg/default.html.

Greenfell, M. (2000) Learning and teaching strategies. In S. Green (ed.) *New Perspectives on Teaching and Learning Modern Languages*. Clevedon: Multilingual Matters.

Long, M.H. and Robinson, P. (1998) Focus on form: Theory, research and practice. In C. Doughty and J. Williams (eds) *Focus on Form in Second Language Acquisition* (pp. 15–41). Cambridge: Cambridge University Press.

Meskill, C. and Ranglova, K. (2000) Sociocollaborative language learning in Bulgaria. In M. Warschauer and R. Kern (eds) *Network-based Language Teaching: Concepts and Practice* (pp. 20–40). Cambridge: Cambridge University Press.

Müller-Hartmann, A. (2000) The role of tasks in promoting intercultural learning in electronic learning networks. *Language Learning and Technology* 4 (2), 129–147. On WWW at http://llt.msu.edu/vol4num2/muller/default.html.

O'Dowd, R. (2003) Understanding 'the other side': Intercultural learning in a Spanish–English e-mail exchange. *Language Learning and Technology* 7 (2), 118–144. On WWW at http://llt.msu.edu/vol7num2/odowd/default.html.

O'Dowd, R. (2006) The use of videoconferencing and e-mail as mediators of intercultural student ethnography internet-mediated intercultural student ethnography. In J.A. Blez and S. Thorne (eds) *Internet-mediated Intercultural Foreign Language Education* (pp. 86–120). Boston MA: Heinle and Heinle.

O'Dowd, R. and Ritter, M. (2006) Understanding and working with 'failed communication' in telecollaborative exchanges. *CALICO Journal* 61 (2), 623–642.

O'Rourke, B. (2005) Form-focused interaction in on-line tandem learning. *CALICO Journal* 22 (3), 433–466.

Pellettieri, J. (2000) Negotiation in cyberspace: The role of chatting in the development of grammatical competence. In: M. Warschauer and R. Kern (eds) *Network-based Language Teaching: Concepts and Practice* (pp. 59–86). Cambridge: Cambridge University Press.

Richter, R. (1998) Interkulturelles Lernen via Internet? *Zeitschrift für interkulturellen Fremdsprachenunterricht [On-line]* 3 (2). On WWW at http://www.spz.tu-darmstadt.de/projekt_ejournal/jg-03-2/beitrag/richter1.htm.

Riel, M. (1997) Learning circles make global connections. In: R. Donath and I. Volkmer (eds) *Das Transatlantische Klassenzimmer* (pp. 329–357). Hamburg: Koerber-Stiftung.

Schneider, J. and von der Emde, S. (2006) At the intersection of telecollaboration, learner corpus analysis, and L2 pragmatics: Consideration for language program direction. In J. Blez and S. Thorne (eds) *Internet-mediated Intercultural Foreign Language Education* (pp. 178–207). Boston, MA: Heinle and Heinle.

Thorne, S. (2006) Pedagogical and praxiological lessons from internet-mediated intercultural foreign language education research. In J. Blez and S. Thorne (eds) *Internet-mediated Intercultural Foreign Language Education* (pp. 2–31). Boston: Thomson Heinle.

Tudini, V. (2003) Using native speakers in chat. *Language Learning & Technology* 7 (3), 141–159. On WWW at http://llt.msu.edu/vol7num3/tudini/default.html.

Ware, P. (2005) 'Missed' communication in on-line communication: Tensions in a German–American telecollaboration. *Language Learning and Technology* 9 (2), 64–89. On WWW at http://llt.msu.edu/vol9num2/ware/default.html.

Ware, P. and O'Dowd, R. (in press) Peer feedback on language form in international telecollaboration.

Warschauer, M. (ed.) (1995) *Virtual Connections*. Manoa: University of Hawaii.

Warschauer, M. and Kern, R. (eds) (2000) *Network-based Language Teaching: Concepts and Practice*. Cambridge: Cambridge University Press.

Zuengler, J. and Miller, E. (2006) Cognitive and sociocultural perspectives: Two parallel SLA worlds? *TESOL Quarterly* 40 (1), 35–58.

Web pages referred to in Chapter 1

IECC Intercultural E-mail Classroom Connections: http://www.iecc.org

eTandem: http://www.slf.ruhr-uni-bochum.de/etandem/etindex-en.html

Ruth Vilmi's homepage: http://www.writeit.fi/ruth/hut/

Reinhard Donath's website for e-mail projects: http://www.schule.de/englisch/email.htm

The Cultura website: http://web.mit.edu/french/culturaNEH/

Chapter 2

Foreign Language Education and the Rise of Online Communication: A Review of Promises and Realities

ROBERT O'DOWD

Introduction

The aim of this volume is to examine how one particular online communicative activity (i.e. telecollaboration or online intercultural exchange) can be successfully integrated into the foreign language classroom. However, before looking at the different aspects of this activity, it behoves us to carry out a more global review of the complex relationship between online communicative technologies and foreign language education and, with the help of the literature, to explore some broader questions in relation to the topic. This chapter aims to explore three key questions. Firstly, in what ways is computer-mediated communication (CMC) being employed in foreign language classrooms around the world? Secondly, how can online communication activity contribute to the language learning process? Thirdly, what social and cultural factors influence the outcomes of online foreign language education? By examining these questions the reader will receive a general insight into some of the issues, dilemmas, promises and challenges that online language learning can entail.

The rise of the internet and online communication technologies over the past 15 years has undoubtedly changed the way people in more affluent parts of the world work, communicate, socialise and learn and has gone a long way to producing what Castells (1996: 21) described as a 'network society'. The availability of high-speed internet connections and communication tools such as e-mail, chats, instant messaging, online telephony and videoconferencing allows people to socialise and communicate with colleagues, friends and family in ways and with a regularity never before thought possible. Furthermore, thanks to powerful tools and resources such as search engines (e.g. Google), video publishing platforms (e.g. MySpace and YouTube), and online encyclopaedias (e.g. Wikipedia), the internet has also become an unrivalled source of information and reference for work, educational and recreational purposes. Finally, a second generation of interactive social networking tools such as blogs (e.g. Blogger) and networking services (e.g. Facebook) are providing users with spaces where they can express and develop their online identities and create interconnected networks of social or professional contacts. The relevance of foreign language education in such an environment is evident. While the internet may have had its origins in the USA, it is clearly becoming a setting for a great deal of intercultural contact and exchange. Crystal (2001: 218) suggests that the days of Anglo-American domination of the internet are quickly coming to an end and that the majority of new websites being published online are no longer in the English language. Furthermore, the international profile of internet users (Global Research, 2004) suggests that learners surfing the internet are likely to encounter users from a great number of different nationalities – each one bringing with it its own cultural-specific beliefs and expectations as to what is appropriate behaviour in CMC.

Against this backdrop, in the field of foreign language education, it is often unclear whether the internet should be seen as a tool for learning foreign languages, or inversely, whether learning foreign languages is simply one of the tools students need to work and communicate on the internet. In either case, the internet opens language teachers to a host of new tools and resources, including a vast amount of authentic materials in the target language as well as communication tools that enable teacher–student or student–student communication in the same classroom or between classes at geographically different locations. There has also been a considerable rise in the use of specific educational online tools often referred to as virtual learning environments (VLEs) (e.g. Moodle, Blackboard or WebCT), which allow students and teachers to organise and reflect on their learning in virtual spaces specifically suited to their classes' needs and requirements. In general, these and other online learning activities have been applied in foreign language educa-tion in two distinct learning scenarios. The first of these is distance learning (White, 2003), in which students learn a foreign language at a distant location to the educational institution without coming into physical contact with their teacher and classmates. The second is referred to as 'blended learning' and describes learning that combines online activity with more traditional periods of face-to-face contact and class-room interaction (Thorne, 2003). In both contexts, the quality of the online language learning appears to be very mixed. Many writers are critical, for example, that the majority of online foreign language learning merely involves the transfer of text-based material to an online format. White explains:

> Some providers tend to focus on the web as a means of getting materials into electronic format, and tend to view the new learning spaces as something to be filled by their printed study materials, with perhaps some links to other sites. This is a very typical approach. In this view the new spaces are used as a means of course dissemination, rather than as a new, rich learning context in themselves. (White, 2003: 216)

While such assessments are disappointing, there is nevertheless a high level of interest among foreign language educators, researchers, administrators and indeed learners as to how networked technologies can enhance the process of foreign language learning. With this in mind, in the following sections of this chapter I will critically examine three key reasons why it is believed that online communication technologies can make important contributions to foreign language education. These include examining, firstly, the relationship between these learners' current online practices and the demands of formal online language learning; secondly, the increased possibilities for communication and learner participation that networked environments can offer; and thirdly, the new opportunities that online tools can offer to teaching methodology.

The first of these issues is related to the widespread use of online technologies by young people today. It is often suggested that the younger generation of language learners will be particularly prepared and suited for online language learning due to their regular use of new technologies for recreational and social purposes. Zemsky and Massy (2004: 48) write in detail about this belief in their critical study of online learning in institutions of higher education in the USA, describing it as the assumption that 'the kids will take to e-learning like ducks to water'. The second key area refers to the increased possibilities for communication and participation and deals with the belief that the internet is a culturally and linguistically 'neutral' environment that provides learners of all different social, linguistic and cultural backgrounds with the same balanced 'playing field' on which they can interact and learn. In the words of Kramsch and Thorne (2002: 85), many believe that in networked interaction ' . . . native and non-native speakers can have access to one another as linguistic entities on a screen, unfettered by historical, geographical, national or institutional identities'. The third area deals with the hope that the use of new technologies will in some way bring about more progressive and innovative approaches to language teaching. As online technologies are seen to facilitate communication and collaboration among individuals, it is often expected that the technology will be adapted for use in foreign language classroom for these same purposes, thereby making language learning more student-centred, collaborative and communicative. The creators of the VLE Moodle, for example, claim that the socioconstructivist principles of their platform mean that the role of the teacher ' . . . can change from being "the source of knowledge" to being an influencer and role model of class culture, connecting with students in a personal way that addresses their own learning needs, and moderating discussions and activities in a way that collectively leads students towards the learning goals of the class' (Moodle, n.d.). In the following sections of this chapter, these issues will be examined individually.

To What Extent is the Younger Generation of Foreign Language Learners Particularly Suited to Online Foreign Language Education?

The internet and its associated communication tools have clearly become one of the main environments of expression, recreation and socialisation for members of affluent societies. This is particularly true for the younger generations who have been socialised in the use of networked technologies since their early childhood. To take the example of this author's present location, recent statistics show that more than 60% of the internet users in Spain are under the age of 34 and that a third of young people in Spain between the ages of 12 and 24 (2.4 million in total) are regular users of Microsoft's instant messaging system Microsoft Messenger. Among this generation of internet users, 34% report using the internet for study and research purposes, while 8.5% already report taking part in 'e-learning' – educational courses offered over the internet (Red.es, 2006). These statistics are quite significant for a country such as Spain, which is still not considered one of the most networked European societies. Indeed, recent data show that Spain ranks no. 14 in the list of global internet users, coming well behind other European countries such as Germany, France, Italy and the UK (Computer Industry Almanac, 2004). These statistics also pale when compared with descriptions of the 'digital natives' or 'net generation' emerging in the USA. A study carried out in 2002 found that 86% of American college students had gone online, in comparison to 59% of the general population in the country (Jones, 2002). It also found that 74% of students used the internet four or more hours a week, while a fifth (19%) used it 12 or more hours a week. Thorne and Payne (2005: 380) go so far as to say that that the new generation of internet users in the USA ' . . . thinks, performs, learns and communicates in ways that qualitatively differ from cohorts born prior to the wide adoption of digital communication and information technologies'.

However, if the learners of today are comfortable socialising, communicating and informing themselves using networked technologies, is it accurate to assume that they will also be both suited and open to learning foreign languages in online environments? A review of the literature suggests that any such assumption should be made with great care for two reasons. Firstly, students' acceptance of online learning activities will depend on whether they see the activity and the particular communication tool being used as appropriate and relevant to themselves and their learning practices. Secondly, a considerable gap may exist between the students' everyday online practices and the online literacies that are required to operate effectively in virtual foreign language learning scenarios.

The first of these factors is a stark reminder that any online learning activity does not exist in a vacuum, but rather belongs in a particular sociocultural context and that its success depends on a complex array of external factors including learners' needs, expectations and lifestyles, institutional requirements and common online practices in a particular society. Any online learning activity will only be taken on successfully by learners if the task and communication tool in question make sense in the learners' particular context. Various reports serve to illustrate this point. Zemsky and Massy (2004), for example, found that one of the main factors for what they perceived as the failure of many e-learning initiatives in the USA was that students were unwilling to miss out on the social aspects of on-campus study. The authors found that when e-learning initiatives involved students working alone and being physically isolated from their classes and their classmates, the courses were inevitably rejected. On the other hand, successful e-learning case studies usually involved group work around computer screens inside classrooms which used online content as a stimulus for face-to-face collaboration and discussion.

However, not only must online activity make sense in the particular learning context, but the communication tool must also be seen as appropriate by the learners for the particular task at hand. Steve Thorne's (2003) work on the theme of 'cultures of use' (2003) suggests that communication tools such as e-mail or instant messaging are not neutral objects but rather are culturally mediated and therefore have certain cultural associations and characteristics that they have acquired from their use in everyday life. To illustrate this point, Thorne uses the example of the use of e-mail in an online intercultural exchange between an American and a French student. He explains how the exchange failed to gather momentum as neither student saw e-mail as an appropriate tool for exchanging informal messages with partners of their own age. E-mail, according to the American student in the study, was suitable for more formal communication between students and teachers, while student-to-student communication was considered more suited to tools such as Microsoft Messenger.

The work of Thorne and others clearly illustrates that while language learners may be open to the use of online technologies for their language learning, it should not be taken as a given that online activity will be taken up without question. Online language learning has to make sense to learners in their particular context and it has to be seen to be making a practical contribution to how they learn. Furthermore, the tasks should be seen to use communication tools in a fashion that is coherent with their habitual uses in society.

Of course, the successful adaptation of learners' to online learning does not only depend on their current online practices and expectations but also on the skills and linguistic knowledge that they use to operate online. While language learners may be active on the internet in social and recreational activity, the interactional and linguistic skills that they require to take part in chats and messaging, the upload and download of videos and music, and the creation of personal profiles for social networking are likely to differ greatly from the skills, attitudes and knowledge they require to carry out typical online tasks in formal foreign language learning contexts. These tasks may involve, for example, establishing contact and developing working relationships with native speakers of the target language, collaborating and reaching agreements with other learners in distant locations in order to complete projects together or working with tandem partners on the correction of their texts in their target language. These tasks may require the use of formal or academic registers in the target language, well developed sociopragmatic sensitivity in text-based intercultural communication and a high level of language awareness about the target language and the L1. As such, there can be a clear difference between the forms of literacy that informal or recreational online interaction may involve and those required by more formal online learning activity. Inevitably, this issue highlights the need for foreign language educators to consider such concepts as the digital divide and electronic literacies.

'The digital divide' is a term that has been used widely in discussions on the use of the internet and society. Very often on governmental and administrative levels, the term has been understood as a reference to the lack of physical access to computer hardware and online technologies by economically disadvantaged parts of a population and therefore the solution is seen to be high levels of financial investment in online computer terminals in disadvantaged areas and schools. However, many researchers have attempted to redefine the digital divide as an absence, not only of financial investment, but also of institutional and societal support as well as a lack of access to training in the skills and literacies of the knowledge society. Warschauer (2002: 5) explains: '. . .a digital divide is marked not only by physical access to computers and connectivity, but also by access to the additional resources that allow people to use technology well'. In short, if members of a society do not receive the support and training necessary in how to use and exploit the technology for social and professional development, then providing them with access to the technology itself will make little difference to their lives. In the context of foreign language learners, the concept of the digital divide serves as a warning that simply providing learners with computer laboratories and online communication tools will not be sufficient to guarantee successful language learning. Learners also require training and support in the intricacies of formal CMC activity.

But what are exactly the skills and knowledge which learners will need to know in order to participate successfully in online foreign language learning? Various models have already been developed of what 'electronic literacy' may involve for foreign language learners and these go some way to establishing what learners need to know in more formal online contexts. Two of these will now be looked at briefly.

Probably the best known model of electronic literacy for foreign language learners is that developed by Shetzer and Warschauer (2000: 177– 178), which is divided into three overlapping areas: communication, construction and research. The area of most interest in this context is communication. Here, the authors identify the skills that foreign language learners need as including how to establish contact with others using the internet, how to collaborate online, how to choose the appropriate communication tools for particular tasks as well as having an understanding of issues such as netiquette (i.e. appropriate politeness and behaviour on the internet), safety and privacy. The authors argue that the internet is an independent medium with its own specific stylistic and sociolinguistic features and thereby brings with it a form of communication that is different to both traditional oral and written communication. The internet, for example, often involves real-time communication that is very often text-based. It also allows, through various conferencing tools, simultaneous contact with different individuals in many geographically dispersed locations.

However, any model of electronic literacy must also take into account that online interaction not only involves dealing with the particular characteristics of the medium, but also requires attention to the cultural characteristics of the online participants. The problem is not merely that learners are communicating in a virtual text-based environment. Instead, the problem is that, firstly, they are in this particular environment and, secondly, that they may come from different cultural backgrounds and will therefore have different expectations as to how communication should be carried out, at what rate it should develop and what content it should contain. In other words, electronic literacy for language learners needs to borrow significantly from models of intercultural communicative competence such as that proposed by Byram (1997). For example, online language learners need to have knowledge of how online behaviour is organised and interpreted in different cultures and they will also need skills, including the ability to interpret online publications and behaviour from different cultures and the ability to interact online with members of different cultures and to elicit the meaning of certain online behaviour for them.

Interestingly, another model of electronic literacy, proposed by Moser (2000), goes a good way to addressing this issue. Moser organises his model into technical, cultural, social and reflexive competences. In the section on cultural competences, the author refers to the need for learners to be able to deal with the 'multicultural character of the internet' and to understand the 'cultural codes and presentation forms in the World Wide Web' (Moser, 2000: 251). Such an awareness of the intercultural nature of online publications and communication is a vital aspect of any model of electronic literacy for language learners.

To conclude this section, it is clear that teachers intending to engage their learners in online communication activities for foreign language purposes need to take into account the current online practices of their learners when planning online learning. Instead of going online based on the belief that such practice is inherently good or progressive, educators have to convince students that online activity is relevant and that the tasks and online communication tools make sense in terms of their goals and current learning practices. Secondly, teachers also need to consider the electronic literacies that students will need to master in order to take part in online language learning. These literacies should include much more than basic technical skills as to how to use internet forums and how to publish in blogs. Electronic literacies for foreign language learners need to include the skills and knowledge necessary to interact, investigate, publish and collaborate appropriately, taking into consideration the characteristics of the medium as well as the cultural and professional backgrounds of one's interlocutors.

Does Online Communication Technology Facilitate Increased Student Participation and Intercultural Communication Between Learners?

One of the principal reasons for the success of online technologies in foreign language education has been the opportunity that it has given to teachers to increase student interaction and thereby to develop fluency in the target language. Online communication in classrooms has taken various forms, including student–teacher contact (e.g. in the case of student mentoring), student-to-student interaction within the same classroom and student contact with others outside of the classroom (e.g. including online intercultural exchanges). To date, the research on online student communication has focussed principally on text-based communication, but improvements in band width and technology means that teachers are turning more to audioconferencing tools (Hauck & Hampel, 2004), videoconferencing (O'Dowd, 2005) and online telephony (e.g. Skype). As it has been the focus of most research to date, this section will concentrate on whether online text-based communication can support communicative opportunities in the foreign language in ways that might not be possible in traditional classroom environments.

Stemming from the theme of online student interaction, a great deal of the earlier literature on CMC in foreign language education claimed that both asynchronous and synchronous forms help to bring about more equal levels of participation between learners than would normally occur in face-to-face interaction. This related to shy and outgoing students, high- and low-level status groups (such as academics and students), male and female participation, and interaction between members of different cultures (Sproull & Kiesler, 1991; Warschauer, 1996). This increase in levels of participation was often attributed to the fact that aspects of peoples' identity such as their race, gender, social class and accent can often be hidden in the text-based environments of online communication. As a consequence, those who may feel uncomfortable about participating in face-to-face interaction or who may be discriminated against in such interaction will have an opportunity to participate more in online learning scenarios (Simmons, 1998; Tella & Mononen-Aaltonen, 1998). Reports also suggested that another important aspect of the internet's limited social dimension was the absence of non-verbal cues such as frowning and hesitating. This factor, it was argued, also contributed to making CMC a less intimidating environment and thereby encouraged those individuals or cultures that are less dominant to play a greater role in interaction (Salaberry, 1996). Warschauer (1997) offered the example of Japanese school children who are usually expected in their culture to take a passive rather than an active role in class and therefore tend not to participate in class discussions. CMC, he claimed, offers these students an opportunity to make a contribution to a discussion without going against this cultural norm.

In the context of online intercultural exchange, this characteristic of CMC, in theory at least, can be seen as advantageous as it implies that groups from different cultures in contact together via text-based communication tools will interact on a more 'equal footing' than they might in a face-to-face situation, thereby increasing the potential for interaction in which neither group is dominated by the other. Simmons (1998: 14) summarised this perceived advantage of working and learning in a virtual intercultural environment in the following way:

> Skin colours and other biases based on visual factors will be minimised. Individuals who by ethnicity or personality are less outspoken in face-to-face situations may contribute more abundantly to news groups and forums [. . .] where they enjoy anonymity or less exposure.

However, there are reasons why this characteristic may not be as advantageous for online foreign language learning as might be initially imagined. Firstly, it has been called into question whether CMC does indeed make interaction more 'democratic' by hiding aspects of identity such as gender, race or culture. Extensive research by Herring (1996) found that interaction on the internet is actually dominated by a male discourse style that is based on the principles of debate, freedom from rules and adversarial argumentation. Furthermore, the author also maintained that internet users generally reveal their gender by their style of interaction online, and that their gender-related characteristics may even be exaggerated in online environments (Herring, 1996: 4).

Similarly, more recent research has rejected the suggestion that there is anything culturally homogenous about the internet and it is suggested that, first of all, the internet itself is based on specific cultural principles and values and that, secondly, users of the internet also bring with them their own cultural values and modes of behaviour which may or may not be compatible with those of other online users. Reeder *et al.* (2004) argue, for instance, that the internet and common standards of online behaviour have been heavily influenced by the values of its Anglo-American creators and online interaction is therefore based on the principles of speed (i.e. quick responses to interaction), openness (as opposed to privacy), debate and informality. Based on their analysis of online interaction involving aboriginal Canadians, non-aboriginal Canadians and immigrants to Canada in a course of online learning, the authors concluded that common online communication tools (such as message boards) and online learning platforms (such as WebCT) operated on Western principles of publicity and efficiency, which may not be suited to international groups of learners. Similarly, Kim and Bonk (2002), in their study of online behaviour of Korean, Finnish and North American students, found Korean students to be more socially and contextually driven online, while Finnish students were more group-focussed and reflective in their online behaviour. American students, on the other hand, were found to be more action-oriented and showed a greater interest than the other nationalities in getting results from their online interactions. The authors warn that online educators should take into account differing cultural attitudes to online collaboration and interaction when planning online learning tasks for groups of international learners. In another study based on online communicative practices in various French and English discussion forums, Hanna and de Nooy (2003) also found that cultural-specific norms and practices are clearly visible not only in the thematic content of online content but also in online communicative practices. However, they warn against simplistic generalisations as to how different cultures can be expected to interact online. Instead, they suggest that the way a culture adapts to a new genre will depend on whether the genre is interpreted as being based principally on a spoken or written model and, the authors argue, this choice is unforeseeable.

In the light of these findings, it is necessary to seriously question any claims that the internet is some kind of 'neutral zone' free of cultural values where learners can interact in ways which they would not be able to in face-to-face situations. Hawisher and Selfe (2000: 5) identify this perception of the internet as a way of erasing barriers to communication as stemming from the American narrative of the global village, a concept that originated in the time of the telegraph and depicts technology as a tool for establishing a global network which erases difference between cultures and establishes a sense of international community and union. The authors are unconvinced by this approach, suggesting that many countries and cultures are liable to see the extension of Western technologies and computer networks as simply another form of cultural colonialism in which Western forms of thinking, working and communicating are imposed on others: 'To citizens in these countries, the Web may seem less a neutral and welcome medium for global communication than a disturbing and unwelcome system for broadening western colonial culture and values' (Hawisher & Selfe, 2000: 9). However they do recognise the potential of the internet as a medium for self-expression and the development of self- and cultural identity. They refer to Haraway (1991), for example, who exploits the metaphor of cyborgs and cyborgian identities to illustrate how virtual text-based activity can offer users a chance to escape gender stereotyping and to shape and become politically active in the networked world in which they operate.

Online communication tools clearly offer students more opportunities than before to interact with their classmates and with distant learning partners and the fact that many of the tools in use in classrooms today are still text-based means that a certain level of anonymity still remains possible. However, it should not be assumed that learners will in some way leave behind the shackles of their own social and cultural identities once they begin to interact online.

Furthermore, I would question the value of increased student interaction that comes about through the disguising or hiding of aspects of one's identity and the consequent avoidance of bias and prejudice, rather than through a constructive dialogue that deals with these issues in a direct and transparent manner. I would argue this for the following reasons. In their theoretical work on the role of media-based communication in dialogism, Tella and Mononen-Aaltonens' (1998) definition of dialogue refers to interaction between individuals or cultures which produces a genuine change or shift in their way of viewing the world. The authors identify mutual respect as a vital element of dialogic interaction, yet they curiously go on to say the following:

> Different kinds of things connected to race, gender, religion etc, can be powerful impediments to dialogism as well. As an example of CMHC [Computer Mediated Human Communication] that does away with various artefacts is email, which lets people communicate across age, gender, geographical barriers etc. (Tella & Mononen-Aaltonen, 1998: 91)

The implication here (and in the work of Simmons cited earlier) appears to be that CMC sometimes facilitates dialogue because the participants may be unaware of aspects of each other's identity. If so, then it is questionable whether mutual respect ever really becomes an issue and whether true intercultural dialogue is ever really achieved. The real challenge of intercultural interaction, online or face-to-face, is to come to terms with the differences found in the other culture which one may initially wish to reject. If these differences remain hidden in the online environment (with the help of text-based communication) then true dialogue, authentic intercultural communication and the consequent changes in the interlocutors' perspective are never likely to come about. An early example of online intercultural exchange from the literature serves to illustrate this point.

Sayers (1995) describes an e-mail exchange between two classes which illustrates these issues quite well. In the exchange, an American group of learners exchanged mails with a group from Quebec for over a year and a half in order to carry out various parallel learning projects. The exchange is reported to have worked extremely well and the American group are said to have considered their Quebecois partners '[. . .] competent and highly-proficient models for learning French' (Sayers, 1995: n.p.). It was not until the two groups met at the end of the exchange that the American students realised that their partner class actually consisted of deaf children who studied in a school for the deaf. No doubt Sayers recounts this anecdote in an attempt to show the ability of CMC to allow communication to take place without it being hindered by the prejudices that learners might have towards handicapped students. However, there appears to be a deliberate attempt on the part of the organisers to hide information from the learners and this may take away from the ultimate value of the project. It is fair to speculate that the American learners would have benefited more from the exchange knowing from the beginning that their partners had a disability but were still going to be able to take part successfully in their project. In any case, CMC can be seen here to have been employed in order to avoid challenging stereotypes and prejudice, rather than in order to confront them.

In contrast to this approach, I would suggest that learners engaged in online interaction should operate on a premise of honesty and that any online activity should be begun by the creation and publication of online photos and biographies in which the students present themselves and their backgrounds. Online communication should provide students with the opportunity to confront and deal with the prejudices, stereotypes and myths that they hold about other social groups and cultures and that others may hold about them. Presenting online communication as a '[. . .] utopian middle landscape [. . .] unfettered by historical, geographical, national or institutional identities' (Kramsch & Thorne, 2002: 85) is, in the long term, inaccurate, unrealistic and fails to exploit the medium to its full potential. With Moore (2002), I would also reject any suggestion that there is something inherent in the nature of CMC which brings about the reduction of prejudice: 'If technology challenges social roles, then it is because social change has allowed those roles to be challenged' (Moore, 2002: 22).

Can the Introduction of Online Technologies Facilitate the Emergence of New Ways of Teaching and Learning Languages?

As noted at the outset of this chapter, much online language learning involves the transfer of current teaching practices and materials into an electronic format. For example, a typical blended course may require students to upload essays to the class platform as opposed to submitting them by hand or to complete multiple choice quizzes online instead of in their textbooks. As for teachers, they may consider the publication of class notes online in powerpoint format instead of their reproduction as printed photocopies. In these cases, the function of online learning is seen as speeding up or facilitating current practices but has little to do with changing the way any learning and teaching actually take place.

This approach may be advantageous due to its practical contribution to the work flow in the classroom but it is often seen as limited as it fails to exploit the communicative and collaborative nature of CMC. For this reason, many educators are aiming to expand and enhance their learners' experience of foreign language learning by introducing activities involving student interaction. These activities include online intercultural exchange with learners in different locations (i.e. the theme of this publication), student participation in public discussion forums based in the target language (Hanna & de Nooy, 2003), engaging in online interactive dialogue about subject content with tutors and classmates (Weasenforth *et al.*, 2002) and the collaborative creation and publication of websites or blogs (Jeon-Ellis *et al.*, 2005).

The use of such CMC activities in foreign language education is essentially based on the belief that in order for cognitive growth to occur, it is necessary for learners to engage in a process of dialogue with peers and tutors, wherein understanding of the subject matter is articulated, challenged and explored. This belief that knowledge is not transferred from tutor to learner but rather constructed through interaction and exchange is known as social constructivism or sociocultural learning and its origins are commonly attributed to the work of the Russian writer Vygotsky (1978). Since then, the contribution of sociocultural theory to online foreign language education has been explored in depth by writers such as Lantolf (2000), Van Lier (1996) and Thorne (2003) and has become one of the primary fields of research in Computer Assisted Language Learning (for an interesting review, see Levy & Stockwell, 2006: 112–139). CMC is considered particularly suited for achieving language learning through interaction for various reasons. The characteristics considered advantageous include:

- The use of online communicative activities gives learners more opportunities to interact together than would be possible within the time constraints of the traditional classroom.
- Online communication tools give learners greater opportunities to come into contact and interact with native speakers of the target language as well as speakers of other languages.
- The asynchronous nature of many communication tools (e.g. e-mail, discussion forums, blogs) allows learners more time to read and understand their partners' perspectives and language input than would be the case in face-to-face communicative situations.
- The text-based nature of many communication tools provides learners with increased opportunities for noticing aspects of how the L2 is structured. This can contribute to increased accuracy and development of the learners' interlanguage (Sotillo, 2000).
- The possibility of printing and saving transcripts of online interaction gives learners a unique opportunity to re-read and study communicative events after they have taken place. Learners can identify structures and vocabulary in the target language that appear in the transcripts and later adapt them to other situations and contexts, thereby increasing the range of constructions they can use in the target language (Appel & Mullen, 2000).
- In distance courses, online communication can provide learners with a sense of support and belonging and reduce feelings of isolation and insecurity, which can be common among distance learners (White, 2003).

While these advantages are significant, it is necessary to be wary of what Bax (2003: 26) describes as the 'sole agent' fallacy, which implies focussing on how the inherent characteristics and functions of a particular communication tool will guarantee successful learning outcomes. Much of the recent research in online language learning has demonstrated that identifying the affordances of the tools used in tasks is insufficient to anticipate how the technology and the learning activity will be taken up by learners and teachers. As an alternative, a sociocultural approach to online research encourages educators to look at technology, not as an independent force that shapes and determines how learners carry out a learning task, but rather as a part of a complex mesh of factors which go to making up any particular learning context. Warschauer (2005: 26) explains: '...technology does not exist outside of a social structure, exerting an independent force on it, but rather the technological and social realms are highly intertwined and constantly co-constitute each other in a myriad of ways'.

In foreign language education, the 'social realm' that shapes the development of online language learning involves a wide variety of factors. These can include, firstly, physical aspects of the social environment, such as levels of student access to technology and the location of computer rooms and buildings; secondly, common online practices, which refers to how often students use technology, what communication tools they prefer to use and for what purposes they use them; and thirdly, common attitudes to technology, which include the importance with which they are attributed in education and what is considered appropriate online activity. Dutton *et al*. (2004), for example, examined the impact of a VLE on an American university and found that although the courseware was highly valued by both faculty and students, the majority of teachers had used the technology in essentially 'traditional' ways, employing it as a substitute for the copier or projector in order to support one-to-many lecture-based instruction. The authors suggest that the lack of innovative teaching techniques using the VLE was due to aspects of the culture of campus-based higher education. These aspects included the difficulties that many students experienced in gaining access to technologies, the negative attitudes of students toward contact classes being replaced by online sessions, and practical problems such as copyright issues when making images and course readings available online.

A further review of the literature on the socioinstitutional factors that influence how technologies are employed in learning reveals two other key factors, these being the teachers' own teaching philosophy and, secondly, the support and opportunities that teachers receive from the educational institution in which they are working. Reinhardt and Nelson (2004), for example, carried out a survey of over 118 teachers who had used an online Spanish language resource in order to identify which factors lead instructors to go beyond simply adopting online resources and instead to find innovative ways of using and integrating the websites into their classes. The study found that teachers often took a limited approach to implementing the online resources due to contextual issues such as access to technology, lack of institutional support and the constraints of assessment preparation. Only one of the three representative case studies referred to in the study was seen to succeed in using the online resources in an integrated, innovative fashion. This teacher was seen to have benefited from support from his colleagues as well as from a rich institutional CALL environment. Similarly, in their study of 20 foreign language teachers who had taken part in a graduate level CALL programme, Egbert *et al*. (2002) found that teachers' unwillingness to use new technologies in their classes was not related to a lack of confidence or interest, but was rather due to a lack of resources and time as well as perceived administrative or curricular restrictions.

In conclusion, the research reviewed here clearly highlights the importance of context, which also emerged in the other sections of this chapter. Online communication is a powerful tool for foreign language education which offers a wide range of advantages for educators who seek to introduce them into their classes, but it should not be seen as a 'silver bullet' that will bring about change and innovation by itself. In order for CMC to make a genuinely new contribution to language learning, its introduction must be part of a wider movement that includes a willingness for teachers to explore new ways of teaching, administrative support and leadership and an attempt to increase awareness of learners' needs and learning practices.

Conclusion

Over the past decade the internet has indisputably become an integral part of modern life in Western society and has impacted on the way people do business, travel, socialise, maintain relationships and learn. For this reason it is perhaps unsurprising that there is often what Healy describes as an ' ... unreasonable and unfounded fascination and belief in ... technology's educational power' (cited in Bax, 2003: 25) and a hope that the internet will make revolutionary changes to the way languages are taught and learned. In this opening chapter my aim has been to recognise the undoubted potential of the internet for foreign language education but also to present what could be described as a 'social realist' approach as to what the internet can actually contribute to the field and what factors will influence its effectiveness.

As a form of summary, I believe a social realist approach to online foreign language education involves the following factors. Firstly, it requires an avoidance of any assumptions that all CMC activity and tools are naturally suited to learners. Rather, activities and tools need to reflect the learners' needs and current online practices and their introduction should also be accompanied with training in the electronic literacies necessary for formal online educational activity. Secondly, such an approach does not attribute to the affordances of the internet's magical powers to change undesirable aspects of society such as stereotyping, group domination or discrimination. The increased potential for inter-cultural contact that CMC activity provides should be used as a tool to confront and deal with these issues rather than avoid or disguise them. Thirdly, a realistic understanding of the internet in education will also involve an appreciation that online learning *per se* does not signify progress or change in foreign language teaching. Innovation through online activity only comes about when, in the words of Kern *et al.* (2004: 255), educators '...use the Internet not so much to teach the same thing in a different way, but rather to help students enter into a new realm of collaborative enquiry and construction of knowledge'. This change is only likely to come about when teachers are given the training, support and time necessary to learn about and try out new approaches to teaching online.

References

Appel, C. and Mullen, T. (2000) Pedagogical considerations for a web-based tandem language learning environment. *Computers and Education* 34, 291–308.

Bax, S. (2003) CALL-past, present and future. *System* 31, 13–28.

Byram, M. (1997) *Teaching and Assessing Intercultural Communicative Competence*. Clevedon: Multilingual Matters.

Castells, M. (1996) The Rise of the Network Society. The Information Age: Economy, Society and Culture (Vol. I). Oxford, UK: Blackwell Publishers Ltd.

Computer Industry Almanac Inc. (2002) *USA Tops 160M Internet Users*. On WWW at http://www.c-i-a.com/pr1202.htm. Accessed 6.4.07.

Crystal D. (2001) *Language and the Internet*. Cambridge: Cambridge University Press.

Dutton, W., Cheong, P. and Park, N. (2004) The social shaping of a virtual learning environment: The case of a university-wide course management system. *The Electronic Journal of E-Learning* 2 (2). On WWW at http://www.ejel.org/volume-2/vol2-issue1/issue1-art3-dutton-cheong-park.pdf.

Egbert, J., Paulus, T. and Nakamichi, Y. (2002) The impact of CALL instruction on classroom computer use: A foundation for rethinking technology in teacher education. *Language Learning and Technology* 6 (3), 108–126. On WWW at http://llt.msu.edu/vol6num3/egbert/.

Franklin, S. and Peat, M. (2001) Managing change: The use of mixed delivery modes to increase learning opportunities. *Australian Journal of Educational Technology* 17 (1). On WWW at http://www.ascilite.org.au/ajet/ajet17/franklin.html.

Global Research (2004) On WWW at http://www.ge.com/research/. Accessed 6.4.07.

Hampel, R. and Hauck, M. (2004) Towards an effective use of audio conferencing in distance language courses. *Language Learning and Technology* 8 (1), 66–82.

Hanna, B. and de Nooy, J. (2003) A funny thing happened on the way to the forum: Electronic discussion and foreign language learning. *Language Learning and Technology* 7 (1), 71–85. On WWW at http://llt.msu.edu/vol7num1/hanna/default.html.

Haraway, D. (1991) *Simians, Cyborgs, and Women*. New York: Routledge.

Hawisher, G. and Selfe, C. (eds) (2000) *The Web, Literacy, and Identity: A Review of Global Literacies and the World-Wide Web*. London: Routledge.

Herring, S. (1996) Introduction. In S. Herring (ed.) *Computer-mediated Communication. Linguistic, Social and Cross-cultural Perspectives* (pp. 1–10). Amsterdam: John Benjamins Publishing Company.

Jeon-Ellis, G., Debski, R. and Wigglesworth, G. (2005) Oral interaction around computers in the project oriented CALL classroom. *Language Learning and Technology* 9 (3), 121–145.

Jones, S. (2002) The internet goes to college: How students are living in the future with today's technology. On WWW at http://www.pewinternet.org/report_display.asp?r=71. Accessed 6.4.07.

Kern, R. and Warschauer, M. (eds) (2000) *Network-based Language Teaching: Concepts and Practice*. Cambridge: Cambridge University Press.

Kern, R., Ware, P. and Warschauer, M. (2004) Crossing frontiers: New directions in on-line pedagogy and research. *Annual Review of Applied Linguistics* 24, 243–260.

Kim, J.K. and Bonk, C. (2002) Cross-cultural comparisons of on-line collaboration. *Journal of Computer-Mediated Communication* 8 (1). On WWW at http://www.ascusc.org/jcmc/vol8/issue1/kimandbonk.html.

Kramsch, C. and Thorne, S. (2002) Foreign language learning as global communicative practice. In D. Block and D. Cameron (eds) *Language Learning and Teaching in the Age of Globalization* (pp. 83–100). London: Routledge.

Lantolf, J. (ed.) (2000) *Sociocultural Theory and Second Language Learning*. Oxford: Oxford University Press.

Levy, M. and Stockwell, G. (2006) *CALL Dimensions: Options and Issues in Computer-assisted Language Learning*. Mahwah, NJ: Lawrence Erlbaum Associates.

Moodle (n.d.) On WWW at http://docs.moodle.org/en/Philosophy. Accessed 6.4.07.

Moore, N.A.J. (2002) Review of E-moderating – The key to teaching and learning on-line. *Language Learning and Technology* 6 (3), 21–24. On WWW at http://llt.msu.edu/vol6num3/review1/default.html.

Moser, H. (2000) *Einführung in die Medienpädagogik*. Opladen: Leske and Budrich.

Nunan, D. (1999) A foot in the world of ideas: Graduate study through the internet. *Language Learning and Technology* 3 (1), 52–74.

O'Dowd, R. (2006) Combining networked communication tools for students' ethnographic research. In J. Belz and S. Thorne (eds) *Computer-mediated Intercultural Foreign Language Education* (pp. 86–120). Boston, MA: Heinle and Heinle.

Parks, S., Huot, D., Hamers, J. and Lemonnier, F. (2003) Crossing boundaries: Multimedia technology and pedagogical innovation in a high school class. *Language Learning and Technology* 7 (1), 28–45. On WWW at: http://llt.msu.edu/vol7num1/parks/default.html.

Red.es (2006) XII Oleada 'Las TIC en los hogares españoles' (December 2006). On WWW at http://observatorio.red.es/estudios/documentos/informe_doce_oleada.pdf. Accessed 6.4.07.

Reeder, K., Macfadyen, L.P., Roche, J. and Chase, M. (2004) Negotiating culture in cyberspace: Participation patterns and problematics. *Language Learning and Technology* 8 (2), 88–105. On WWW at http://llt.msu.edu/vol8num2/reeder/default.html.

Reinhardt, J. and Nelson, B. (2004) Instructor use of on-line language learning resources: A survey of socio-institutional and motivational factors. *ReCALL* 16 (2), 280–292.

Salaberry, M. (1996) A theoretical foundation for the development of pedagogical tasks in computer mediated communication. *Calico Journal* 14 (1), 5–34.

Sayers, D. (1995) Language choice and global learning networks: The pitfall of Lingua Franca approaches to classroom telecomputing. *Educational Policy Analysis* 3 (10). On WWW at http://epaa.asu.edu/epaa/v3n10.html.

Shetzer, H. and Warschauer, M. (2000) An electronic literacy approach to network-based language teaching. In M. Warschauer and R. Kern (eds) *Network-based Language Teaching: Concepts and Practice* (pp. 171–185). New York: Cambridge University Press.

Sotillo, S.M. (2000) Discourse functions and syntactic complexity in synchronous and asynchronous communication. *Language Learning and Technology* 4 (1), 82–119.

Sproull, L. and Kiesler, S. (1991) *Connections: New Ways of Working in the Networked Organization*. Cambridge, MA: MIT Press.

Tella, S. and Mononen-Aaltonen, M. (1998) *Developing Dialogic Communication Culture in Media Education: Integrating Dialogism and Technology*. Helsinki: Media Education Publications.

Thorne, S. (2003) Artefacts and cultures-of-use in intercultural communication. *Language Learning and Technology* 7 (2), 38–67. On WWW at http://llt.msu.edu/vol7num2/thorne/.

Thorne, S. and Payne, J. (2005) Evolutionary trajectories, internet-mediated expression, and language education. *The CALICO Journal* 22 (3), 371–397.

Van Lier, L. (1996) *Interaction in the Language Curriculum*. London: Longman.

Vygotsky, L.S. (1978) *Mind in Society: The Development of Higher Psychological Processes*. Cambridge: Harvard University Press.

Warschauer, M. (1996) Comparing face-to-face and electronic discussion in the second language classroom. *CALICO Journal* 13 (2), 7–26.

Warschauer, M. (1997) Computer-mediated collaborative learning: Theory and practice. *Modern Language Journal* 81 (3), 470–481.

Warschauer, M. (1999) *Electronic Literacies. Language, Culture and Power in On-line*. New Jersey: Lawrence Erlbaum Associates.

Warschauer, M. (2002) Reconceptualizing the digital divide. *First Monday* 7 (7). On WWW at http://www.firstmonday.org/issues/issue7_7/warschauer/.

Warschauer, M. (2003) *Technology and equity: A comparative study*. Paper presented at the Annual Meeting of the American Educational Research Association, 24 April 2003, Chicago, IL.

Weasenforth, D., Biesenbach-Lucas, S. and Meloni, C. (2002) Realizing constructivist objectives through collaborative technologies: Threaded discussions. *Language Learning & Technology* 6 (3), 58–86. On WWW at http://llt.msu.edu/vol6num3/weasenforth/.

White, C (2003) *Language Learning in Distance Education*. Cambridge: Cambridge University Press.

Zemsky, R. and Massey, W. (2004) *Thwarted Innovation: What Happened to e-Learning and Why*. Pennsylvania: University of Pennsylvania.

Web pages referred to in Chapter 2

Google: http://www.google.com
MySpace: http://www.myspace.com/
YouTube: http://www.youtube.com/
Wikipedia: http://en.wikipedia.org/
Blogger: http://www.blogger.com/
Moodle: http://moodle.org/
Blackboard: http://www.blackboard.com/
WebCT: http://www.webct.com/

Part 2

Models of Online Intercultural Exchange

Chapter 3

Models of Telecollaboration (1): eTandem

BREFFNI O'ROURKE

Introduction

As the enormous importance of language and communication technologies in foreign language pedagogy is easily forgotten, it is instructive to bring to mind the language-learning experience of those who went to school as recently as 50 years ago. Let us put ourselves in the shoes, for example, of a Dublin secondary school student learning French as one of her state Leaving Certificate subjects in 1958. She has had five or six years of instruction, with primary emphasis on the explicit learning of grammar. She has practised translation into and from French, and in the final two-year cycle before the all-important state examination, she has read the mountaineering novel *Premier de cordée*, perhaps learning passages from it by heart. This typical pupil has never visited France – and neither, quite possibly, has her teacher. She has never met a native speaker of French. It is quite possible that she will sit, and pass – maybe even pass handsomely – her Leaving Certificate French examination without ever having heard the sound of French spoken as a mother tongue. Should such a young woman subsequently find herself in France, perhaps living with a French family while minding their children, we can easily imagine the sense of overwhelming disorientation she must surely feel in her first experience of real people actually chatting, arguing, joking – chaotically, fluently, above all incomprehensibly – in a language that in school seemed to have all the vitality and contemporary relevance of Classical Greek.

Tape recorders promised to change such austere language-learning experiences beyond recognition. But if the advent of affordable audio recording and playback technology ought, from today's perspective, to have heralded a classroom revolution, the revolution was initially side-tracked by the duties imposed on the machines by the prevailing pedagogical model. The audio-lingual method predated the widespread availability of tape recorders, and the new and – in hindsight –

revolutionary technology had to fall in with it. As deployed in the audio-lingual method, the native-speaker voices that finally echoed through language classrooms were nothing like those to be heard in target-language communities. Their utterances were drained of all personal meaning and of virtually all cultural meaning and served up in dry, unappetising slices, packaged as structure drills. Though it was technically true that native-speaker voices were being heard for the first time – and on the level of form and phonology, this was of course a significant advance – recordings used in this way were poor, two-dimensional representations of the vibrant reality of personal and social expression.

The point is that whatever a new technology appears to promise, it does not bring about worthwhile pedagogical innovation in and of itself. That is not to deny the ultimate impact of technologies: rather, it is to say that they may make their presence felt in more subtle but very significant ways, by pointing to new possibilities and opening up new avenues, whether or not teachers feel ready to avail of them. Thus, though there are many well-known reasons why the communicative approach came to dominate thinking and practice, it seems likely that the very availability of audio and video technologies, and their potential to mediate authentic, meaningful language-in-use, was vital in stimulating consideration of the roles of authenticity and meaningful input in learning once the ideological climate was propitious.

The same is likely to be true of computer-mediated communication (CMC). There is no denying its enormous potential (after all, prior to the internet it was impossible to facilitate regular, fast, streamlined interaction between foreign language learners and native speakers), but its full effects on our pedagogical frame of reference may not yet have been fully felt. If CMC has yet to be widely adopted in the classroom, it is perhaps because the dominant pedagogical environment is not currently suited to its full exploitation.

The model of telecollaboration dealt with in this chapter, tandem language learning, is one that is underpinned by a particular view of pedagogy, that of learner autonomy. In view of the foregoing observations, one could argue either that tandem learning over the internet is likely to succeed best in classroom and institutional environments that already value autonomy, or that tandem learning might have a kind of washback effect on the practices of teachers, encouraging them to be more sensitive to the need to yield responsibility to learners. Whatever the case may be, I hope to show that Tandem learning has the potential to make native speaker voices a central part of the language learning experience – where 'voice' is to be understood as a metonym both of the target language as authentically used, and of the expression of personal and cultural meanings.

Origins and Theoretical Underpinnings

History

At its simplest, tandem learning means reciprocal support and instruction between two learners, each of whom is a native speaker of the other's target language, be it through face-to-face or any other mode of communication. In this broad sense tandem learning has likely existed in informal arrangements since people first sought to learn foreign languages. Tandem learning was thus not originally a theoretically driven *method* so much as a widespread *practice*, independently 'discovered' many times over by individuals wishing to learn the language of an acquaintance and prepared to offer their own native-speaker expertise in return. When such a learning opportunity presents itself, the self-evident possibilities that open up are likely to override whatever convictions one might have about how languages are best learned. What committed learner would turn down the chance to try out, on a regular basis, his or her developing language skills on a native speaker, particularly if the native speaker is willing to provide explicit guidance, correction and support?

If this kind of more or less ad hoc arrangement was practised long before it was given the name 'tandem', though, what is a recent development is the theorisation and systematic exploitation of tandem as an open learning method. Brammerts (1996) cites a number of precursors to later initiatives which provided experience of tandem learning in diverse contexts: French–German youth meetings of the late 1960s, partnerships in the 1980s between tourists and native speakers and between university students, and tandem training courses for professional peers resident in different countries. The earliest publications referring to tandem by that name appeared in the early 1980s (Wolff, 1982a,b), and the Language Learning in Tandem Bibliography (Brammerts, 2003) shows that tandem learning continued to be an active field through the 1980s and early 1990s.

But it was in 1992 that tandem learning was first attempted over the internet, and from these seeds grew funded projects that sought to promulgate the idea of tandem learning, to set out its fundamental principles and explore its potential, and to provide practical support and resources for individual and institutionally based Tandem partnerships. In that year the Ruhr-Universität Bochum and the University of Rhode Island set up an e-mail forum called RIBO-L and arranged individual student e-mail partnerships (Brammerts, 1996) for their students. Following this

Bochum instituted the International E-Mail Tandem Network, later called the International Tandem Network, in partnership with the universities of Sheffield and Oviedo. The Network, which was founded with the support of the European Commission, established a number of bilingual 'subnets' and a service for finding Tandem partners (initially called the Tandem Dating Agency, now simply the Tandem Agency). A follow-on project, also EU-funded, was called eTandem Europa; eTandem is becoming established as a standard term for internet-based forms of tandem (e.g. Cziko, 2004).

Theoretical underpinnings

We have seen that what came to be known as tandem learning had historically been an ad hoc, opportunistic practice; but the goal of firmly establishing, further developing and widely disseminating tandem as a powerful learning tool required that its hitherto implicit, unanalysed theoretical roots be exposed and carefully explored. Open learning of all kinds are based on the premise that learners can take control of and responsibility for their own learning; and this is the fundamental insight of learner autonomy (Holec, 1981; Little, 1991), the educational theory that has become a central plank in contemporary discussions of tandem learning. Learner autonomy – which is not to be confused with self-access or self-directed learning – proceeds from the claim that autonomy, defined as 'a *capacity* – for detachment, critical reflection, decision-making, and independent action' (Little, 1991: 4), is the hallmark of successful learning processes and of successful learning outcomes. This means that autonomous learners are able to operate on the metacognitive level to regulate both their own learning processes (cognitively, organisationally, etc.) and the use of target skills and knowledge outside the classroom. In language learning, this of course means a developing capacity to think analytically about language itself, and about the target language in particular, both in learning and in using it. This in turn implies an important role for written language, a point to which we shall return below.

But learner autonomy is not a kind of radical individualism that sees no role for teacher guidance or peer collaboration. First, it is worth stressing again that autonomy is best thought of as a capacity, or as a goal to be pursued, rather than as a behaviour or a permanent, steady state (Little, 1991: 3–4). Learners do not become autonomous automatically, especially those who have been acculturated to a transmission model of education – i.e. teaching as simple transfer of knowledge from one mind to another. Teachers must prepare the ground for autonomous modes of working and encourage the development of reflective patterns of thought in their learners. Second, all human behaviour based on higher mental functions takes place within a social context, in obvious ways (interaction and collaboration with others) and less obvious ways (thinking and acting are mediated by the symbolic, linguistic and physical tools given to us by our society and culture; Vygotsky, 1986). Finally, reflective, critical and analytical attitudes are often fostered by collaborative activity, in which private thoughts are made explicit – and thus more easily available for critical inspection – and modified in conversation with peers (Mercer, 2000).

The making explicit of thought is in fact a key mechanism in the pursuit of autonomy. Critical reflection is possible only where there is distancing, and distancing from one's own thoughts is made much easier when thoughts are externalised through language. And so we return to the question of metalinguistic awareness in language learning itself, where we can see that the same argument applies: it is easier to reflect on language when we are distanced from it, something that is not easily accomplished in speech. This and similar considerations have led Little (1997; 1999a, b) to argue that writing should be central to any autonomy-focussed pedagogy, since it acts as a focus for metalinguistic reflection. Indeed, it has been cogently argued by, among others, David Olson, that it was only upon the invention of writing that it became possible to bring language to consciousness in the first place (Olson, 1994a, b; 1995). He argues that the same is true of individuals: children learn to perceive language through the prism of writing, rather than coming to the learning of writing pre-equipped with metalinguistic skills (Olson, 1995). Furthermore, it seems possible, and it has certainly frequently been argued (e.g. Kitade, 2000; Ortega, 1997; Pellettieri, 2000; Smith *et al.*, 2003; Tudini, 2003), that synchronous text-based communication (chat, Instant Messenger and similar applications) affords increased chances of attention to linguistic form in the course of primarily meaning-focussed interaction. This possible effect of the electronic written medium of much CMC has further encouraged experiments and research in online tandem learning.

To summarise, tandem language learning is not a model derived from a theory, but a long-standing practice whose usefulness has been recognised by many generations of language learners. What recent years have given us is a range of related initiatives that have unified research around the 'tandem' label and around the pedagogical perspective of learner autonomy. The advent of the internet has given further impetus to this kind of telecollaboration, mainly because it has made finding and communicating with partners incomparably easier, but in part too because of the hypothesised potential of the written medium to promote reflection on language form.

Principles

Successful tandem learning is founded on two principles: the principle of reciprocity and the principle of learner autonomy. We have already considered what learner autonomy means in general, but what precisely does it mean in relation to tandem learning? In considering this we must bear in mind that tandem is a form of open learning, and that, in contrast to the Cultura model (see Suárez & Crapotta, this volume), it does not prescribe a particular structure, or even imply any particular conversational content. Thus, tandem learners typically have a great deal of freedom to decide what to talk about, in what depth, when to talk about it, what other tasks or activities they might wish to engage in, what kind of language feedback or error correction they wish to give and receive, and so on. The successful establishment and continuation of a tandem partnership will therefore demand considerable self-awareness. Learner autonomy in this context means that learners must decide on, and be clear about, their goals and their preferred means for achieving them. In order to sustain the learning focus, they must also monitor and evaluate both objectives and means, being prepared to alter both in the light of experience. Brammerts (1996: 11) points out that this level of learning awareness is all the more important in tandem learning, as it is rare that both partners share precisely the same objectives and preferred way of working, and it would be easy for partners to slip into a compromise habit of working that meets the expectations of neither.

Thus autonomy in Tandem learning interacts with the principle of reciprocity, i.e.

> the reciprocal dependence and mutual support of the partners; both partners should contribute equally to their work together and benefit to the same extent. Learners should be prepared and able to do as much for their partner as they themselves expect from their partner. They should not only dedicate the same amount of time to each language: they should also invest the same amount of energy in preparation, in the interest they show in the learning success of their partner, and in their concern for their partner's success in speaking and understanding their language. (Brammerts, 1996: 11)

Reciprocity is the particular strength of tandem learning: each partner at different times takes the role of learner and of expert, so that both sides of the learning process are constantly in focus. Indeed, research by Appel (1999) found that some tandem learners felt they benefited as much from taking the role of native-speaker expert and assisting their partner as they did from their work in the role of learner. This is because explaining points of language and usage to the partner involves verbalising and thus making explicit what is otherwise unanalysed, intuitive knowledge. Tandem work thus has the potential to raise learners' general sensitivity to language. Beyond considerations of metalinguistic awareness, of course, affective and interpersonal issues also loom large in tandem partnerships. To remain effective and satisfying, a tandem partnership will need to negotiate matters of 'face' (Brown & Levinson, 1987) – i.e. communicative incidents, some trivial, some less so, that have the potential to impinge upon self-esteem and mutual respect – and to manage frustration and maximise motivation. These can be tricky areas, and of course there will be considerable variation across individuals and across tandem pairs. But the nature of the tandem learning situation inherently mitigates threats to 'face' and to motivation, to some degree at least: both partners are in the same boat, facing similar, if not identical, challenges in communicating in their target languages. They are thus more likely, on average, to display understanding of their partner's difficulties and concerns.

I have been using the terms learner and expert in relation to the roles that each partner takes at different points in Tandem interaction, though the implications of the term 'expert' need to be examined carefully. Clearly the term 'teacher' in relation to the role of the partner using his or her native language at a given moment is inappropriate: the native-speaker partner is meant to be a source of meaningful and well-formed target language data, and also a source of metalinguistic insight into the nature of his/her language in various general aspects and in relation to particular usages (vocabulary, multi-word units, structures, slang, etc.). But although increased consciousness of language, one's own and that of one's partner, is supposed to be one of the benefits of tandem, (a) a high level of general awareness cannot be presupposed from the very outset, and (b) we cannot presume that in the specific explanations they offer their partners, native speakers will be either strictly or, in some cases, even approximately accurate, or precise enough to be useful. Consider Example (1), an extract from the Trinity College Dublin–Ruhr-Universität Bochum e-mail tandem project reported in Little *et al.* (1999):[1]

(1) **GE1:** I have done a Physics test last week. It was no good.

    IR1: [*correcting the above*]**:** I [have done] (did – I think it's because you put a time in the sentence. Usually you don't put the past perfect and a time clause together. I only just noticed that!) a Physics test last week.

The Irish partner's correction is inaccurate at the level of metalinguistic labelling: the structure is present perfect, not past perfect, and 'last week' is an adverb phrase, not a clause. However, whether or not the German partner is familiar with these grammatical terms and spots the mistakes, the essential point should be clear enough. The rule of thumb given is quite a robust one, though it overgeneralises a little: temporal adverbs like 'all day' can modify clauses with perfect aspect. The next example, also from IR-GE-mail, is a generalisation about the German partner's errors that is surely too vague to be of much use to him:

(2) **IR4:**   Is the way I corrected your (very few) mistakes alright with you? The only general comment I can add is that your tenses are a bit mixed up.

This generalisation is not quite as vague as it seems, as it follows seven specific corrections/reformulations, but in fact only one of these corrects an error of tense.

The point is that native-speaker 'expertise' is just the implicit competence of someone who normally speaks their language unreflectingly; it is not the analytical expertise of the language teacher or linguist. Native speakers can usually be relied on to make reliable judgements as to grammaticality and idiomaticity; generalised explanations for these judgements are likely to be considerably less trustworthy. This is not to say, though, that metalinguistic discourse that attempts to reach a level of generality is not useful. In making language the content of discourse, such discourse is apt to raise the partners' shared level of metalinguistic awareness, and in the course of a partnership which may last months (or in principle even years), learners can negotiate, explicitly or implicitly, the depth of analysis that they find most useful, from vague generalisations like (2) to precise points of grammar like (1). It is doubtful whether grammatical explanations, accurate or not, are likely to 'stick' in precisely the form in which they are expressed. The benefit is more likely to be in the cumulatively acquired habit of thinking about and analysing language form.

One important precept that falls out of the principle of reciprocity is that of language balance: for both partners to have a reasonable expectation of profiting equally, communication should normally be divided evenly between the two languages. What this means in practice will depend on the means of communication: in face-to-face tandem, each meeting can simply be split between the two. In e-mail, on the other hand, as time is not a factor, it is simplest to devote half of each e-mail to each language. In synchronous CMC (SCMC) modes, matters can be more complicated. Differences in proficiency can lead to considerable differences in the amount of language produced per minute; a simple 50–50 time split can result in a gap between the actual amount of one language produced compared to the other. A further and more significant threat to language balance in SCMC is the 'lingua franca effect' (O'Rourke, 2002; 2005; Schwienhorst & Borgia, 2006), in which partners drift into the habit of using the target language of the more L2-proficient learner. We shall return to this in 'Strengths and Weaknesses'.

In short, the important difference between tandem learning and other less theoretically grounded forms of one-to-one telecollaboration lies in learner attitude and conduct, and specifically in the constant, explicit presence of a language-learning focus. This kind of focus, if maintained, means critical monitoring of the learning processes and outcomes and continuous reflection on language – the latter in particular being facilitated by text-based modes of communication.

The Tandem Model in Practice

Organisational choices

Tandem learning can be employed in a wide range of institutional and pedagogical situations. We have seen that, historically, tandem arrangements were typically an initiative of individual learners rather than teachers; the internet generally, and the Tandem Agency in particular, have made this kind of one-to-one arrangement much more accessible. The kind of arrangement that I will focus on, though, is one in which there is some degree of involvement by teachers. There is a continuum of degrees of integration of tandem into a language course. At the least integrated end, a teacher may simply recommend to students that they find a tandem partner and point them in the direction of the Tandem Agency or some similar clearing-house; or, somewhat more supportively, a teacher may devote class time to introducing learners to the concept of tandem learning, encourage them to find partners, and perhaps act as a kind of tandem consultant or advisor, helping students at their initiative when they run into linguistic or interpersonal difficulties. These kinds of arrangement are unlikely to meet with consistent success: the tandem partnership is unlikely ever to be seen as a priority, initial enthusiasm (if any) will flag unless initial communications are highly engaging, and partnerships may quickly find themselves becalmed.

For reasons like this, it is usually more fruitful to incorporate tandem more tightly into classroom work. Integration implies in the first place a specific role for tandem activities within an existing course: for example, learners may be asked to draw on their partners' cultural knowledge in researching aspects of target-language society and culture in group or class projects (Little *et al.*, 1999), to draw on their partner's native-speaker intuitions in researching points of language, or to have their partners reformulate draft texts of one kind or another in more idiomatic language. In such cases it might be found necessary to have learners submit e-mails or chat logs as evidence of their active participation in tandem. This is of course not wholly desirable: students are rarely pleased to feel monitored, as the following extracts suggest:

(3) **GE10:** Den beiden 'Big-Brothers' frohes Gelingen bei der Aus-
      wertung unserer Post.
      PS: Man fühlt sich schon irgendwie beobachtet
      *Every success to the two 'Big Brothers' [the organisers, one
      on each side of the exchange] in their evaluation of our
      correspondence*
      PS: You do feel watched somehow.

[From IR-GE-mail].

Similar concerns arose in a synchronous (MOO) exchange in which session logs were automatically 'harvested'. (A MOO is a text-based virtual environment with a wide range of functionality; however, for present purposes it can be considered a kind of chat program.) Each user 'transmission' is automatically prefixed with the phrase '[username] says, ', and some users break their 'utterances' over two or more lines, as in this example.

(4) GE17 says, 'as this communication is watches (big brother!!!!)'.
      GE17 says, 'i will send you an email to tell you something ...'

Such monitoring may well inhibit the character of communication and thus the development of interpersonal relations between the partners. This can be mitigated somewhat by requiring students to submit only a specified number of messages or logs, which they are free to select, and perhaps also to edit.

Integration of this kind is likely to be feasible only where the teacher and students can be reasonably confident of a similar level of commitment from the partners on the 'other side', which is rarely the case when each student finds his or her own partner separately. For this reason, group partnerships offer the best prospect of stability over the course of a tandem project. Groups that are matched as closely as possible in terms of proficiency level, age, interests, expectations, etc., are on average more likely to produce effective and stable tandem partnerships. Beyond these learner variables, though, the exchange organisers – normally the teachers – have themselves a great deal of preparatory collaborative work to do before launching the partnership. For reciprocity at the tandem-pair level to be meaningful, both partners should be engaged in the enterprise for more or less the same reasons; if the partners are not motivated by similar considerations and incentives, then any perceived discrepancy in effort between partners will be felt all the more keenly. This means that the way the tandem exchange is integrated into the course on each side – whether it is compulsory, whether there is a required level of participation or of message length, whether participation carries marks, whether tandem messages are submitted as required coursework, and so on – needs to be matched as far as institutional constraints will allow. Naturally, the content of the tandem exchange needs to be agreed between the organisers. In many cases it will be appropriate to set particular tasks which may be linked to classroom activities; for example, researching a classroom project with the help of the partner, preparing a report on an aspect of life in the partner's community, or reformulating a text more idiomatically in the target language. Alternatively, a menu of activities can be provided, from which each pair chooses the particular activities they wish to pursue and the order in which they wish to pursue them. In such a menu, however, some kind of preliminary task to assist learners in getting to know each other is often useful as a warm-up. Whether this kind of guided approach is taken or whether it is left up to the learners to determine the content, plenty of time and space should be left for learners to converse freely. It would dilute the essential character of tandem to specify how they are to spend their time beyond a certain point.

As the nature of tandem learning demands learning awareness and self-management skills, and may in some cases involve the use of CMC systems that are unfamiliar to students, it will usually be important to provide at least one introductory session. Matters that should be addressed include the principles of reciprocity and autonomy, stressing in particular the need for partners to negotiate working methods and approaches to linguistic feedback; how the project relates to the course in which it is embedded (marking, coursework, frequency of communication, etc.); and technical details of the CMC system to be used.

A further choice that needs to be made is how to match students with each other. If matching students by variables such as interest, sex and age is seen as a priority, then teachers might pair students on the basis of brief personal sketches submitted by the students. Alternatively, one side might submit personal sketches while the other side gets to pick their partners; this has been done in the past, but it is rather reminiscent of a 'marriage market' in which there are winners and losers; and on what principled basis does one choose which learners 'sell themselves' and which side gets to choose? Particular difficulties arise when the group sizes do not match; this will be further discussed in 'Strengths and Weaknesses'. It may be considered best in the final analysis to match learners randomly.

Choice of communication mode

Of the various kinds of communication channel, I will focus on just two categories: asynchronous e-mail and synchronous text-based CMC. The latter category encompasses a number of types of program (notably Instant Messenger, chat, MOOs), but I will assume that they have enough in common for present purposes to be treated as a single category.

The choice between synchronous and asynchronous modes is likely to be determined in large part by practical considerations. Unless they are confident that their students have the time, technical resources and discipline to engage in synchronous tandem sessions in their own time, organisers are likely to want to integrate tandem activity into timetabled class sessions, which means that one class hour must be shared between both sides, taking account of any time-zone differences. In addition, of course, a computer suite must be available at that time on each side of the exchange. If this choreography proves too complex, then asynchronous communication – usually e-mail – is the only option.

But assuming that the teachers have the luxury of choice, then a number of issues will have to be factored in to the decision. Choice of mode will affect the kinds of activities that learners can engage in, perhaps the nature of the relationships that emerge, and certainly the kind of language used, the way in which it is processed, and the way in which language itself comes into focus in the course of interaction. The remainder of this section will focus on the metalinguistic implications of CMC modes.

The potential benefits of text-based CMC derive from two properties: short-term retrospective availability and long-term retrospective availability. Long-term availability – or 'archivability' – refers to the fact that, in contrast to oral communication, a textual record of individual contributions or entire interactions is available for inspection after the interaction is over. This allows the learner, at his leisure, to reflect on whichever aspects of the dialogue or language are of interest to him. This is a property of both synchronous and asynchronous communication, assuming that there is a mechanism for storing the output of the synchronous system in question. On the other hand, short-term avail-ability – perhaps better termed 'real-time visibility' – means the visibility of the dialogue and linguistic units within the dialogue while the dialogue is still taking place. Real-time visibility allows the conversational partici-pant (i) to review and perhaps revise his own productions before actually 'uttering' them by pressing the Enter key; (ii) to critically monitor his own output after uttering by re-reading what he has typed after hitting the Enter key; and (iii) to review and perhaps recycle his (conversational) partner's utterances by looking back in the dialogue, by scrolling if necessary. The benefits entailed by these two properties are of course of two very different kinds from the point of view of linguistic processing. The learning benefits of real-time visibility are a matter of real-time processing under pressure of time and attentional resources, requiring a rapid switching back and forth between the short-term communicative goal (the need or desire to convey a particular meaning at a particular moment) and momentary concern with linguistic form. The learning benefits of archivability derive from the ability to reflect – *without* immediate pressure – on linguistic form, either in itself or as it relates to communicative purpose.

The asynchronous mode of e-mail brings with it three advantages in particular. First, learners can take their time over the drafting of their own messages, revising them, incorporating responses to their partner's conversational initiatives, and perhaps drawing on linguistic reference resources and teachers' or peers' expertise before sending. Second, they are not under urgent pressure to respond to e-mails, so that they have time to make sense of their partners' messages; ideally, they should examine them linguistically as well as for content, perhaps copying and pasting unfamiliar features into a note-file. Third, they can give corrective feedback to their partners that is as broad (covering several points) and/or as deep (detailed) as desired.

In contrast to the asynchronous mode, synchronous CMC (SCMC) proceeds under immediate pressure of time. Individual contributions to a chat-style interaction may be less carefully crafted, less linguistically diverse, and metalinguistically less penetrating. On the other hand, unlike e-mail, SCMC shares with face-to-face communication the fact that discourse is collaboratively constructed. Partners co-construct meaning and negotiate content and tone; each utterance is contingent on nearby utterances. This commonplace proposition is sometimes misconstrued as a Pollyanna-like assertion that conversational interlo-cutors are always agreeable towards one another. This is clearly not the case. The point is that all kinds of talk must respect certain implicit and shared conversational rules if it is not to lead to bewilderment (instead of the desired provocation, or solidarity, or amusement, etc. Even hostile talk, if it is to work as hostility, must be implicitly cooperative. It is in this less obvious sense that interlocutors negotiate meaning, topic, face-threatening acts, etc.). In this situation, error correction will typically be sporadic and superficial. But a different kind of metalinguistic focus emerges: as in face-to-face communication, partners must manoeuvre their way around communication difficulties in order for communication to succeed. Interactionist theory (e.g. Gass, 1998; Gass & Varonis, 1985; Long, 1983; Pica, 1994; Swain, 1995; Swain & Lapkin, 1995) has it that these episodes of 'negotiation of meaning' lead to a focus on linguistic form *in the course of* expressing meaning, rather than separately from meaning.

The following examples – the first from IR-GE-mail, the second from IR-GE-chat, give a sense of the differences between the negotiation of cultural and lexical meaning in the two modes:

(5) **IR1** (*27 November*): [...] I'd better go now, I've just finished training for the evening and am about to toddle off home for the night. (I play camogie and do Karate after college, by the way) [...].

　　GE1 (*1 December*): [...] Da ich gerade bei den Fragen bin, was ist 'camogie'.
　　　　[...] *While I'm asking questions, what is 'camogie'.*

　　IR1 (*3 December*): [...] Camogie ist eine Irische Sport, wo viele Leute laufen in einen Sportplatz mit Schläger ('hurleys') um ein kleines Ball ('sliotar' – das spricht sich 'shlither' aus. Es ist ein Irisches wort.) zwischen ein Tor zu schlagen. Das ist ähnlich zu shinty (Schottisch) oder veilleicht, (einige sag' es aber ich glaube es nicht) wie Hockey. Camogie ist ein 'mädchen's' sport, weil die Männer spielen Hurling. Hurling und Camogie sind die gleiche, aber, Hurling ist, normal-erweise schneller als Camogie. Die beiden sind gefährlich ab und zu, aber. [...]

　　　　[...] *Camogie is an Irish sport where a lot of people run around on a playing field with bats ('hurleys') to hit a small ball ('sliotar' – that's pronounced 'shlither'. It's an Irish word.) into a goal. It's similar to shinty (Scottish) or maybe, (some say but I don't believe it) like hockey. Camogie is a 'girl's' sport, because men play hurling.*

> *Hurling and camogie are the same, but hurling is normally faster than camogie. Both are dangerous now and then, though. [...]*

(6)   IR4 says, 'how was my German?'
         [...]
         GE33 says, 'hmmmmm it was what we call *holprig*'
         IR4 says, 'holprig?'
         [...]
         GE33 says, 'let me see... it was not fluently to read, and many different mistakes..... mostly concerning the verbs'
         IR4 says, 'holpring means all that?:)'
         GE33 says, 'holprig is a road, with many holes and hills... so you cannot drive without stopping'
         IR4 says, 'here in Ireland, we call it a "boreen"'
         GE33 says, 'ah, and something is boreened ...?'
         IR4 says, 'no it's not a verb. just a road.'
         GE33 says, ' ahhhh i understand:)'

In both cases what is at issue is the meaning of certain words (Irish English *camogie* and *boreen*, German *holprig*). In the case of the e-mail exchange the word *camogie* is addressed in a highly structured way across three successive e-mails: IR1 uses the word in context, GE1 asks what it means, IR1 explains at some length, and the topic ends without further formalities. The synchronous exchange is more complex, and the fact that the problem word (*holprig*, 'bumpy, clumsy, jerky') is negotiated between the participants means that that explanations are briefer, additional communicative difficulties arise, and in negotiating these difficulties a further question of word meaning (this time Irish-English) comes into play (*boreen*, a small country road, usually of poor quality).

Focus on language is manifested in e-mail tandem primarily as error correction, which may take the form of a specific reformulation either without elaboration (Example 7), or accompanied by an explanatory generalisation about the language system or lexicon (8), or accompanied by generalised feedback about the learner's interlanguage (9):

(7)   *GE6 quotes IR6 and reformulates:.*
         > Es tut mir furchtbar leid, daß ich nicht für so lange schreiben habe.
         I'm terribly sorry that I haven't written for so long [subordinate clause grammatically incorrect]
         ..., daß ich so lange nicht geschrieben habe.
         [provides grammatically correct version of subordinate clause]

(8) **GE3:** I did not really understand the meaning of the sentence 'Ich lerne seit 6 Jahren Deutsch, aber habe schlechte Verstandnis von der Sprache!' [. . .] Im Deutschen wird Verständnis nicht direkt als Substantiv von verstehen benutzt. Dies wäre eher 'das Verstehen'. 'Verstehen' ist etwas globales. Ein schlechtes Sprachverständnis hat jemand, der Sprachen schlecht lernt, der unbegabt ist.

I did not really understand the meaning of the sentence 'Ich lerne seit 6 Jahren Deutsch, aber habe schlechte Verstandnis von der Sprache!' *[. . .] In German* Verständnis *[understanding] isn't really used as the noun of* verstehen *[to understand]. That would really be* 'das Verstehen'. 'Verstehen' *is something global.* Ein schlechtes Sprachverständnis *is said of someone who is bad at learning languages, who isn't talented.*

(9) **GE12:** Mir fällt auf, daß Du manchmal falsche Artikel verwendest. *I notice that you sometimes get articles wrong*

Synchronous CMC may also have explicit feedback and correction, but the kind of linguistic episode that predominates is in fact 'negotiation of meaning', in which comprehension difficulties arise and are repaired jointly:

(10)   IR17 says, 'o god, ich kann nicht [*]kontresiert'
         IR17 says, 'o god, I can't kontresiert'
         GE17 says, 'hä????????????????????????????'
         IR17 says, 'he he'
         IR17 says, 'how do you say concentrate?'
         GE17 says, 'konzentrieren'
         IR17 says, 'that is what I meant'
         GE17 says, 'na gut'
         GE17 *says, 'right then'*
         IR17 says, 'ich kann nicht konzentrieren'

One notable aspect of negotiation in SCMC is that nearly all instances focus on meaning, at either the word or the utterance level, and rarely on idiom, morphosyntax or pragmatics (O'Rourke, 2005). There are instances too of other kinds of language-related episode, such as self-repair, and spontaneous and elicited correction (i.e. where communication has not failed). The use of spontaneous correction in particular needs to be a matter of agreement between partners; if done too much, it can cause the corrected partner to lose face:

(11) IR12 says, 'Okay. You're making me feel very insecure with all
those corrections'
IR12 grins
GE12 say, 'ohoh'
GE12 blush[es]
GE12 says, 'well'
IR12 says, 'I'm sure your concern is genuine'

The character of a tandem project is thus determined by a number of
fundamental choices that must be thought through carefully. In particular, although the mere fact that learners have the opportunity to
communicate more or less freely with native speakers of their target
language brings its own rewards, it is important to keep in mind the kind
of language input that learners will be exposed to and the ways in which
the communications medium will enable them to process it.

Strengths and Weaknesses of Online Tandem Learning

In setting up learning partnerships between people who are previously unacquainted with one another, success is far from guaranteed.
For example, partners may not share the same level of enthusiasm or
commitment, or the same interests, or the same sense of humour. The risk
that these will become issues that might lead ultimately to the failure of a
tandem partnership can be minimised through the kind of organisational
precautions discussed in 'Organisational choices'; in particular, by
ensuring that there are incentives on both sides for the partnership to
succeed. Naturally, one cannot legislate for the vagaries of human
relationships, but having conceded that, one must also recognise that
not all problems are reducible to individual factors or the dynamics of
individual partnerships. Common causes of failure – from individual,
through classroom, to institutional factors – are closely analysed and
categorised by O'Dowd and Ritter (2006). The following discussion
focuses on some of the vulnerabilities arising specifically from the
tandem configuration.

At the organisational level, one variable that can cause particular
difficulties is mismatch in group size. It will rarely be possible to match
learners one-to-one with no learners left over on one side. If partners
have been selected by their peers rather than randomly assigned by
teachers, then being one of the 'left-overs' is surely not an agreeable
feeling; and in any case, the question arises of what precisely to do with
unmatched learners. One solution to this is to use groups of three or
more as necessary; this is likely to assure more lively and sustained

interaction, but it infringes the basic one-to-one assumption of tandem learning. One consequence might be that less confident or less proficient learners might find themselves marginalised within their group. It might also be the case that a fifty–fifty language split is harder to sustain in a small group than in a pair. In the case of non-compulsory courses, student drop-out on one side can also lead to a mismatch in numbers, with some learners on one side of an institutional partnership left high and dry. Considerations such as these underline the need for careful institutional planning and sustained cooperation between organisers, not to mention contingency planning for the event that some partnerships fail for one reason or another.

There are also various linguistic issues that can work against the success of tandem. One is the implications of a mismatch in proficiency. This can lead to what I have called a 'lingua franca effect' (O'Rourke, 2002; 2005): if the Italian partner can communicate more fluently in Czech than the Czech partner can in Italian, then it is quite likely that Czech will come to be the pair's effective lingua franca, with the result that the Czech partner benefits considerably less than the Italian partner. This is a risk particularly in synchronous interactions, where the need to keep communication flowing takes priority over considerations of linguistic accuracy and pedagogy, and where it is not as easy to keep track of the relative proportions of each language being used. A software tool called the Bilingual Tandem Analyser has been developed that analyses MOO logs and reports to users on language balance, which is intended to keep the issue in the foreground and allow corrective action to be taken if necessary (Schwienhorst & Borgia, 2006). This tool was based on a similar system developed for a web-based tandem toolkit called Electronic Tandem Resources (Appel & Mullen, 2000). Aside from such tools, maintaining language balance in spite of mismatches of proficiency is a matter for awareness-raising on the part of teachers and autonomy on the part of learners.

Two further linguistic factors need to be mentioned. First, as codeswitching is always a viable communication strategy in tandem (and is certainly pervasive in SCMC; O'Rourke, 2002), it may be that there is less perceived need, vis-à-vis typical native speaker/non-native speaker situations, to produce comprehensible output – i.e. to produce language that is as grammatical and idiomatic as possible (Swain, 1985; 1995; Swain & Lapkin, 1995). Second, Crystal (2001) points to 'the constraining effects of multi-person interaction on language, such as shorter sentence length and uncertain turn-taking' and argues that utterances in synchronous environments 'represent only a small part of the grammatical repertoire of a language'. This consideration may become increasingly pertinent as Instant Messenger interaction continues to grow and abbreviating linguistic and discourse conventions becomes more firmly established.

These vulnerabilities all arise to one extent or another from the openness of tandem learning by comparison with a prescribed-lesson model like Cultura; but that openness is also its central philosophy, and the source of its strengths. Tandem learners may grow into a sense of their control over their own learning, which may positively affect their attitude towards language learning beyond the Tandem exchange. A successful partnership can be enjoyable and intellectually stimulating, and inculcate a readiness to take risks in communicating in the target language. It can also increase a learner's general sensitivity to the way language in general works, and how the target language in particular works, while also yielding insights into the partner's culture. These are all enormous boons to the learner in the foreign-language classroom in particular, where such access to the target language and its speakers cannot otherwise be taken for granted. Not least, experience shows that tandem learning can lead to friendships that transcend language-learning. In short, tandem at its best offers a uniquely vibrant, engaging, open and authentic interaction with individual native speakers as representatives of their culture, of a kind that technologies have otherwise failed to deliver. The work that tandem demands of teachers and students alike in setting up an exchange and keeping it on track is more than compensated for by the rewards that it can deliver.

Note

1. This project will be referred to as IR-GE-Mail. Partners are designated by their country of residence and the numerical designator given to their partnership in the data; hence, GE1 = tandem pair number 1, German partner; IR1 = tandem pair number 1, Irish partner. The students were not necessarily German or Irish by nationality, but 'German' and 'Irish' will be used for convenience.

References

Appel, C. (1999) *Tandem language learning by e-mail: Some basic principles and a case study* (CLCS Occasional Paper no. 54): Dublin: Trinity College Dublin.

Appel, C. and Mullen, T. (2000) Pedagogical considerations for a web-based tandem language learning environment. *Computers and Education* 34, 291–308.

Brammerts, H. (1996) Tandem language learning via the Internet and the International E-Mail Tandem Network. In D. Little and H. Brammerts (eds)

A guide to language learning in tandem via the internet (pp. 9–22). CLCS Occasional Paper no. 46. Dublin: Trinity College Dublin.

Brammerts, H. (2003) *Language Learning in Tandem Bibliography*. 13 October. On WWW at http://www.slf.ruhr-uni-bochum.de/learning/tanbib.html. Accessed 6.4.07.

Brown, P. and Levinson, S.C. (1987) *Politeness: Some Universals in Language Usage*. Oxford: Oxford University Press.

Crystal, D. (2001) *Language and the Internet*. Cambridge: Cambridge University Press.

Cziko, G.A. (2004) Electronic Tandem language learning (eTandem): A third approach to second language learning for the 21st century. *CALICO Journal* 22 (1), 25–39.

Gass, S.M. (1998) The role of input and interaction in second language acquisition. *Modern Language Journal* 82 (3), 299–307.

Gass, S.M. and Varonis, E.M. (1985) Task variation and nonnative/nonnative negotiation of meaning. In S.M. Gass and C.G. Madden (eds) *Input in Second Language Acquisition* (pp. 149–161). Cambridge, MA: Newbury House.

Holec, H. (1981) *Autonomy in Foreign Language Learning*. Oxford: Pergamon.

Kitade, K. (2000) L2 learners' discourse and SLA theories in CMC: collaborative interaction in internet chat. *Computer Assisted Language Learning* 13 (2), 143–166.

Little, D. (1991) *Learner Autonomy 1: Definitions, Issues and Problems*. Dublin: Authentik.

Little, D. (1997) The role of writing in second language learning: some neo-Vygotskian reflections. In R. Kupetz (ed.) *Vom gelenkten zum freien Schreiben im Fremdsprachenunterricht* (Vol. 3, pp. 117–128). Frankfurt: Lang.

Little, D. (1999a) Developing learner autonomy in the foreign language classroom: a social-interactive view of learning and three fundamental pedagogical principles. *Revista Canaria de estudios ingleses* (38), 77–88.

Little, D. (1999b) Metalinguistic awareness: The cornerstone of learner autonomy. In B. Mißler & U. Multhaup (eds) *The Construction of Knowledge, Learner Autonomy and Related Issues in Foreign Language Learning: Essays in Honour of Dieter Wolff* (pp. 3–12). Tübingen: Stauffenberg.

Little, D., Ushioda, E., Appel, M.C., Moran, J., O'Rourke, B. and Schwienhorst, K. (1999) *Evaluating tandem language learning by e-mail: Report on a bilateral project* (CLCS Occasional Paper no. 55). Dublin: Trinity College Dublin.

Long, M.H. (1983) Native speaker/non-native speaker conversation and the negotiation of comprehensible input. *Applied Linguistics* 4 (2), 126–141.

Mercer, N. (2000) *Words and Minds: How We Use Language To Think Together*. London: Routledge.

O'Dowd, R. and Ritter, M. (2006) Understanding and working with 'failed communication' in telecollaborative exchanges. *CALICO Journal* 23 (3), 623–642.

Olson, D.R. (1994a) Literacy and the making of the Western mind. In L. Verhoeven (ed.) *Functional Literacy: Theoretical Issues and Educational Implications* (pp. 135–150). Amsterdam: John Benjamins.

Olson, D.R. (1994b) *The World on Paper: The Conceptual and Cognitive Implications of Reading and Writing*. Cambridge: Cambridge University Press.

Olson, D.R. (1995) Writing and the mind. In J.V. Wertsch, P. del Río and A. Alvarez (eds) *Sociocultural Studies of Mind* (pp. 95–123). Cambridge: Cambridge University Press.

O'Rourke, B. (2002) Metalinguistic knowledge in instructed second language acquisition: a theoretical model and its application in computer-mediated communication. Unpublished Ph.D. thesis, Trinity College Dublin, Dublin.

O'Rourke, B. (2005) Form-focused interaction in on-line tandem learning. *CALICO Journal* 22 (3), 433–466.

Ortega, L. (1997) Processes and outcomes in networked classroom interaction: Defining the research agenda for L2 computer-assisted classroom discussion. *Language Learning & Technology* 1 (1), 82–93.

Pellettieri, J. (2000) Negotiation in cyberspace: The role of chatting in the development of grammatical competence. In M. Warschauer and R. Kern (eds) *Network-based Language Teaching: Concepts and Practice* (pp. 59–86). Cambridge: Cambridge University Press.

Pica, T. (1994) Research on negotiation: What does it reveal about second-language learning conditions, processes, and outcomes? *Language Learning* 44 (3), 493–527.

Schwienhorst, K. and Borgia, A. (2006) Monitoring bilingualism: Pedagogical implications of the Bilingual Tandem Analyser. *CALICO Journal* 23 (2), 349–362.

Smith, B., Alvarez-Torres, M.J. and Zhao, Y. (2003) Features of CMC technologies and their impact on language learners' on-line interaction. *Computers in Human Behavior* 19 (6), 703–729.

Swain, M. (1985) Communicative competence: Some roles of comprehensible input and comprehensible output in its development. In S. Gass and C. Madden (eds) *Input in Second Language Acquisition* (pp. 235–253). Rowley, MA: Newbury House.

Swain, M. (1995) Three functions of output in second language learning. In G. Cook and B. Seidlhofer (eds) *Principle and Practice in Applied Linguistics: Studies in Honour of H.G. Widdowson* (pp. 125–144). Oxford: Oxford University Press.

Swain, M. and Lapkin, S. (1995) Problems in output and the cognitive processes they generate: a step towards second language learning. *Applied Linguistics* 16 (3), 371–391.

Tudini, V. (2003) Using native speakers in chat. *Language Learning & Technology* 7 (3), 141–159.

Vygotsky, L.S. (1986) *Thought and Language*. Cambridge, MA: MIT Press.

Wolff, J. (1982a) TANDEMadrid – du hilfst mir lernen, ich helfe dir lernen, und so verstehen wir uns besser. *Spracharbeit* 1, 21–26.

Wolff, J. (1982b) Von der wirklichkeitsnahen Organisation des Unterrichts zur lernfördernden Organisation der realen Kommunikation-Tandem-Kurse. *Zielsprache Deutsch* 3, 21–28.

Web pages referred to in Chapter 3

The Tandem Server: http://www.slf.ruhr-uni-bochum.de

Service for finding e-tandem partners: http://www.slf.ruhr-uni-bochum.de/email/stats-eng.html

Chapter 4

Models of Telecollaboration (2): Cultura

JESÚS SUÁREZ GARCÍA and JAMES CRAPOTTA

Introduction

Over the last decades the relationship between language and culture has become one of the most important issues in the field of foreign language teaching and learning. The teaching of culture, once a subordinate element in the hierarchy of skills we thought students needed as they moved towards greater communicative competence and proficiency, has become a more central element in our pedagogical thinking and classroom practice. Our very definition of culture has broadened and multiplied as we now ponder what cultures we should teach and how we might teach them.

Perhaps Hymes's work in the 1970s might be taken as the point of departure in this reconsideration of the place of culture in the language curriculum. In his critique of Chomsky's model of language acquisition, Hymes proposed the notion of communicative competence. He argued that first language acquisition involves more than just grammatical competence and that chief among the many other competences a learner needs to master is the sociolinguistic, the ability to use language appropriately. Going one step further, Hymes maintained that linguistic and cultural competence develop in tandem:

> From a finite experience of speech acts and their interdependence with sociocultural features, (children) develop a general theory of speaking appropriate in their community which they employ, like other forms of tacit cultural knowledge (competence) in conducting and interpreting social life.
>
> . . .
>
> From a communicative standpoint, judgements of appropriateness may not be assigned to different spheres, as between the linguistic and the cultural; certainly the spheres of the two will interact. (Hymes, 1972: 279, 286)

Although Hymes's main focus was the analysis of social interaction and communication within a monolingual social group using its first language, his ideas contributed to the development of the communicative approach to foreign language teaching. Nonetheless, the sociocultural component would continue to play only a secondary role in foreign language pedagogy for quite some time; communicative language teaching turned its attention elsewhere: to speech act theory in the 1970s (van Ek, 1975; Widdowson, 1978), to discourse analysis and notions of social variety in the 1980s (Canale & Swain, 1980; Widdowson, 1990) and to task-based learning in the 1990s (Zanón & Alba, 1994). As a consequence, communicative approaches focused more on the sociolinguistic than on the sociocultural, and communicative competence became defined more as appropriate language use rather than competence in the social and cultural practices of the community that speaks the language.

But the profession was to undergo yet another paradigm shift in response to the social and technological transformations of the waning years of the 20th century. The notion of the 'global village' was everywhere palpable, with the internet making cultures immediately accessible and present in everyday life, and with globalisation and new waves of migration rendering societies increasingly multiethnic and multilingual. The importance of intercultural communication and of the profession's need to tackle this issue head-on could not be ignored.

Now, well into the new century, culture has acquired a more central role in the foreign language curriculum. The notions of 'cultural learning', 'cultural studies', 'sociocultural competence', 'intercultural competence' and 'intercultural communication' are present in policy initiatives on language learning in the UK, France, Germany and a number of other European countries, as well as in the USA, Canada and Australia and in documents of international bodies such as the Council of Europe and UNESCO (Roberts *et al.*, 2001). Language learners are often described as 'cultural mediators', 'border-crossers', 'negotiators of meaning' or 'intercultural speakers'. From this new perspective the acquisition of a foreign language is seen as 'the acquisition of the cultural practices and beliefs it embodies for particular social groups' (Byram, 1997), and communication in a foreign language is described as a process that 'involves mediating and establishing relationships between one's own and other cultures' (Roberts *et al.*, 2001).

This new focus on the development of learners' social competence means that foreign language teaching must focus on equipping learners with tools to develop their intercultural understanding. Instead of simply providing factual information about history, institutions, etc. and descriptions of generalised beliefs, values and attitudes presented in an unproblematic way, as has often been the case in foreign language teaching and textbooks. The objective is to develop the learners' ability to access and analyse cultural practices and meanings.

The model of telecollaboration described in this chapter, *Cultura*, is one whose focus is precisely that of intercultural competence. Its methodology integrates culture into the language classroom by facilitating the direct communication between two groups of learners from different cultures and the comparison of those cultures. We will describe the principles and practices of *Cultura* and examine its implementation in an ongoing exchange between classes at Barnard College in New York and the University of León in Spain.

The Original *Cultura* Model

Cultura is a web-mediated model of telecommunication that, as its name suggests, focuses on the integration of culture into the language classroom. It was created and developed in 1997 by Gilberte Furstenberg, Shoggy Waryn and Sabine Levet of the Department of Foreign Languages and Literatures at the Massachusetts Institute of Technology (MIT), with major funding from the National Endowment for the Humanities and the Consortium for Language Teaching and Learning. It was first used in an exchange between students of French at MIT and students of English at the Institut National des Télécommunications in Evry, France (for more details see the list of weblinks at the end of this chapter) and since then it has been adopted by other institutions, including the two that are the subject of this chapter, Barnard College (USA) and the University of León (Spain).

Principles

The theoretical underpinnings of the *Cultura* project are grounded in thinking about the nature of culture and cross-cultural communication and their relationship to the new wired world.

The creators of the project take as a point of departure the idea that cultural competence involves much more than accumulating facts about another culture: history, traditions, holidays, etc. Instead, it entails an understanding of embedded cultural concepts, beliefs, attitudes, and ways of interacting and looking at the world, and is an 'ongoing dynamic process of negotiating meaning and understanding differences of perspective' (Fustenberg *et al.*, 2001). Furthermore, cultural comparison is the best way to understand other cultures. As different studies and experiences suggest (Byram, 1997; Zarate, 1997), viewing side by side elements from two different cultures allows the observer immediately to notice similarities and differences embedded in the respective cultures that otherwise might be difficult to perceive.

If cultural comparison suggests an active and ongoing engagement between cultures, then the World Wide Web and web-based tools are natural vehicles for entering into international and intercultural dialogue. The internet allows students in different cultural settings to communicate directly and facilitates immediate and authentic intercultural exchange. The internet provides students and teachers with a tool to understand and analyse a globalised world, develop analytical and critical-thinking skills and communicate directly with their peers in another culture.

A project grounded in the *Cultura* model brings together two groups of students from two different countries who study in similar school settings and who are students of the language spoken in the other country. These two groups share a set of cultural materials, some of which are produced by the students themselves (answers to questionnaires, postings in forums, essays) and some of which are external sources (online media and links, films, articles) that are made available at a common project website. This material then becomes the basis for an extended and ongoing cross-cultural dialogue as students compare, analyse and discuss their observations both with the partner group and within the classroom.

Stages of *Cultura*

In *Cultura* the work of cross-cultural analysis is a gradual process that develops over a series of stages that introduce learners to progressively more complex cultural concepts as they broaden the scope of their inquiry. These are the stages:

Stage 1: Questionnaires (online)

Students complete web-based questionnaires that have been designed to reveal basic cultural differences. They deal with topics such as politeness and social behaviour, perceived representative elements of each culture, every-day life, etc. Questionnaires are of three types:

- Word associations. In these students see a list of individual words (police, family, work, etc.) and, in a process of free association, are asked to write the first two or three words (nouns, adjectives or verbs) that come to mind.

- Sentence completion. Students complete sentences of the type: 'A good citizen is someone who. . .'. Students may write more than one answer for each sentence if they wish.
- Reactions to hypothetical situations. Students respond to a series of hypothetical situations (e.g.: 'You see a student next cheating on an exam') by stating the first thing they would think, feel or do.

Questionnaires are presented in the native language of the students (e.g. English for the American group and Spanish for the Spanish group) and they likewise record their responses in their native language. After students complete these responses, the results from both sets of students are compiled and presented online side by side. These juxtaposed sets of answers provide first-hand ethnographical information about the contrasting cultures and will become the point of departure for intercultural dialogue and analysis, both in the forums and in the classroom (Figure 4.1 and Figure 4.2).

Stage 2: Analysis of questionnaires (in the classroom and at home)
Each group of students, under the guidance of their teachers, analyses the juxtaposed lists of responses in order to find differences and similarities between the two groups' responses. They also look for and comment on such features as positive and negative signs of approval or disapproval, contradictions, categories that receive fewer or more responses and indications of basic underlying cultural assumptions. They carry out this work in the target language (Spanish in the American institution and English in the Spanish institution, for example) both individually and collectively in their respective classes.

Stage 3: Exchanges and forums (online)
Following the individual and group analysis of the questionnaires in the classroom, students from both groups meet in online message boards accessible to all participants. There they exchange observations, communicate their first reactions, preliminary findings and conclusions and address questions and doubts raised by the information. Their goal here is to get a better understanding of the cultural values and beliefs that lie behind the differences they have observed. These exchanges in forums mark the beginning of an ongoing dialogue as the students in both groups engage in a collaborative process of intercultural analysis.

The online forums are an essential and central component of *Cultura*. They provide a continuous thread throughout the whole process of intercultural analysis. Forums are where students enter into a real dialogue, exchanging viewpoints and asking and answering questions.

list of topics/lista de temas | bios/biografías | background texts/textos informativos | images/imágenes
tools/herramientas | data/cifras | media/medios | library/biblioteca | credits | feedback | help/ayuda

Español	English
	USA
Extenso, eclectico, contradiccion	America, freedom
patriotismo, poder, guerra	power, diversity, misguided
curiosidad, enorme, desconocido	dangerous, home, varied
diversidad,	My home
llamativo, diferente, potencia	war, McDonalds, endless roads across the country
diferente, grande, desconocido	George W. Bush, democracy, English
enorme, variedad, rascacielos	diverse, eclectic, Americans
yankis, libertad, bush	Patriotism, Nationalism
poder, globalización	opportunities, patriotism
potencia, globalización, exageración	Major world power, potential to be a more responsible leader
yankis, michael moore	bush, iraq, unipolarity
conservadurismo, armas, prepotencia	fat, basketball, pizza
	arrogant, powerful
	home, country, flag
	diverse, george bush, rich
	Home, War, Freedom
	democracy, young, strugglin
	arrogant, powerful
	country, america
	mixed, difficult, freedom

Figure 4.1 *Cultura* questionnaire based on the keyword 'USA'

list of topics/lista de temas | bios/biografías | background texts/textos informativos | images/imágenes
tools/herramientas | data/cifras | media/medios | library/biblioteca | credits | feedback | help/ayuda

Español	English
A friend of yours who is 25 years old is living with his/her parents.	
Probablemente sea por causa de la inseguridad laboral no porque el no quiera irse de casa	I talk to my friend that he/she needs to become self-sufficient at some point and help my friend if he needs me to get a job or move out.
me parece bien yo creo que es normal	I would probably be a little resentful that they were being taken care of financially.
Le digo que espavile y se busque la vida, que ya es hora.	I would feel very very bad for him or her.
no es muy raro...	that person is not independent
si el está contento no digo nada.	I may be in the same situation in a few years so I don't see the big deal.
si es feliz me parece muy bien	
lo vería absolutamente normal, dada la situación en mi país de encontar un buen trabajo.	I would pity them, as they would be doing themselves an injustice by not getting out into the world and living their own independent lives.
Es algo normal en este país, si con 25 años no tienes un trabajo decente ni dinero para marcharte de casa, ¿dónde vas a vivir mejor que estando en casa con tus padres?	There is nothing wrong with that. He's still young, as long as he is working and giving his parents some money.
le intento explicar que tiene que hacer su vida	They need to grow up and move out.
la mayoria lo hacen. la vida está muy cara	I would feel sorry for this friend--by 25 years old, you should be out on your own, supporting yourself and beginning your own life.
¿hay alguno q a esa edad no viva con ellos?	
seguramente no ha encontrado un trabajo digno con el que gane suficiente dinero para independizarse. no tiene otro remedio.	If the parents are good people, I would invite myself over for dinner on a regular basis. I would also do my best to accomodate my friend at my place either permanently or whenever necessary.
	its her choice.
	I would suggest they move out, unless they can't afford to.
	I would understand his circumstances and let him do what he thought is best. He is probably doing it for economic reasons, so its not a big deal.
	That's odd but may be explained by circumstances.
	I joke with him that he should start his own life.
	you annalyze the situation to see if it is necessary and then if not, help them find a way to move out.
	I don't judge.
	Nothing wrong with that.
	Inwardly I would not have as much respect for him/her.
	I don't consider this strange as long as he or she has job and is considering moving out as soon as he or she has a steady job and income.

Figure 4.2 *Cultura* questionnaire based on the theme of living with one's parents

In trying to make sense together of the materials they analyse, they cooperatively construct an understanding of each other's culture. The originators of *Cultura* conceived of these forums in the native language of the students (e.g. American students write in English and Spanish students in Spanish). We will discuss the use of languages in forums in further detail later on.

Stage 4: Analysis of the forums/further discussion (in the classroom)
Students bring the messages in the forums back into the classroom for more discussion. There, with the guidance of the teacher, they analyze the language and the content of the exchanges. The new questions and ideas that this analysis raises are posted back again to the forums. In this way the dialogue in the forums and the work in the classroom are linked, each serving as feedback for the other.

Stage 5: Broadening the fields of exploration and analysis (online and in the classroom)
At a later stage, learners are also supplied with other related target-language resources: polls, surveys, news articles, films, etc. These materials allow them to broaden the scope of their inquiry and re-examine their conclusions. They then discuss their new findings in class and online with their partners.

Underlying pedagogical and working principles

The creators of the *Cultura* model have suggested a set of guidelines or working principles that they believe will lead to a successful launching of a *Cultura* interchange.

Perhaps the most important principle is that the two schools involved in the *Cultura* partnership should be similar so that students can work with partners of the same age and with similar life experiences. This makes more possible a choice of topics that will be more or less of equal interest to both groups.

An online exchange between two groups whose native and target languages are the exact opposite requires decisions as to which language to use in different parts of the exchange. If, on the one hand, it is a truism that students can write more fluently in their native language, it is equally important to recognise that the reason they are in the classroom is to learn the target language. The designers of *Cultura* thought long and hard about this issue before advising that students use the target language for class discussion and written analytical essays but use the native language for questionnaire answers and discussions in the online forums. It is important to understand that there are two languages in use in the forums; Spanish students, for example, ask questions of their American partners in Spanish but receive responses from those partners in English. In other words, in the forums students write in the native language but read the target language. The creators of *Cultura* explain their choice of the native language in the forums in the following way:

> (1) it eliminates possible dominance by a group or individuals with respect to differing proficiency levels in the foreign language (L2) and puts all students on an equal linguistic footing; (2) it enables students to express their views fully and in detail, formulate questions and hypotheses clearly, and provide complex, nuanced information because they are not bound by limited linguistic abilities; and (3) it enables the creation of student-generated authentic texts, which serve both as L2 input for the foreign partners and new objects of linguistic and cultural analysis. (Bauer *et al.*, 2005: 35)

Another working principle that plays itself out in the project is that the interaction in the forums needs to be asynchronous. Unlike synchronous exchanges (chat rooms, IMs), which encourage immediate, if unreflective, responses, the time delay in the exchange allows for reflection and analysis before posting a response. (And of course, in cases where the partner schools are in different and distant time zones, the asynchronous mode is also the only one realistically available.)

The creators of the original project also underline the principle that *Cultura* be completely integrated into the very core of the course curriculum and that a large part of the work take place in the classroom. *Cultura* is not simply the proverbial Friday-afternoon add-on activity but at the very core of the class. Teachers are exhorted to find connections between the work done in the online exchange project and the rest of the class syllabus.

Finally, as *Cultura* is a process and not a product, the project needs to take place over a sufficient period of time to develop fully and to produce valid analyses. The minimum recommended time is eight weeks.

Roles of teacher and student

In *Cultura* students themselves construct their own learning and understanding of another culture. Once the teacher has set up the tasks students take centre stage. They are the ones observing, inquiring, investigating, hypothesising and interpreting, tasks they undertake jointly with their cross-cultural partners. In this process the teacher is not the authoritative storehouse of knowledge. Instead (s)he learns with the students and becomes another participant in the process.

However, at the same time, the teacher's role is crucial. It is the teacher who chooses the questionnaire topics, sets up the calendar, establishes the rhythm, organises class activities, chooses outside sources of supplementary data and ensures that everything stays on schedule. The teacher has an important role as a guide and facilitator who helps, encourages and further challenges students in their construction of hypotheses and cultural understanding. The teacher who uses *Cultura* must be flexible, as the set syllabus of the traditional classroom is replaced by a dynamic and fluid process that can take many turns. As the intercultural dialogue and new themes develop, or as issues or misunderstandings between the groups arise, the teacher must find ways to guide and arbitrate without intruding or usurping student initiative.

Language and culture

While culture is the explicit focus of a *Cultura* exchange, the linguistic component does not disappear; students learn the language as they learn about the culture, not the other way around. Throughout the project, students work on thematic vocabulary appropriate to the topics under discussion. In like manner, linguistic functions and grammatical features of the target language are examined not abstractly but within a cultural and communicative context for the purpose of improving communication and understanding. Students thus perceive an immediate practical purpose for improving their language skills as they see that some language errors can lead to misunderstandings or be mistaken for slights or attacks on the other culture.

In the original *Cultura* model, the questionnaires and forums are a source of authentic target language readings. And as we shall see, in cases such as ours where students at times also write in the target language and where clear communication is essential, the need to be understood can spur them on to improve their linguistic skills and, when achieved successfully, help improve their confidence.

Adapting the Original Model: *Cultura* at Barnard/León

Exchange background

The Department of Spanish and Latin American Cultures at Barnard College and the Department of Modern Languages at the University of León, Spain, have been engaged in a *Cultura* exchange since the start of the 2003–2004 academic year, in which Barnard students enrolled in an intermediate level Spanish course are paired with León students studying English in the fourth and final year of their major in English Philology.

A number of decisions had to be made before this interchange could get under way. The first, and most immediate, was how to manage the different academic calendars of the two schools. Barnard, like most American colleges, works on the semester system, with little if no continuity of students between the Fall and the Spring semesters of a course; the University of León, on the other hand, follows the European model of year-long courses. Additionally, the American academic year starts in September, breaks in December, and then starts with new classes in January, while León classes start in October and have different intersession breaks. On the purely technical side, technicians on the Barnard/Columbia side were still constructing the *Cultura* engine and adapting the original interface used at MIT and Brown so that it would mesh seamlessly with the existing Barnard/Columbia networking system.

We were able to turn these issues to our advantage by launching a trial run of the project during the month of November. During those four weeks students in a Fall semester Barnard class and students from León engaged in a limited exchange of a few questionnaires and subsequent forums. This allowed instructors from both schools to identify and work out issues they had not foreseen and fine tune some elements of the project before a full-fledged exchange would begin in January, the start of Barnard's second semester.

Changes in model application

The trial period made clear that while the original methodological foundations of the *Cultura* project were sound, some changes and additions were in order both to meet the needs of our institutions (for example, León students had less access to computers at home, making it necessary for some class time be used for questionnaires and forum responses) and to test what would happen if some of the original methodological assumptions were modified.

Thus, the Barnard-León project includes various features at the start of the exchange not present on the original MIT *Cultura* model. One is a section of student autobiographies, in which students at each school write personal narratives (in the target language) with accompanying photos to present themselves to their partners. Another new section is entitled 'Background texts' where students create short texts and videos (also in the target language) on topics such as their local town, home university and educational system. The aim of these new sections is to help the participants get to know their partners more personally at the very beginning of the exchange and to make each group more aware of the sociocultural environments in which they and their partners live and study. Also, as the type of work they will be doing in *Cultura* will most likely be new territory for our students, during the first days of classes they engage in preliminary activities designed to introduce and sensitise them to the notion of cross-cultural understanding.

As in the original model, students answer the questionnaires in their mother tongue. But while the MIT model prescribed assigning ten items for each questionnaire category – words, sentences and situations – we reduced this number with the belief that the exact quantity mattered less than the choice of items in each category. It was also evident from the trial run that there would not be enough time to work in depth with a large number of topics. We took care to choose items that we hoped would elicit a range of varied, and maybe even unexpected and contradictory, attitudes, values and beliefs within the target culture, provoke lively dialogue and discussion in the forums and challenge preconceived cultural stereotypes.

The next step closely follows Stage 2 of the original *Cultura* model: once the students have completed the questionnaires they begin preliminary analysis of these data. Their examination is both cross-cultural and linguistic as they focus both on the content (cultural values and assumptions) and the language (vocabulary, expressions, structures) of the responses of the two groups. As in the original model, this work is carried out in the target language in and outside of class, individually and in groups.

The observations, questions and preliminary conclusions drawn from this comparison and discussed in class are then posted to the online forums, marking the beginning of Stage 3 of the original model. And it is here that our use of *Cultura* differs markedly from that model and its insistence on the use of the mother tongue for all forum entries. Our decision to swerve from this directive was dictated at first by institutional concerns. As León students of English had little access to home computers and, consequently, had to use class time to post to the forums, the León instructor was under pressure from the university to justify the allocation of instructional time for students writing in their native language. This pragmatic concern led to a solution that has given surprisingly rich results: half of the forums were to be in English, with both groups communicating in English, and the other half were to be in Spanish, with the common use of that language from both groups.

Contrary to the concerns of the creators of *Cultura* that the use of the target language in the forums would inhibit students from responding freely and with nuance and lead to the domination of one group over the other (see 'Underlying pedagogical and working principles'), we found that the use of the target language did not significantly change the level and quality of participation in the forums. At the end of the first trial semester we administered a questionnaire to determine how participants evaluated the use of native and target languages in the forums. An analysis of their responses indicates that a significant majority of American students supported the option of writing and reading in Spanish (66.7%), while in the Spanish group 88% reported preferring the option of writing and reading in English. Clearly, both groups felt comfortable writing and reading in the target language on the message boards. Moreover, some Barnard students in the final interviews and evaluations of the course reported that their confidence grew upon discovering that their counterparts understood them and that they were able to keep a discussion going in Spanish.

Another change that we have introduced is to group topics of the questionnaires into four general categories: 'This is me/This is my life', 'Here and There: Attitudes towards USA culture/Spanish culture', 'Moral and Social Behavior' and 'Rights, Duties and Citizenship'. And in place of a forum for each individual item of the questionnaires we reduced the number of forums to four, one for each of these major thematic groupings. In this way, from the very beginning students have to look for wider patterns and identify new and unexpected relationships. We have also begun to use online voice forums alongside the written ones. Here students can hone their oral communication skills as they record and listen to messages related to forum topics (Figure 4.3).

Supplementing the online *Cultura* exchange: Live class visits abroad

A unique feature of the Barnard-León *Cultura* exchange has been our incorporation of a live exchange into the project. In the early stages of conception of our project, we were able to secure a commitment of support from both institutions in the form of a formal agreement to explore ways to promote the exchange of students, faculty and resources. Part of that support was the allocation of some limited institutional funding to allow for a live exchange of some students participating in the *Cultura* project. With this funding six Barnard students and six León students, along with their respective instructors, travelled abroad to spend a week with the students of the partner school. The visits occurred in mid-semester after the online interchange had long been under way,

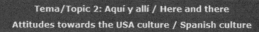

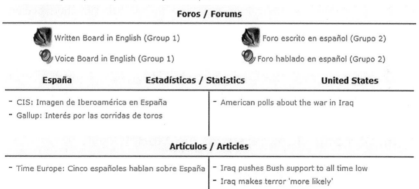

Tema/Topic 2: Aquí y allí / Here and there
Attitudes towards the USA culture / Spanish culture

Questionnaires / Cuestionarios

- Spain / España
- USA / Estados Unidos
- Hispanic / Hispano
- Bull fighting / Corrida de toros
- Family / Familia
- The biggest problem of my country is... / El principal problema de mi país...
- The best thing of my country is... / Lo mejor de mi país es...

Foros / Forums

Written Board in English (Group 1)	Foro escrito en español (Grupo 2)
Voice Board in English (Group 1)	Foro hablado en español (Grupo 2)

España	Estadísticas / Statistics	United States
- CIS: Imagen de Iberoamérica en España - Gallup: Interés por las corridas de toros		- American polls about the war in Iraq

Artículos / Articles

- Time Europe: Cinco españoles hablan sobre España	- Iraq pushes Bush support to all time low - Iraq makes terror 'more likely'

Figure 4.3 Resources and tools for Barnard-León *Cultura* project, including both oral and written message boards.

with each group making its visit during its Spring break (mid-March for Barnard students and late April for the León students).

The trips were designed to be very intensive periods of field work in the target culture rather than simply fun trips abroad. Students chosen for the trip were expected to interact fully with the host culture and gather new material and insights to be used in class on their return. As these visits would be relatively short, we had to be sure that each group would take to the new cultural setting relatively quickly and here the online autobiographies, texts about the respective cites and universities and, above all, weeks of online exchanges in the forums were key. On their arrival at the host institution participants were greeted as old friends; Barnard students lived with the families of the León students who would be visiting New York (León students were later housed in Barnard dormitories) and bonding between partners was immediate.

The visit of the partner group became the focus of classes during the week of the trip as the visiting students gave cultural presentations about their country and engaged in group discussions and class debates. (As we would be working in two languages a set of rules had to be established: all work in class would be in the language of the visiting group, while all other exchanges, even those among members of the visiting group, would be in the language of the host country.) Activities outside of class time focused on interviews with natives of various ages and experiences (these were arranged beforehand by the host instructors) for the purpose of gathering ethnographic and cultural data that would later be used to question and explore further the data culled from the online forums.

On their return to their home classes, these students then became resident 'experts' as they presented – via formal presentations, essays, blogs, videos and photo journals – the results of their interviews and experiences to their classmates. Thus, these visits abroad enriched the cultural input of the project with first-hand observations which, in turn, became the subject of further online and in-class discussion, questioning and analysis.

Strengths and Weaknesses of the Model

Challenging cultural stereotypes

Our overall experience using *Cultura* has been very positive. The dialogue between the two groups of students has been fluid and the results in general encouraging. The exchange has helped our students in many cases to change previous ideas and attitudes towards the other culture and to think differently about it. The following examples from student exchanges on the topics of bullfighting, terrorism and politics illustrate such a process.

The discussion in the forums on bullfighting led the American students to question their stereotypical images of the Spanish fascination for the *corrida* as they read comments such as the following from the Spanish group:

> A mí es que esto de los toros siempre me ha dado bastante vergüenza ajena, vamos que no es lo mío, y creo que España sería un país mejor si nos desprendiéramos ya de una vez de esta costumbre paleta ... Nunca me ha gustado que el torero y los toros sean uno de los principales símbolos españoles de puertas hacia fuera.

> This bull fighting thing has always made me quite ashamed for other people – I mean, it's not my thing – and I think Spain would be a better country if we unhitched ourselves of this provincial custom

once and for all . . . I've never liked the idea that bullfighters and bulls are one of the main symbols of Spain for the rest of the world.

Such postings obviously surprised the American students, as this response clearly indicates:

Estuve sorpresa [sic] que algunos estudiantes de León creen que la corrida de toros es crueldad. Yo creía que todos los españoles estaban a favor de este tema, pero yo estoy contento que hay algunas personas que no están a favor de este tema.

I was surprised that some students from León believe that bullfighting is cruel. I thought that Spaniards were in favor of this topic but I am happy that there are some people who are not in favor of this topic.

In their final essays American students made frequent references to how the exchange had challenged their ideas about Spain. One student explained that she '. . .was surprised with responses in the "bullfighting" topic. I thought all Spanish people liked the idea of bullfighting but it turned out to be the opposite'. Others referred to the emphasis which the Spaniards had placed on the issue of terrorism in the Basque country, a topic about which our students had been virtually ignorant. One American wrote that he had learned a lot about 'nationalism – País Vasco, terrorism and how Spanish people are affected by this', while another suggested that she had '. . . learned about what it is like to live in a country with terrorism' (this in post-9/11 New York!).

On the other side, the Spanish group was surprised by the Americans' reactions to political themes such as 'If I could change one thing about my country. . .' and 'Your government does something immoral'. Comments like 'I would also change "the president" of the US. George Bush sucks and he is dumb. Yes, I know, a very sophisticated observation. He and his administration have absolutely ruined US foreign relations' made the Spanish students reassess their attitudes to Americans in general.

In their final feedback, the Spaniards concluded that their partners were '. . . leading a change towards changing traditional American stereotypes' and that '. . . not all Americans are the same – New York students are tolerant and open-minded'.

The potential of such *Cultura* exchanges to further cross-cultural understanding and contest cultural stereotypes might best be summed up in this final observation from the Spanish side:

There were a lot of things about the USA that I didn't know, talking to the young people there cleared up many things for me such as their way of thinking and the difference between the reality over there and how we see them.

Institutional constraints and logistics

Cultura provides a flexible yet very structured model of telecollaboration. The carefully calibrated series of stages (questionnaires, analysis, forum discussion, etc.) prescribed by the model's creators serve as a step-by-step guide for teachers and students, taking much of the guesswork out of how an institution might put into practice such a collaboration. Their guidelines map out ways to set up the programme, the schedule and the activities, and are particularly helpful for the early stages of the exchange.

However, at the same time this structure requires a great deal of coordination between the two participating institutions. Instructors must collaborate on the construction of the questionnaire topics and on the timing of each stage well before the first class begins. And all during the exchange the instructors must make sure that their groups stay on schedule as a missed or delayed response on one side will have repercussions for the progress of the whole exchange. The process of collaborative investigation that is the essence of *Cultura* can easily come to a halt if one side does not participate in the discussion forums fully, or if it does not respond on schedule. Instructors must also be in regular communication with each other to deal with any unforeseen technical or scheduling problems.

Institutional constraints such as academic calendars (the two institutions will most surely construct their semester start and end dates, vacation and exam periods differently), instructor teaching loads and other duties, material that must be 'covered' in certain classes, and accessibility to instructional technology must all be taken into account before embarking on a *Cultura* exchange. How the participating institutions sort out and resolve these constraints could, as O'Dowd (2005) and others have pointed out, determine the success or failure of the entire undertaking. Therefore it is essential that participants on both sides – teachers and institutions alike – be equally committed to the success of the project from the very beginning and throughout its run. (O'Dowd (2006) explains in detail the process of negotiation and adaptation that took place in the Barnard-León exchange. Bauer *et al*. (2005) also describe the logistics involved in establishing a Russian/English *Cultura* exchange.)

Another important aspect when deciding whether to implement *Cultura* is the time element. *Cultura* interchanges require a minimum of several weeks. Therefore, whether *Cultura* be its own course, as in the Barnard-León setup, or part of a pre-existing course, it cannot be relegated to the proverbial 'Friday afternoon' class filler. It is necessary that students and teacher dedicate a considerable amount of time in and out of class for the project to bear fruit.

From the point of view of logistics, then, *Cultura* is more demanding than other models of telecollaboration. At the same time it is a flexible framework open to adaptations that suit particular academic contexts. Its success or failure depends much more on effective faculty collaboration, well planned scheduling and invested classroom interaction than on its technology.

Interpreting culture: Risks and remedies

Our initial research findings into *Cultura* have also shown that students' initial analysis of the *Cultura* materials can lead to facile cultural misinterpretations, particularly in the early stages of the project. The problems are of three types:

(a) Students run the risk of over-generalising and forming quick and ready interpretations of both the target and native cultures that can become rigid and difficult to undo, as these two examples illustrate:

Student 1:

Of the surveys I thought the one defining a polite person showed the biggest differences between the Spaniards and Americans. In Spain a polite person is, in general, someone who respects others and knows how to behave. Whereas, in the US we believe that a polite person is well mannered and says 'please' and 'thank you.

Student 2:

Me interesa que los estudiantes norteamericanos dijeron que una persona buen educada es una persona que dice 'por favor' y 'gracias' pero los estudiantes españoles no lo mencionaron. Parece que a los norteamericanos les importan los costumbres sociales, pero a los españoles les importa los sentimientos que motivan las acciones.

I think it is interesting that the American students said that a well-mannered person is someone who says 'Please' and 'Thank you' but that the Spanish students did not mention this at all. It seems that Americans give importance to social customs while Spaniards give importance to the feelings behind the actions.

(b) Knowing that their objective is to compare and contrast cultures, students may be tempted to overemphasise the differences between the cultures and pass over the similarities, thereby creating an artificial binary between the two:

Student 1:
Cuando leí los cuestionarios los semejanzas no me sorprendieron mucho, pero las diferencias me interesaron.

When I read the questionnaires I was not very surprised by the similarities but I found the differences interesting.

Student 2:
I have read your answers about the questionnaire we all had to do, and I have found it quite interesting, because of the different answers we, the Spanish, and you, the Americans have written.

(c) The fact that the students act as informants and perceive themselves as representatives of their culture could influence the sincerity and spontaneity of their answers. In our project some students mentioned in the forums and in their final essays the concern that their awareness of their role as cultural ambassadors might have affected their answers and that, for example, in some cases they eschewed answering from a personal perspective and responded with what they considered to be a more widespread or positive position. As one participant commented, 'I think that sometimes when I respond (and possibly when others respond as well), I am trying to overcompensate for the stereotypes that Americans tend to have (for example, that Americans are materialistic)'.

Such concerns argue strongly for the need to allow the *Cultura* project to unfold and develop as a process over a sufficient period of time. When this process is given sufficient time to develop, it becomes clear that the *Cultura* model can, instead, overcome or at least minimise the risk of stereotyping and over-generalising.

For one thing, *Cultura* offers an environment where the students from both countries collectively construct their own learning and understanding of their cultures over time. Participants help each other by posting reflections, comments and questions in the forums in an ever-expanding dialogue that goes beyond first impressions. This constant dialogue, the analysis that takes place in the classroom (which includes the teacher in the role of Socratic gnat) and the iterative process of reassessing conclusions in the light of new information help directly counteract the risks of cultural misapprehension, as all observations are open to ongoing scrutiny and critique. In other words, conclusions are always provisional and never fixed. The cross-pollination offered by outside sources is also important here, as more 'objective' or 'authoritative' texts (articles, polls, movies, etc.) bring in new elements to enrich and problematise their new assumptions.

The results of our Barnard-León exchange and those of the American–Mexican partnership described in Bauer *et al.* (2005) indicate that *Cultura* can foster an increasingly complex sense of national identities and cultural heterogeneity. It can also help make learners aware of the fact that they constitute a group with particular characteristics within their own native culture that in some ways might be different from other sectors of their culture; in turn, this may provoke students to question to what degree the partner group can stand in for its culture as a whole.

Thus, messages like the following, taken from the Spring 2005 Barnard-León exchange, are quite common:

I also worry about our making generalizations about 'Spain' and 'Spaniards' based on the responses of a few students. Take the business of cutting in line – does the fact that a lot of people said they would speak up really tell us anything about Spanish or American culture? Or do we just happen to have a group of people here who are either particularly gutsy or particularly conscious of injustice?

The point is that, as you say, America is huge and if there's one thing one cannot definitely do is generalizing. Maybe some people are very religious and put in practice their strict beliefs, but other people may do this together with crazy parties every night, or not, or are not religious at all, or, or . . . there are so many ways of life within the 'American way of life' that it's impossible to state firmly anything.

With regard to the danger of overemphasising cultural differences, many students in their final essays concluded that there are more similarities than differences between the two groups of students and between the two cultures than they thought before the exchange began. As one student wrote, 'As we have seen, there are some cultural differences between both countries but we also have some things in common'.

To conclude, the dynamic process of negotiating meaning and understanding differences of perspective over time that is central to *Cultura* can counteract the problem of cultural misconstruction. *Cultura* does not ask students to reach definitive conclusions but to engage in a process of investigation and understanding. In the words of one student in her final evaluation of our project: 'I learned a lot about Spaniards in terms of having a place to start thinking about how different issues are perceived in another country that otherwise I wouldn't have thought about'.

Conclusion

The development of intercultural competence in language learners has become one of the top priorities of the language curriculum. The *Cultura* model of telecollaboration described in this chapter constitutes a powerful tool for realising that objective.

The notion of culture fostered by such a project challenges the concept of culture as it has been framed in the traditional foreign classroom, replacing a static series of facts and generalisations about the other country and its people with a process of discovery of a living culture mediated through direct, if virtual, intercultural exchange. In the *Cultura* class culture is positioned as a dynamic, unstable and sometimes contradictory set of values and attitudes. And as participants construct their own learning environment, both individually and collectively, they become independent and critical learners whose goal is not to arrive at fixed and definitive conclusions about another culture but to learn to interpret and analyse.

In contrast to the *Tandem* model, which does not prescribe a particular structure or imply any particular content (see O'Rourke, this volume), *Cultura* clearly establishes a series of stages that the exchange should follow. On the one hand such a structure could serve as a guide for the development of a syllabus grounded in a *Cultura* project. On the other hand, the need to follow the stages of the model poses problems of coordination, requiring clear timetables and the synchronisation of calendars and tasks between the participating classes and instructors. But in spite of a structure that on first examination might seem overly to guide and restrict, results are not foreseeable or predictable. No two groups of students approach their investigation in the same way and conclusions, and even the success of the exchange, many vary widely from one group to another.

The essence of *Cultura* lies more in the process than in the contents or the results. It sets in motion a process very similar to that of ethnographic investigation – the compilation of first-hand cultural data and its organisation, analysis and interpretation – and then guides learners through a process of discovery and investigation. In such an environment students can actually interact in a meaningful way with their peers in another culture.

To return to the words of the creators of this project:

No one academic experience will 'produce' interculturally competent students. However, a project like *Cultura* can affect this process substantively. (Bauer *et al.*, 2005)

References

Bauer, B., deBenedette, L., Furstenberg, G., Levet, S. and Waryn, S. (2006) Internet-mediated intercultural foreign language education: The cultura project. In J.A. Belz and S.L. Thorne (eds) *Internet-mediated Intercultural Foreign Language Education* (pp. 31–63). Boston, MA: Heinle and Heinle.
Belz, J.A. and Müller-Hartmann, A. (2003) Teachers negotiating German–American telecollaboration: Between a rock and an institutional hard place. *Modern Language Journal* 87 (1), 71–89.
Byram, M. (1997) *Teaching and Assessing Intercultural Communicative Competence*. Clevedon, UK: Multilingual Matters.
Canale, M. and Swain, M. (1980) Theoretical bases of communicative approaches to second language teaching and testing. *Applied Linguistics* 1, 1–47.
Cultura Homepage (2006) 29.11.06. On WWW at http://web.mit.edu/french/culturaNEH. Accessed 6.4.07.
Furstenberg, G. (2003) Constructing French–American understanding: The cultura project. *Politics, Culture, and Society* 21 (2), 111–121.
Furstenberg, G., Levet, S., English, K. and Maillet, K. (2001) Giving a virtual voice to the silent language of culture: The cultura project. *Language Learning and Technology* 5 (1), 55–102. On WWW at http://llt.msu.edu/vol5num1/furstenberg/default.html.
Hymes, D.H. (1972) On communicative competence. In J.B. Pride and J. Holmes (eds) *Sociolinguistics*. Harmondsworth: Penguin.
Müller-Hartmann, A. (2000) The role of tasks in promoting intercultural learning in electronic learning networks. *Language Learning and Technology* 4 (2), 129–147. On WWW at http://llt.msu.edu/vol4num2/muller/default.html.
O'Dowd, R. (2000) Intercultural learning via videoconferencing: A pilot exchange project. *ReCALL* 12 (1), 49–63.
O'Dowd, R. (2003) Understanding the 'other side': Intercultural learning in a Spanish–English e-mail exchange. *Language Learning & Technology* 7 (2), 118–144. On WWW at http://llt.msu.edu/vol7num2/odowd/.
O'Dowd, R. (2005) Negotiating sociocultural and institutional contexts: The case of Spanish–American telecollaboration. *Language and Intercultural Communication* 5 (1), 40–56.
O'Dowd, R. (2006) The use of videoconferencing and e-mail as mediators of intercultural student ethnography internet-mediated intercultural student ethnography. In J.A. Blez and S. Thorne (eds) *Internet-mediated Intercultural Foreign Language Education* (pp. 86–120). Boston MA: Heinle and Heinle.
Roberts, C., Byram, M., Barro, A., Jordan, S. and Street, B. (2001) *Language Learners as Ethnographers*. Clevedon: Multilingual Matters.
van Ek, J. (1975) *The Threshold Level*. Strasbourg: Council of Europe.

Widdowson, H. (1978) *Teaching Language as Communication*. Oxford: Oxford University Press.
Widdowson, H. (1990) *Aspects of Language Teaching*. Oxford: Oxford University Press.
Zanón, J. and Alba, J.M. (1994) ¿Qué es la enseñanza del language mediante tareas? *Hispanorama* 68.

Web pages referred to in Chapter 4

The MIT Cultura website: http://web.mit.edu/french/culturaNEH/
The Cultura Community site: http://www.culturacommunity.org/drupal/
The Cultura Teacher's Guide: http://web.mit.edu/french/culturaNEH/guide/index.html
The Barnard–León Cultura Website: http://www2.ccnmtl.columbia.edu/cultura/login.pl

Chapter 5

Models of Telecollaboration (3): eTwinning

ANTONIA DOMÍNGUEZ MIGUELA

Introduction

This third model of telecollaboration, referred to as eTwinning, differs from the previous models as it does not propose a specific set of guidelines as to language use, thematic content or exchange structure. Instead, the eTwinning model is essentially a network of schools and educators within the European Union which avails of the tools and platforms provided on the eTwinning portal to engage their students in collaborative cross-curricular international projects. Although this model is being employed in European schools, there are no reasons why the projects and activities described here could not be applied to other geographical contexts.

eTwinning projects are open to a wide variety of people and schools. Teachers in any subject can participate, as well as headmasters, librarians and other school staff. The project is open to primary and secondary schools (the indicative age bracket is usually 3– 19 year-olds) from countries belonging to the European Union countries, Bulgaria, Norway and Iceland. There are no requirements as regards the aims, duration or scope of activities, except the pedagogical relevance of the project for the school and its pupils and the use of information and communication technology (ICT). These projects always originate within the framework of the eTwinning portal (see the list of weblinks at the end of the chapter). It is very easy to find partner teachers and schools using the eTwinning portal, which is full of extremely useful tools such as the partner search tool. Statistics confirm the growing popularity of this model of tele-collaboration. In November 2005 there were 10,000 registered schools and in May 2006 the number had reached 15,000.

eTwinning has grown in popularity among educators and students in recent years for various reasons. The concept of online interaction and collaborative project work with students in other countries has proven to be very motivating and attractive to students and eTwinning has provided a well developed network and collection of tools for teachers interested in getting their students involved in such activity. Teachers have also found that students take to the online environment quite quickly and are willing to use foreign languages to communicate with their peers using the online tools that the portal provides. The following comments by a teacher in one eTwinning project reflect this belief quite well:

> What still amazes me is the way the students very quickly took to the eTwinning platform and started to consider it as their own place. For many of the students it is a 'virtual street corner', where they can hang out with their friends, have a chat, do exercises and read and write messages at the same time. From an educator's point of view, it is really fantastic. The students willingly spend time in a completely English environment studying and learning English in their free time. (The Learning and Sharing Project Website)

In the following sections, the origins and principles of eTwinning will be outlined and, following that, the reader will be introduced to how the model works, the tools that the portal offers and the different steps that educators need to take in order to set up an eTwinning project with colleagues in other locations. The common problems that emerge in eTwinning projects will also be examined and a sample project will be outlined.

Origins and Principles

eTwinning was created as a framework for schools to collaborate with partner institutions in other European countries. It is the main action of the European Union's e-learning programme[1] Decision No 2318/2003/ EC of the European Parliament and of the Council of 5 December 2003 adopting a multiannual programme (2004–2006) for the effective integration of ICT in education and training systems in Europe (eLearning Programme). The programme aims to encourage schools to co-operate, exchange information and share learning materials on an ongoing basis for a specific goal or purpose. eTwinning broadens the scope of the pedagogical opportunities that are offered to teachers and students, motivates to learn and opens the classroom to Europe using a foreign language to communicate.

The structure of the model is a complex one and support is supplied to participants on different levels. There is a Central Support Service (CSS) and a National Support Service (NSS). The CSS, formed by members of the European Schoolnet (EUN) in Brussels, plays a fundamental role coordinating the European Commission eTwinning action and ensuring the coherence of the model on a European scale. It also provides a team of advisors and online services that complement those of the National Support Services. The NSS is the first national contact for any teacher interested in using the eTwinning collaborative model, providing information and dealing with teachers' needs and questions. Together with the CSS, the NSS also selects examples of excellent projects awarding the National Quality Label and other annual eTwinning Prizes.

One of the main objectives of the eTwinning model of telecollaboration is to integrate a feeling of European identity as well as an awareness of the continent's linguistic diversity into the learning process. That is the reason why eTwinning can be so powerful in the foreign language classroom: it helps students to use a foreign language in a real context to communicate with other students in foreign countries.

There are also four main technological and pedagogical principles that are constantly reflected in eTwinning projects: the integration of ICT and of the concept of a European identity into schools, pedagogical innovation through teachers' associations and exchange of ideas, the establishment of a European school network and, finally, the strengthening of students' intercultural awareness. The pedagogical and theoretical basis for eTwinning can be found in the European Commission's e-learning programme which promotes two important aspects: the use and integration of ICT in education and training programmes and, secondly, the development of intercultural understanding among European peoples using the languages of the continent. The European Commission encourages cooperation, networking and exchange of good practice through the eLearning Initiative and Action Plan. The eLearning programme focuses on a set of actions with a strategic relevance to the modernisation of Europe's education and training systems.

The eTwinning initiative has the following main objectives: firstly, to create networks among European schools; secondly, to encourage students and teachers to participate in educational projects with their counterparts in other European countries and thirdly to foster a European dimension in education. The initiative also aims to promote awareness among young people of the European model of a multilingual and multicultural society, to improve intercultural dialogue and mutual understanding through internet-based learning communities and finally, to help update teachers' and trainers' professional skills in the pedagogical and collaborative use of ICT.

Background Theory

eTwinning is essentially based upon the premise that the internet and new communication tools provide an ideal environment for a new model of online collaborative learning and exchange. The internet and online technologies facilitate not only access to general knowledge but also facilitate the exchange of information among students and thus, the possibility of carrying out projects together using different languages. Online technologies can easily be used within the primary and secondary classroom to develop collaborative work and learning and to exchange ideas and experiences. Digital communication and the integration of office suites as tools for collaborative work allow for more complex and useful techniques in online collaborative learning than those existing years ago.

Collaborative learning implies a sharing of authority and acceptance of responsibility among students working in a common project. They need to reach a consensus through cooperation and therefore cooperative learning encourages students to interact together in order to accomplish their goal or to design a final product (Panitz, 1996). Collaborative learning is therefore the most important pedagogical implication of eTwinning but it is necessary to take into account that collaboration is not only about making students work in groups. This type of learning is based on the theory of 'situated constructivism' developed by Vygotsky (1978) and Young's 'situated knowledge' (1997). According to this theory, situated constructivist learning takes place when 'meanings emanate from the patterns of our individual and unique social experiences that occur over time in a contextual, situated, and continually changing synthesis' (Kanuka & Anderson, 1999). Interaction among students and with the teacher is highlighted in the process of knowledge construction incorporating the social dimension of learning to constructivist theory.

The eTwinning model is an interesting new way in which technology, together with the appropriate teaching methods, can situate learning and include important social and cultural aspects. It combines collaborative learning and technology, providing opportunities to connect students and classrooms with the rest of the world. Through the eTwinning projects, students can compare similar materials from their cultures and then exchange viewpoints about these materials or work together towards a final product on cultural topics. Language and culture are very closely related and 'through the use of technology, students in diverse classrooms can come to know each other's culture while also practicing the target language' (Butler-Pascoe & Wiburg, 2003: 63).

The eTwinning model is based on technology-mediated collaborative learning and indeed these are the two most outstanding features of eTwinning projects: collaboration between groups of students takes place necessarily through the use of ICTs and a common foreign language. Working together acquires a new meaning when we use ICTs because it opens the doors to new resources, people and non-traditional means of communication. For instance the 'Twinspace' tool provides an always-accessible virtual work space where files and documents can be shared, stored, corrected by students and teachers in distant schools. This type of learning needs to be designed well in advance and activities should be integrated in a curriculum based on project learning (a key theme in eTwinning telecollaboration), appropriate materials and special teacher control over the development of planned activities, students' participation and roles, etc.

Structure of eTwinning Exchanges

eTwinning projects can take many forms, including partnerships on school level, school management level or teacher level. The manner in which schools and classes are twinned or linked together may be related to previously established town twinning agreements or to long-term student–teacher exchanges, to other Socrates actions (Arion visits, Comenius or Minerva projects), or may simply be based on new partner-ships.

School management twinning may involve a peer-to-peer project facilitating mutual exchange and dialogue on decision-making issues and on the organisation of a whole school twinning project. Teacher twinning may take the form of a curricular option in which teachers of the same subject in different countries bring a European dimension to their pedagogy, a cross-curricular option in which teachers of different subjects tackle a theme where their subjects complement one other, or it may be based on a joint activity that involves two teachers setting up a common collaborative event, like a concert, a match, an exhibition or a play.

There is also the possibility of having a group of teachers in one geographical location working collaboratively with another team. In this case, teacher team-twinning can take the form either of a curricular option in which two or more sets of teachers of the same subject work together on a common theme and compare different approaches linked to cultural and curricular differences or of a cross-curricular project in which groups of teachers of different subjects work together on a common theme. Librarians, educational advisors and counselling committees can also take advantage of eTwinning by working together with other people in similar positions. However, the most common kind of projects to be used by foreign language teachers are those where students from different countries work together on a common project exchanging information about a specific topic and doing common tasks.

In order to carry out an eTwinning project with a partner school, teachers need to be aware how such project work may effect the organisation of their classes. For instance, teachers may perceive initially that they have lost authority since they are not now the only source of information and, furthermore, that they have lost control over their students' work. These feelings usually disappear progressively as the students assume the new class rules and as the teachers carry out a carefully planned organisation of the work to be done with computers. Thus, they soon assume their new role as facilitators and organisers of their students' work.

An important curricular aspect to consider is the careful preparation of a curriculum based on projects that cover the objectives the teachers want to achieve. Projects usually conclude with the elaboration of final products such as dossiers, graphic material and presentations using traditional or multimedia/digital tools. Technology is also crucial because it is necessary to be aware of the technological possibilities and limitations of the schools and classrooms. Projects need to be designed taking into account the availability of the necessary technological tools and most importantly, how familiar the students are with them before the project starts. Tasks should be based on the collaborative learning principles in most cases so it is important that students are aware that it is necessary not only to exchange information with their foreign partners but also to interact with them and strive for the achievement of common goals and pedagogical objectives.

Even though it is not strictly necessary, working in groups in the classroom is something that clearly facilitates the development of eTwinning projects. Even though working in groups may imply less time to cover all curricular topics, these students are usually more skilled at solving problems, understanding materials and being autonomous. When organising and designing students' group work it is always crucial to let them know about the importance of working in groups as well as establishing the advantages of group work.

eTwinning Tools

When looking at how an eTwinning exchange functions, it is necessary to distinguish between the eTwinning *desktop* tools, which have been specially designed for this type of exchange and come as an integrated part of the exchange portal, and other external tools which are openly available on the internet. The *eTwinning desktop* is a private area on the portal that any registered school can use. In the desktop you can create your profile, look for partners, communicate with them in a private and safe environment, look for and upload learning resources, etc. When a partnership is approved, schools can use some more tools to apply for the eTwinning Label, enter the partnership's collaborative workspace called *Twin Space* and check the *Progress Card* to keep track of project activities. Furthermore, the *desktop* enables users to communicate with partners using an internal messaging system in a safe virtual environment (Figure 5.1).

Desktop tools

Desktop tools are those utilities included in the private section of a member's desktop that facilitate communication with other partners and the development of projects. These tools are the profile, the Twinfinder, the internal messaging system, the chat and the Twinspace. All of these will now be described briefly.

Profile

The Profile section contains the information about the teachers and their schools that they submitted when they registered in the portal. It is possible to register different teachers of the same school as the school has its own registration information. This information can be modified at any time. The profile also contains information about the partner schools. Teachers can manage their projects and eTwinning users by editing, removing or adding new partners and schools.

Twinfinder

This is an extremely useful tool that enables teachers to find partners that match the eTwinning preferences they included upon registering. The Twinfinder tool also allows users to refine their search by including more specific criteria such as country, languages used in the project, subject, age group, use of ICT. Alternatively, they can search from the Twinfinder map by simply clicking on a specific country.

Internal messaging system

Using this tool, teachers can send messages to other teachers and school staff involved in eTwinning. Messages can only be sent to the e-mail addresses of registered users.

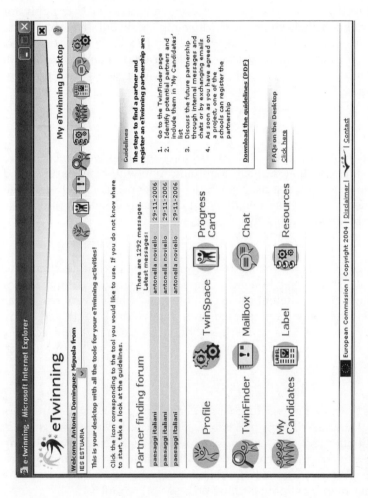

Figure 5.1 The eTwinning desktop

The chat

This is open only to registered eTwinning users. There are two types: the public chat rooms that are available to all registered users, and the private chat rooms that can be booked for specific talks with a potential partner.

Chat and e-mail are used in most eTwinning projects by students to exchange information about their tasks. A clear example could be the project 'L'Eau dans la Ville' (see list of related websites at the end of this chapter) where students from two schools tried to describe, analyse and compare the influence of water on their cities in Belgium and Portugal. The two groups compared results obtained from year to year, using the chat and e-mail tools to communicate and share their findings. The students completed their project by organising an exhibition meeting in Belgium.

The *TwinSpace* is a collaborative workspace developed specifically for eTwinning activities. All schools registered in eTwinning have a private workspace on the web which can be used to collaborate with partners. The Twinspace is available from the personal desktop and it is a space where files, documents and links can be shared between partners. It has an internal messaging system and chat room where teachers and students communicate in a closed network. It is browser-based and works with all operating systems. Many precautions have been taken to make sure that the Twinspace is a safe virtual environment. Schools can communicate and work together on this platform without interference from the outside (Figure 5.2).

External publishing tools

Apart from the tools provided by the eTwinning portal, there are some other external publishing and communication tools that can be very useful when working on an eTwinning collaborative project. Some of the publishing tools available to educators include blogs, MagazineFactory, wideboards and Media Synchrone. A blog is a personal web space, a journal, a diary, a space for schools or interest groups that can be used to describe activities and progress in a project. Anything, starting from ideas, news, links to pictures and videos, can be published. Teachers can set up a team blog and use it as a platform for collaboration in their partnership. Students can then contribute and comment on the items posted on the blog. The Central Support Service (CSS) now offers a blog for registered schools in eTwinning. However, teachers can also use other

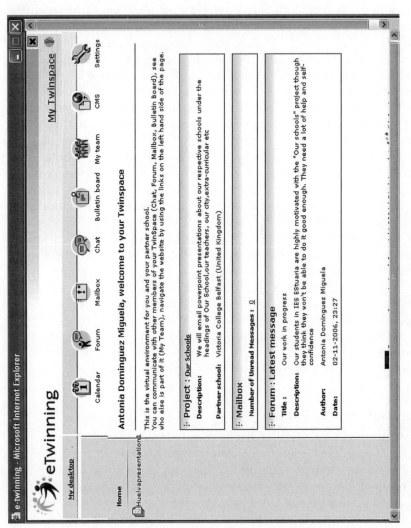

Figure 5.2 The Twinspace tool in the eTwinning portal

free blogging services like Blogger, blogia.com, etc. (See Dooley, this volume for more on blog use in telecollaboration.)

MagazineFactory is a versatile concept for developing web magazines for various purposes and contexts. The web magazine may be a single project or a magazine that is edited continuously throughout the school year. MagazineFactory is a free, easy and enjoyable publishing tool that provides teachers and pupils an opportunity to work as editorial staff in the class and to publish a web magazine of their own. The teacher is the editor-in-chief, while the pupils are journalists. To use MagazineFactory, it is necessary to be registered with eTwinning. Once an account has been opened, the tool will then be available from the eTwinning desktop.

Wideboards are large, virtual two-dimensional surfaces on which any type of object can be placed. All users see changes on the board online in real time. A board is persistent, which means that it keeps its objects until the board owner erases it. The board is web-based and platform-independent and also runs on Personal Digital Assistants (PDAs) and mobile phones. To use the ChatFiti wideboard, it is necessary to be registered with eTwinning and to contact the European Schoolnet to get an account. An example could be the wide board created by Christian Perrier (see list of weblinks at the end of the chapter), which can be used in such a way that students can insert text and images and work together correcting other people's texts.

Media Synchrone is web-based software that facilitates the easy production and publishing of rich media and open-content materials. Teachers can work on a variety of media components in any format: audio, pictures, PowerPoint presentation, existing video files, and texts linked with resources, web links, etc. Media Synchrome automatically does the technical tasks such as encoding, digitisation and online publishing. The user does not need to have any knowledge about formats, conversion, standards, etc. This tool can be used in projects where students create media materials about a specific topic and then share it with their partners in the other country. Good examples of this kind of project are videos included in electronic journals that are exchanged with the other school, such as the one carried out by students in Slovakia and Germany entitled 'D&L eMag' where students not only included videos about school news but also articles, pictures, sound recordings, etc.

External communication tools

Many of the online communication tools that teachers are already familiar with can also be very useful for eTwinning projects. Some of these include popular synchronous tools such as Skype and MSN Messenger. Skype is a computer tool that you can use to call other people on their computer or phone. While using Skype to call phones involves a charge, computer-to-computer calls are free. The tool also allows instant messaging, the transfer of files, as well as conference calls. To use Skype, it is necessary to download software and have a headset, speakers or a USB phone. Perhaps a better known tool is MSN Messenger, which enables synchronous chatting as well as audio- and videoconferences. Messenger also allows users to share photos, files and backgrounds.

Both tools are useful for projects where videoconferences and text-based chat take place. Students feel highly motivated using these tools to exchange information about how they are working on their common tasks or simply to talk about their projects and experiences. There are many eTwinning projects that have used or are using these tools, but it always depends on the availability of this kind of technology in the schools (webcams, microphones, good internet connection, etc.).

The Model in Practice

Registering

The first step to participate in an eTwinning project is to register in the eTwinning network on its web page. While registering, the teachers need to fill in a form that includes information about the school, the students, their partner preferences, etc. Then they can enter the desktop and use desktop tools to search for a partner and then to set up and manage partnerships. When announcing one's intended project, it is important to describe the idea clearly so that possible future partners will understand the proposal. There are no requirements as to the aims, duration or scope of activities (Figure 5.3).

Finding a partner

As mentioned above, the *Twinfinder* tool available in the eTwinning desktop enables teachers and school administrators to find partners for their classes. Once a possible candidate has been found, there is also the option of examining the qualities of the partner by establishing contact with the teachers and learning more about them. Teachers can add as many schools as they wish to the section 'My Candidates'. When choosing the best partner for an eTwinning project it is advisable to ask candidates to fill in a form about themselves, their school and their students. This form should include questions related to the

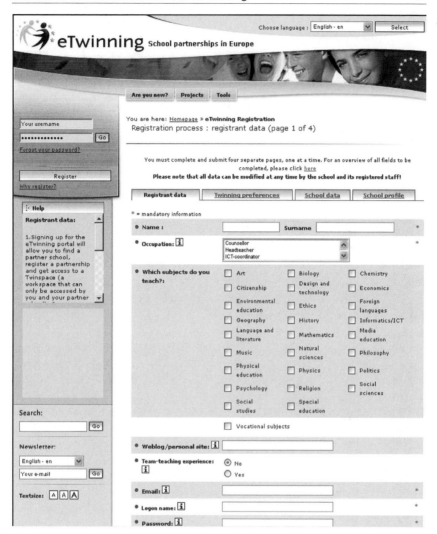

Figure 5.3 The registration process in the eTwinning portal

curriculum, to school organisation, type of school, social and economic background, students' age, language competence, etc. This information will be very valuable when it comes to deciding on valid potential partners (Figure 5.4).

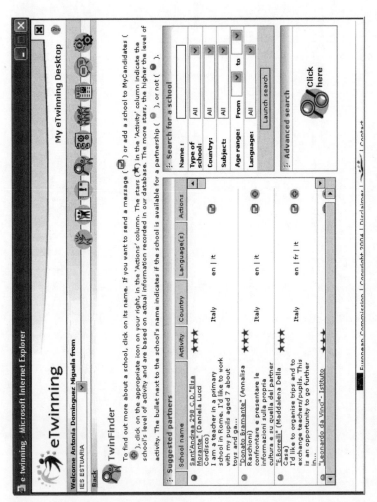

Figure 5.4 The Twinfinder function in the eTwinning portal

Preparing a project

The next stage in the process is to design a project which both teachers and students want to work on. It is recommended that eTwinning projects share most of the features of cooperative learning methods, many of which have been outlined by Slavin (1995). For example, the project needs to be flexible so that it will also cater for the other school's needs. Some of the organisational aspects that need to be taken into account include the project timetable, holidays, ICT tools available and the characteristics of each group of students. Regarding duration, projects can take many forms, for instance: a short project lasting one month where you focus on a specific part of your curriculum; a three-month project teaching your pupils how to set up a common website and present information in a foreign language; a school-year project on European history, mathematics or art, which is integrated into the curriculum and eventually forms part of final examinations; a project that sets up a cooperation framework with one or more partners.

Before starting a project, teachers need to have a clear idea of what they want to achieve from the virtual collaboration. Many aspects and elements in eTwinning projects may need to be modified as teachers move on to the second phase of mutual planning of the project with their partners. At this time it will be necessary to deal with the three essential elements of a collaborative project: content (themes, topics, issues to be dealt with), context (why our schools/students want/need to collaborate and what our objectives are) and process. This last element is one of the most important ones because it is in the process where the aims and activities are established, giving emphasis to interacting, sharing of information, communicating and working collaboratively online. When organising and planning project-oriented activities, teachers need to bear in mind the power of the computer. As de Szendeffy (2005: 117) reminds us, computers in project-oriented activities '...give rise to student interaction, discovery, and creativity combined with acquisition of content knowledge, computing, and other skills in a process they feel ownership of and with a tangible product to show for it'. Even though these activities are usually more rewarding for students, they also require more careful teacher planning, preparation, involvement and follow-up.

When organising the project participants need to establish a number of common objectives, which should be agreed upon by both partners. They also need to agree on the issues that are going to be dealt with and how they are going to be addressed or worked on in the project. Tasks are another important part of the project and both partners should be clear in their allocation and should agree on the deadlines for having those tasks completed. Collaboration is essential but clarity and a good understanding between the partners is the sin qua non condition for successful collaboration.

The role of language use is obviously very important in these projects. Particularly in the case of language projects, the linguistics objectives and the role of language learning are crucial for both partners. This is the case of two partners using a foreign language (for instance a Spanish school and a Polish school using English to communicate) or two partners using each other's language as a foreign language (for instance a Spanish and a British school using English and Spanish depending on the language they want to improve).

The actual development of a project depends on the schools, the students' workload, the time available for this project in our schedule, the access to ICT tools, etc. What is most important is to have a clear planning and timing of all the tasks in our project so that both partners know what they have to do at any time. The distribution of tasks among groups of students, how they respond to the tasks, and the exploration of problems are all issues that need to be returned to constantly throughout the process. Thus, it will also be necessary to have a constant evaluation of the project itself in order to detect emerging problems and find solutions as soon as possible. On-going evaluation will be carried out by the teacher not only by evaluating students' performance but also by observing the quality of collaboration with the partners. Students can also provide some feedback in evaluating forms as a final evaluation of the project.

Regarding the methodology, there are some issues that both partners need to discuss apart from the objectives, content and timeline. These are related to how students and teachers are going to communicate with each other and share information necessary for the project. In this case, it is necessary to consider the ICT tools available in the classrooms and schools and it is also necessary to decide about how to present and exchange information along the project, for instance the eTwinning Twinspace, using e-mail exchange, using a blog, using a web page where both partners publish their results, etc. At this point it is necessary to keep in mind the risks of publishing students' personal information on the internet, especially when teachers are working with children and young learners. In relation to this, Dudeney (2000: 134) suggests: 'Most people agree that it is sensible to have students (or their parents and guardians) sign a release form – giving the school or institution permission to publish student writing – before publishing their work'.

All the work that is done within an eTwinning project should be properly exhibited in both schools so as to create an atmosphere of international collaboration. A good idea is to publish the project's results in the school web page, print the most important products and display them all over the school boards. The teachers should also inform other colleagues, the head teacher and parents about the project and if possible, make them get involved in it.

A Sample Project

The European eTwinning helpdesk, together with teachers from different countries, has designed many sample projects for teachers who are looking for concrete ideas on how to implement a European collaborative project. Each kit or project relates to a theme and provides information on the target group, objectives and pedagogical value of the activities. The following is a basic example of a possible eTwinning project but the reader should bear in mind that the range of possibilities is very large and depends on the needs and interests of teachers and students.

This particular project is very suitable for the foreign language classroom. In this case, teachers of a foreign language and their pupils, from at least two different countries, work together to create an e-journal (a common online diary, newspaper or magazine). This project aims mainly to encourage language learning and intercultural dialogue. In this project pupils learn how to write collaboratively with both their classmates and partners abroad and how to publish articles online about their own cultures and their daily lives. The pedagogical objectives that are pursued in this project are mainly to improve writing and reading skills in a foreign language, to develop collaborative writing and proofreading skills and to refine critical thinking skills when looking for, selecting and organising relevant information on the chosen topic. Students also have the opportunity to write different types of articles (interviews, news reports, photo-commentaries, advertisements, surveys, reviews and announcements), to take digital pictures and use them in articles and to use ICT collaborative tools for publishing, editing, commenting and, if available, rating articles. Generally speaking, the most suitable students for this type of projects are students from 10 to 19 years old and the project can last from one month to a school year depending on the number of objectives and tasks included in the project. Many different tools can be used in a project like this, such as the Twinspace (websites, folders, files), word processing, chat, e-mail, digital camera and internet.

During the project, teachers in both schools need to work together in order to establish a common set of elements in their projects. Therefore they need to agree on the involved pupils' age and level of competence in the foreign language, to link both the topics and the type of articles to the foreign language curricula in both countries, to concur on time lines and on ICT tools used in the project, to share their ideas on how to teach a foreign language through collaborative writing and reading, to share activities and exercises that will enable their pupils to write articles in a foreign language and finally, to decide on how pupils will collaborate together.

Pupils can write the article about their own school and, once published online, they share and discuss it with partners abroad. However, they can also work on the article with their partners abroad dealing with a specific topic from the outset. As they work on the project students will learn to use the communication tools and publishing tools like the Twinspace, and other ICT tools needed for the project (word processing, e-mail, digital camera and the internet). Depending on the age and the maturity of pupils, the teachers decide on how much freedom the pupils will get in the e-journal creation process and on how complex their e-journal will be.

Once the project theme has been agreed, the students have to select and organise material on the chosen topic together with the students in the other school. They can do that through online exchanges using e-mail, chat and videoconferencing. They can brainstorm their ideas and prepare drafts of the article, respecting the journalistic approach they have chosen and decide on the layout of the article and on the pictures, which will illustrate the ideas expressed in the text. During the process teachers monitor pupils' work, guide them through the process and help them cope with the challenges of collaborative writing in a foreign language.

When writing the final version of the article, pupils take into account the comments made by the other members of the team concerning the quality of the language, content, layout and pictures. They should quote the sources of information provided in the article properly and insert the article in the Twinspace. Finally, teachers as administrators make their articles public.

With this kind of project students learn from the exchanges and learn with and from each other. Pupils read their partners' or other teams' articles, they exchange comments and consider the quality of the language, content, layout and the relevance of the pictures. The articles are put together in an online e-journal. They decide and agree on e-journal design (logo, front page) and organise available articles according to the sections they agreed on at the beginning. Finally they try to find common features and differences in the perception of the chosen topic in their countries. Online exchanges can take many forms but it is usually advisable to organise classroom time for periods of online exchange as a class as well as requiring students to work on the exchange outside of class.

In a final stage articles in a foreign language are published online and in the e-journal, with an organised structure and containing articles written by all teams involved. Pupils may decide to create a paper version of their magazine and that way they can learn about the differences between online and paper magazines. They may also create a real cover for their e- or paper journal with the help of the specialised publishing software available online (see list of weblinks below). They may translate the most interesting articles into their mother tongue, publish them on the school website or print them, and make them available at school or in the local community. (An example of a project by Slovenian and Portuguese students that followed this structure, Ejournal Bridges, can be found in the list of links at the end of this chapter.)

Strengths and Weaknesses of eTwinning

eTwinning projects provide a wonderful opportunity for European schools to work collaboratively with other schools and for students to expand their knowledge of other cultures and languages. Even when the project is not a linguistic project itself, all projects have a linguistic component that helps develop a plurilingual competence in our students. eTwinning European telecollaboration also provides a new dimension to teaching and motivates teachers and students to develop their inter-cultural competence and communication skills and to improve their ICT skills.

However, it is also clear that many problems may arise when groups are working on a project. Problems can arise due to various issues including differences in curricula in schools, the lack of collaboration between teachers, low levels of motivation in students, different levels of language skills and the lack of equipment or technical support in schools. Some solutions to these problems may be agreement of a common curriculum, methodology and objectives from the very beginning, giving greater support to collaborating teachers and to team work, finding interesting and appealing topics for our students, providing more training in foreign languages and, finally, involving an ICT coordinator in our project.

Note

1. Decision No 2318/2003/EC of the European Parliament and of the Council of 5 December 2003 adopting a multiannual programme (2004–2006) for the effective integration of ICT in education and training systems in Europe (eLearning Programme).

References

Butler-Pascoe, M.E. and Wiburg, K.M. (2003) *Technology and Teaching English Language Learners*. New York: Pearson Education.
Central Support Service for eTwinning (2006) Learning with eTwinning. On WWW at http://www.etwinning.net/ww/en/pub/etwinning/helpdesk_and_tools/css_helpdesk.htm. Accessed 6.4.07.
Chapelle, C.A. (2003) *English Language Learning and Technology*. Amsterdam and Philadelphia: John Benjamins Publishing Company.
De Szendeffy, J. (2005) *A Practical Guide to Using Computers in Language Teaching*. Ann Arbor: University of Michigan Press.
Dudeney, G. (2000) *The Internet and the Language Classroom. A Practical Guide for Teachers*. Cambridge: Cambridge University Press.
Kanuka, H. and Anderson, T. (1999) Using constructivism in technology-mediated learning: Constructing order out of the chaos in the literature. *Radical Pedagogy* 1, 2. On WWW at http://radicalpedagogy.icaap.org/content/issue1_2/02kanuka1_2.html.
Panitz, T. (1996) A definition of collaborative vs. cooperative learning. On WWW at http://www.city.londonmet.ac.uk/deliberations/collab.learning/panitz2.html. Accessed 6.4.07.
Slavin, R.E. (1995) *Cooperative Learning*. Massachusetts: Allyn & Bacon.
Vygotsky, L.S. (1978) *Mind and Society*. Cambridge, MA: Harvard University Press.
Young, G.D. (1997) *Adult Development, Therapy, and Culture*. New York: Plenum Press.

Web pages referred to in Chapter 5

The eTwinning homepage: http://www.eTwinning.net

The Learning and Sharing eTwinning Project: http://www.elearningeuropa.info/index.php?page=doc&doc_id=7327&doclng=6

'L'Eau dans la Ville': http://www.agers.cfwb.be/prof/dossiers/etwinning/laureats2005/eau.asp

A wideboard by Christian Perrier: http://macg4.eun.org/~thomas/CPerrier/

'D&L eMag': http://www.divina-lindlar.net

Magazine Publishing Software: http://flagrantdisregard.com/flickr/magazine.php

Ejournal Bridges: http://ejournal.eduprojects.net/Bridges/

Part 3

Issues and Questions in Online Intercultural Exchange

Chapter 6

Grammar and Feedback: Turning to Language Form in Telecollaboration

PAIGE D. WARE and MARIA LUISA PÉREZ CAÑADO

Introduction

Much of the current research in telecollaboration is directed either at the development of intercultural competence (Belz, 2003; Belz & Müller-Hartmann, 2003; O'Dowd, 2003; Thorne, 2003; Ware, 2005; Ware & Kramsch, 2005) or at promoting conversational fluency and negotiation of meaning for linguistic development (Appel & Mullen, 2000; Levy & Kennedy, 2004; Schwienhorst, 2000). In the first of these areas of inquiry, significant strides have been made in understanding how cultural, social and institutional variables impact online communication across linguistic and geographic lines (see the chapters by Belz and O'Dowd in this volume). In the second area, research focuses on what happens in transcripts of real-time interaction and extrapolates from that how particular types of communicative language functions take place and the extent to which linguistic gains are achieved.

In this chapter, which grows out of the findings of each of these research bases, we provide a rationale for turning to a focus on language form in telecollaboration. We suggest that foreign language students can use their online forums, not only as opportunities for promoting their second language (L2) fluency and for deepening their cultural understanding, but also as spaces in which to develop metalinguistic awareness about grammar and to provide their partners with feedback on linguistic accuracy and complexity. We start by examining some of the key issues in grammar instruction and peer feedback in general, and then turn to five specific areas that language teachers might want to consider as they prepare for a telecollaborative exchange that includes a specific focus on language form. Throughout this chapter, we provide authentic examples from our own work with telecollaboration, including excerpts from students' transcripts and sample activities and prompts from previous and ongoing projects.

Why Focus on Grammar in Telecollaboration?

How grammar has been conceptualised as part of classroom teaching has changed across the last few decades. In linguistics, an early perspective on grammar saw it as a body of knowledge accessible to an idealised native speaker. Grammar was viewed as a logical system governed by a discrete set of underlying rules (Chomsky, 1964, 1965). Within a decade, however, informed by fields such as anthropology and second language acquisition, such a static characterisation of language was soon replaced with a view of grammar as learning how to *use* language rules for communicative purposes (Hymes, 1972). Building on this distinction, language education theorists in the 1980s situated grammatical competence as one of four components of language proficiency, including discourse, strategic and sociolinguistic competence (Breen & Candlin, 1980; Canale, 1983; Canale & Swain, 1980). In the two decades since then, the emphasis in much of foreign and second language instruction has built on this notion of four pillars of 'communicative competence'. From the momentum generated by more than 20 years emphasising communicative approaches to language teaching, it is not surprising that early implementations of online writing collaboration across cultures were directed at promoting students' motivation and developing their communicative fluency in the target language (Kern, 1995, 1996; Warschauer, 1996). The grammatical pillar, however, has largely been pushed to the side (Segalowitz & Lightbown, 1999; Swan, 1985a, 1985b; Ur, 1996).

In this chapter, we suggest that a language-based focus can be a justifiable component of telecollaborative projects. In the currently popular communicative view, language is often seen as a conduit for carrying and encoding ideas from one individual to another, but rarely as an object of inquiry in and of itself. Thus, fluency is valued, often at the expense of developing students' linguistic accuracy and complexity in using the target language. And yet, in the context of many foreign language classrooms, particularly at the upper intermediate and advanced levels, students must not only possess sophisticated knowledge about the language, but also be confident in their use of these rules. In many language teaching contexts at the post-secondary level, alignment with institutional and curricular goals alone provides sufficient justification for integrating a stronger focus on language form in telecollaboration.

Taking a broad literacy-based view of language instruction reframes the purpose of language study as that of learning a discrete set of isolated language skills into one of promoting students' critical thinking abilities, their metacommunicative awareness, and their ability to analyse and reflect upon language (Kern, 2000). From this perspective, peer feedback on language form and use makes an important contribution to students' development as advanced language users. Peers not only offer formative feedback on one another's language use, but they also provide an audience for discussing texts, obtaining multiple perspectives, and using the target language as a dynamic, ongoing process. Second and foreign language learners have been found to be less invested in their self-worth in L2 writing than are L1 writers (Leki, 1991), and are therefore not necessarily discouraged by receiving feedback on their language use; in contrast, they often welcome the opportunity to receive individualised feedback.

Integrating a Language Focus into Telecollaboration: Pedagogical Considerations

A student of ours recently pointed out that in her language classes, a focus on grammar typically occurred in the margins of activities, or what she referred to as 'grammar boxes'. Such a decontextualised treatment of language-focused activities, however, is precisely what we aim to avoid by integrating a focus on grammar and feedback into telecollaboration. Instead, our intention in the following sections is to emphasise the need for teachers to integrate a focus on language in authentic ways that do not replicate the common textbook approach of slicing grammar off as a separate set of discrete skills that can be practised in isolation from any ongoing communicative or reflective use. In our view, peer feedback in telecollaboration can become part of the ongoing interaction, not an added-on activity that students complete in order to practise static language rules. The following sections will help teachers who are interested in integrating a focus on language into telecollaboration as they consider some important preliminary questions: What is the context of the telecollaborative exchange? Who are my learners? What are the purposes of the feedback? What activities best promote my pedagogical goals? When and how should students provide feedback?

What Is the Context of a Telecollaborative Exchange?

The first area of consideration is that of context, which includes choices of both the medium and genre of the online writing. Kern (2000: 243) has summarised a comparison of the predominant features of synchronous, or real-time, interaction with those of academic writing. In online chatting, the emphasis is on fluency and interaction among multiple perspectives across multiple topics, marked linguistically by what are often considered both 'oral' and 'literate' forms of communication, including varying degrees of aspects such as informality, topic shift markers and adherence to orthographic conventions. In contrast, in academic writing, students typically write for a single audience, and the emphasis is placed on formal accuracy, the use of conventional discourse forms and coherence markers, and sustained attention to a particular topic that is developed through multiple revisions. Kern has suggested that the features of both academic writing and synchronous writing can be exploited to promote overall literate competence in the target language. Such a tandem approach can be useful when learners are able to log on at the same time, as is often the case in a within-class configuration or in circumstances in which students are not separated by several time zones.

In many cases of international telecollaboration, however, the logistical constraints of organising a real-time exchange between students in different countries have led instructors toward the choice of asynchronous, or delayed-time, exchanges. An added benefit of asynchronous writing is the time available to students to reflect upon and compose a thoughtful response without the pressure of having to formulate an immediate response in real time. Asynchronous messages typically allow students to compose longer messages, and they hold the potential for helping students to engage in a wider range of communicative purposes such as informing, requesting, persuading, narrating and describing. Although the specific medium of e-mail often mirrors the informality, speed and relaxed conventions of synchronous writing, instructors interested in promoting more attention to linguistic form and genre have had success with setting up online asynchronous platforms such as the freeware provided by Moodle (Robb, 2004) or commercial products such as Blackboard and WebCT. These forums tend to provide a pedagogical overlay to the interaction, making it easier for instructors to request that students write using the more formal conventions found in academic writing.

Who Are the Learners?

Most of the recent research on telecollaboration has typically involved at least two groups of post-secondary foreign language students who are partnered together to interact on a weekly basis as part of their intermediate to advanced language classes. In these constellations, students alternate their roles of native and target language speakers in an ongoing bilingual dialogue. Our own experience with telecollaboration tends to reflect this same configuration, but by no means is such a structure the only one possible. Given the vast diversity of potential online partnerships, we suggest that teachers consider several variables including learner background, levels of proficiency and first language influences as they decide on when, if and how to integrate peer feedback on language form into online international writing exchanges.

In considering learner background, we turn to a distinction made by Reid (1998) between 'eye' learners and 'ear' learners. Typically, international students who grow up learning a foreign language in their home countries are 'eye' learners, as their exposure to the language consists mainly of textbooks and classroom instruction. They are usually familiar with grammar rules and terminology and are readily able to explain rules of the target language. Such a cognitive grasp of the formal rules, however, does not always translate into their ability to use the rules with ease. 'Ear' learners, on the other hand, are those who grow up using the target language; they can be native speakers of the language or permanent residents who have learned English as a Second Language without the formal instruction of 'eye' learners. 'Ear' learners recognise what sounds right in a language but rarely have the metalinguistic terminology to explain why a particular word choice, grammatical form or language function is correct.

Interestingly, in telecollaboration, 'eye' and 'ear' learners mix together, each possessing a sophisticated knowledge of the formal system of rules and terminology for their target language, but not necessarily for their own native language. Thus, learners may find themselves at a loss for explaining how their own language works, and might well be frustrated that their partners cannot explain the target language in metalinguistic terms such as 'present perfect tense' or 'subjunctive clauses'. Teachers, given this mixture of learner background, will want to decide on the extent to which they will ask students to use metalinguistic terminology in their online feedback. By using simple questionnaires or examples, teachers can decide if their students are able to function at a more technical level, given some extra support.

In terms of levels of proficiency, Brown (1994) has developed a heuristic for categorising learners into several types that are likely (or not) to benefit from direct language feedback. At the 'random' and 'emergent' stages, learners are still puzzling together very basic language patterns such as spelling rules, verb conjugations or basic sentence word order. In such cases, language feedback may well be less fruitful. By the time learners move into the 'systematic' and 'stabilisation' stages, in which they are actively building an interlanguage of patterns, they are more likely to benefit from feedback that alerts them to their own errors and assists them in becoming more reflective and self-reliant in their editing. Telecollaborative partnerships can be very productive contexts for helping learners become more reflective as they refine and edit their writing in a low-stakes communicative environment as part of an ongoing system of formative feedback.

The influence of the first language (L1) is a final consideration. Typically, telecollaboration has focused on foreign language learners, comprised of two groups of language students who all share a single native language and a single target language with their group. Unlike many second language learning contexts, in which as many different first languages can be represented as there are learners in the classroom, such a clear division of languages can be used as a resource. For example, in an exchange involving learners of Spanish and English, teachers can systematically introduce their students to a contrastive analysis of the two languages across phonetic, morphological, lexical and syntactic domains. English-speaking students can learn why Spanish-speaking students often confuse 'make' and 'do', on the one hand, and why they themselves often leave out necessary pronouns in Spanish. Such metalinguistic priming can help students become more aware, not only of how to help their partners correct certain errors, but also how to better attend to their own mistakes.

What Are the Purposes of Providing Feedback?

The purposes of providing peer feedback on language form vary in type and intensity. In many previously documented projects, the language focus could best be described as *peripheral*. In many telecollaborative exchanges, students interact to foster communicative fluency (Lee, 2004), to explore intercultural learning (Belz, 2003; O'Dowd, 2003; Ware & Kramsch, 2005) or to negotiate meaning in real time (Kötter, 2003; O'Rourke, 2005). To varying degrees, depending on either the individual students' preferences or on the instructor's use of the online transcripts for in-class reflection, learners may or may not choose to exploit their online writing as a context for developing their linguistic accuracy or complexity. In general, however, attention to language form has not emerged as a dominant feature characterising telecollaborative exchanges (Schwienhorst, 2000).

Interest is growing in developing ways that online writing might foster greater language *proficiency* in students' formal writing – that is, in fluency as well in grammatical accuracy and syntactic complexity (Pellettieri, 2000; Sotillo, 2000). The focus ranges from ways that telecollaboration might foster metalinguistic awareness by providing consistent language feedback and peer modelling to ways that it might develop students' interest in risk-taking with new forms and their ability to self-edit their texts.

A third area, still in its infancy, is the use of feedback-focused telecollaboration for *pedagogical* purposes in teacher training programmes. In this type of project, the online interaction typically takes place in only one language, and the roles of the participants are not those of bilingual partners switching out native and target speaker status. Rather, pre-service or in-service language instructors are matched with foreign or second language learners to assist them in tutorial roles with their language development. Each group has a different set of purposes for engaging in the interaction, and the benefits to each are unique. The language students receive individualised feedback on their writing, usually in a much more intensive manner than a single classroom teacher can provide, while the future language teachers are provided multiple authentic opportunities to learn about language pedagogy and feedback strategies under the trained guidance of the supervising course instructor. Ros i Sole and Truman (2005), for example, documented how online tutors provided three main types of feedback strategies: (1) *correction* of errors in which partners merely marked mistakes by providing a metalinguistic label for the type of error made; (2) *specific feedback*, in which partners provided the correct answer for mistakes or made suggestions for improving style and syntactic complexity; and (3) *commentaries*, in which partners not only corrected or pointed out errors but also provided extended metalinguistic commentaries justifying the suggested revisions.

What Activities Best Promote the Pedagogical Goals?

Telecollaborative projects have been organised around multiple themes, among them, joint literature discussions (Belz, 2003), intercultural exploratory projects (Furstenberg *et al.*, 2001; Kern, 1996; O'Dowd, 2003) and media comparisons (Ware, 2005). Because no research has yet addressed how peer feedback on language form is systematically integrated into such projects, there is currently not a recommended set of task types or activities that dominate the research base. There are, however, definite trends in the types of online activities that tend to occur in telecollaborative exchanges, so we review three categories here with suggestions for how a language-based focus can be integrated.

Reinforcement activities

At the highly structured end of an online exchange, instructors establish a sequence of activities that works with the course goals for both instructors and both groups of students. The online component of the coursework complements what happens in the classroom, and vice versa. Such an approach lends itself well to instruction that attempts to integrate the online exchange at multiple levels. Instructors can introduce a discussion topic, text or language-related lesson in their face-to-face time, and students can continue the exploration and practice with their international partners. Subsequent class time can be utilised to download excerpts of students' transcripts for further follow-up discussions. This sequencing of activities requires a great deal of collaboration and agreement between professors and relies on a strong time commitment to the online component of the exchange.

Language exploration activities

Another way to integrate language is to have students periodically use their online forums for a direct exploration of language. The activities do not necessarily rely on systematic integration into the ongoing coursework, but can form part of an overarching approach to infusing the language class with exercises in developing metalinguistic awareness and awakening in students a curiosity of the similarities and differences between their native and target languages. An example would be genre transformation activities in which students rewrite a short newspaper report, for example, into a narrative and then examine with their partners how the language style shifts. More specifically, they can be asked to isolate features of particular genres, such as the person in which the text is written or the way in which instances of reported speech are realised. Attention can also be drawn to the existence of common patterns in sentence initial elements or, in the case of longer texts, to the appearance of a larger discourse and/or information structure. Other possibilities include translation tasks, contrastive rhetoric activities and vocabulary building activities. As they complete these activities, students can be asked to go to particular websites for resources that might contain, for example, lists of useful idioms, brief grammar explanations or lexical fields.

Examples

- Genre transformation activity. All students will read a text and will rewrite it in a different genre (examples: letter to a friend, newspaper story, fiction story, report, etc.). The tutors will provide feedback on the following for the students:

  a) level of formality;
  b) use of prepositions;
  c) use of punctuation.

- Translation activity. Choose a short text (song lyrics, article, letter, etc.) in your native language and translate it into your target language. Without seeing the original text, your partner needs to correct the translation to make it as appropriate and 'natural-sounding' as possible. Discuss the errors your partner made in their translation and try to explain why it 'sounds wrong'.

Communicative activities

A final way to integrate a focus on language is to follow models used in second language writing classrooms, in which students offer one another peer feedback on their writing. The extent to which students need to revise and rewrite their texts based on this feedback would, of course, vary depending on the course goals and instructor's preferences. On one end of the continuum, students can simply provide feedback and hope that their partner will use it in the future. At the opposite extreme, the instructor can require that their students rewrite their texts based on the feedback. Wherever they are on the continuum, students essentially engage in writing about different topics, as they focus primarily on an exchange of ideas and perspectives. Embedded in each of the weekly messages, however, is the directive for students to provide explicit feedback on one or two specific aspects of their partner's language use on an as-need basis.

Example

- Writing a short composition. Students choose one of the three topics and write a short essay:

  a) A typical day in the life of a Spanish college student
  b) The different types and influences of current popular music in your city

c) Types of entertainment for different generations in your city/region

Tutors will ask elaborating questions and will help with style/syntax/vocabulary. Students should ask for specific areas on which they would like feedback.

When and How Should Students Provide Feedback?

Given the lack of evidence from research in telecollaboration on grammar and peer feedback, we turn briefly to research findings from L2 writing. Peer response has been viewed as helpful for providing students with formative assessment, but research findings are quite mixed. A study by Paulus (1999) found general improvement in students' writing after peer feedback, while Connor and Asenavage (1994) found only minimal improvement. Mendonca and Johnson (1994) reported that students used at least half of their peers' comments in subsequent revisions, but a study by Keh (1990) suggests that the feedback typically centres on surface-level errors and not on substantive issues of meaning. In one of the few studies conducted on online peer review, Liu and Sadler (2003) recently reported similar results that students tended to focus on surface-level errors online, whereas in face-to-face interaction, the participants had more fruitful interactions. In general, in face-to-face peer response, research does tend to point toward students' preference for teacher feedback over peer feedback, even when they also evaluate their experiences with peer feedback positively (c.f. Zhang, 1995).

As with most pedagogical initiatives, however, decisive factors for the success or failure of an activity like peer response have more to do with how it is integrated, what its purposes are, what the participants' individual goals are and how well both affective and cultural factors are addressed. For these reasons, telecollaboration remains a very interesting area to explore, as it upends many of the constraints of the traditional classroom. What is clear, however, is how important participant preparation becomes when introducing peer feedback into a telecollaborative exchange. In a traditional classroom context, for example, Horowitz (1986) found that students can offer misleading advice if they do not know how to identify errors. In such face-to-face contexts, training students to give feedback has been shown to help all of those involved – both those who receive and give feedback (Berg, 1999) – especially if students are trained to give concrete advice (Stanley, 1992).

Most instructors will not have the time or freedom from institutional constraints to implement an intensive mentoring project, so we have compiled a set of guidelines that can be useful for training students how to make decisions about when and how to provide feedback. We divide these guidelines into two types of feedback strategies: language-related feedback and interpersonal interaction strategies.

Language-related feedback

On the extreme end of the debate on how to provide language-related feedback are advocates of a 'correction-free approach' who argue that feedback on form has little or even no place in second and foreign language teaching and learning (Krashen, 1984; Truscott, 1996). They argue that no short- or long-term gains are incurred when teachers provide explicit feedback on grammatical form. Rather, language learners are believed to cycle through a natural progression of grammar acquisition through exposure to the language over time. However, evidence from studies integrating different degrees of form-focused instruction shows positive results, particularly in accelerating students' mastery of some grammatical forms (White *et al.*, 1991). Longitudinal studies have shown long-term gains (Ferris, 2002; Ferris & Roberts, 2001), and a short-term study by Chandler (2003) documented how simply underlining and providing direct feedback reduced errors in subsequent student writing.

Within these larger debates, instructors can look to how terminology is used to describe grammar, as these labels provide an indication of how language-related feedback is conceptualised and evaluated. The expression 'error correction', for example, often implies a narrow range of language forms focused mainly on more surface-level mistakes and errors. 'Form-focused feedback', on the other hand, is a phrase common in cognitivist approaches that examine language acquisition through negotiation of meaning. When turning to telecollaboration, we prefer the term 'language-related feedback' as a way to encourage instructors and students to think about a wide range of areas for metalinguistic reflection and action. In short, students can provide feedback on many areas of language use, from grammatical mistakes to stylistic and usage choices. In this spirit of viewing grammar as including a range of aspects from orthographical accuracy to idiomatic expressions, we forward the following advice for providing students with specific strategies for offering feedback within the context of telecollaboration. To illustrate, each guideline is followed by an example of students carrying out the advice in authentic online exchanges.

Distinguish between 'global errors' and 'local mistakes'

Students can learn to ask, 'How important is this error or mistake?' While both errors and mistakes might merit feedback in the context of a particular telecollaborative project, students should be encouraged to understand the difference between the two and to elicit their partners' preferences on whether or not they would like feedback on both types.

Examples

- It would be nice that you tell me about mistakes in the text.
- Please tell me about anything that doesn't sound quite right to you!
- Please, if I have any mistakes, can you correct me? It will be great to improve my English. Thanks.
- Correct all my mistakes please. I don't mind if you correct all of them because it is good for me, though I can feel like a fool that doesn't know anything.
- I'll be glad if you could correct the lots of mistakes that I'm sure I have in the text.

Provide indirect feedback

Students can look for *patterns* in the way their partner uses language and provide 'indirect feedback'. In other words, instead of simply writing in the correct answer for their partners, a form of direct feedback, they can use a different font colour to highlight in their partner's text all of the errors of a particular type.

Example

- I am supposed to highlight the mistakes I find. The words in italics are misspelled. The grey-highlighted words are grammar, word order or word choice mistakes.

Cati is from Mengíbar. She has house very big and nice. She owns two houses, the nicest one is in the country. There you can take fresh *our*. In the summer, she invites me to the swimming-pool. We enjoy walking together, talking about our problems and sunbathing. She also is very skilled and she studies at university. Ah!! I forgot, she is very pretty. One thing I really admire about her is her family *relationship*. They are very joined and they are always celebrating parties.

Selectively address language forms

Research indicates that when teachers provide feedback on just one or two *types of errors* per message (for example, verb tenses or comma usage, but not on every error), students are more likely to recognise the pattern and act upon it in subsequent writing. The following example focuses on comma usage:

Example

She is small and slim but now, my sister is plump because is pregnant. She has a beautiful smile. Her eyes are intense and brown. She has long curly red hair and dark skin. (...) Sonia is funny but moody when she is angry with someone.

Reformulate 'awkward' syntax in the partner's writing

Students can select two or three sentences to rewrite for their partners, thereby providing a basis of comparison for their partner to analyse. Language learners can compare their first version with their partner's 'native-sounding' version, a useful activity for building metalinguistic awareness of L1 and L2 transfer issues.

Examples

- The following are fine, but I have reworded them to sound more fluent:
  - As I am a second-year student I haven't got much free time.
  - *As a second-year student, I don't have a lot of free time.*
  - As we know, English is becoming a universal language on our planet.
  - *As we know, English is becoming a global language.*
  - One person out of six in the world knows English nowadays.
  - *One out of six people in the world knows English.*
  - And in the nearest future
  - *And in the near future*

Give examples to exemplify a point

When students attempt to explain a grammar rule or a vocabulary word, they should provide multiple examples of how this rule is invoked or how the word can be used across other contexts so that their partners have a larger context for assimilating the new rule or expression.

Examples

- Here is my tip of the week:
  - When you talk about some one's age you say he/she IS, I AM, they ARE _____. In Spanish some one HAS age: Yo tengo 21 años. But it does not translate that way in English.
  - Example: I am 21.

- So, go through and correct this sentence:
- I have two brother's one of my brother have 14 years old and my little brother have 3 years old.

- 'He also had two dull sons by the first wife, Flo, and was up to his neck in alimony and child support.' This should be, 'He had two sons by **his** first wife...' This is because it is possessive. For example, you would say 'his bike' or 'his mother'.

Ask clarification questions

To avoid the problem of students offering misleading advice, students should be encouraged to rely on a default strategy of asking for clarification if they do not understand a particular sentence or if they think there might be multiple meanings.

Examples

- However, I do not quite understand the phrase 'she's got fringe too'. Could you please elaborate that for me?
- I am not sure what you mean by 'Blow it!' Do you mean 'Darn it?'

Provide 'mini-grammar lessons'

Time permitting, and student interest pending, instructors might find it helpful to invest class time in explaining frequently used language patterns of the students' native language that students can then draw upon when writing to their partners. These mini-lessons are better viewed as teaching patterns and reasons, not necessarily rules (Larsen-Freeman, 2003).

Example

- It seems to me that the best thing to practice for this paper is comma rules – where and when can a comma be placed. If you would like me to send you a mini tutor session on it, I would be more than glad to, just let me know.

  - A paragraph is usually about four or five sentences. Try to make long and short sentences. In your long sentences use at least one of the following words:
  - For And Nor But Or Yet So
  - This way you can use the comma punctuation. Make sure to insert the comma before any one of those words when they join complete sentences.

Interpersonal interaction strategies

A significant amount of research has examined issues of individual preferences and cultural differences in providing language-related feedback. Villamil and Guerrero (2006), in a long-term study of revision, conclude with the advice that teachers be receptive to and open up class discussions about differences in how students conceptualise writing, how they respond to advice, and how they view their audience's role. In an earlier study (1996), they focus on the importance of affectivity as defined by 'camaraderie, empathy, and concern for not hurting each other's feelings' (p. 65). Hyland (1998) has addressed an important potential difference between teacher feedback and peer feedback, pointing out that teachers take into account the students as writers, not just the writing itself, when they make comments. Whether peers writing in the context of telecollaboration are able to skilfully negotiate the differences in responding to both the writer as well as the writing has yet to be explored.

The degree to which peers are trained to take such interpersonal and cultural factors into consideration, therefore, clearly needs to be addressed. Hyland and Hyland (2001) point out that sometimes teachers' strategies of mitigating their comments through hedges and questions might well go to the opposite extreme of downplaying the feedback to such an extent that their students either misinterpret the feedback or do not act upon it. The question remains whether or not students will err on the side of overly sweetening their feedback. With these caveats in mind, we provide the following suggestions for how students might draw upon some interpersonal interaction strategies. Again, we provide student data to illustrate.

Request help with specific areas for feedback

It is often easier to provide feedback when the recipient explicitly states what they would like help with. Given that many foreign language students are 'eye' learners, they should be able to specify areas of the language upon which they would like to improve.

Examples

- Could you please read this and comment on how I'm using the subjunctive?
- As you read this, will you write down any more sophisticated vocabulary words that come to mind? I think mine are still very simple. Please ignore accent marks this time!

- I'd like to learn more idioms – as you read this, do any come to mind that I might use?
- I cannot seem to distinguish between when to use present perfect and when to use simple past. Can you read this and comment on how I'm using these tenses?

Praise specific points; do not just make general comments

Students can encourage one another by providing positive feedback. Keeping the tone of the exchange upbeat helps both partners from getting self-conscious and also supports them in taking risks as they try out more complicated and sophisticated target language writing.

Examples

- I really like how descriptive you are – you have such a wide range of vocabulary!
- I really enjoyed reading your essay! Your sister seems like a wonderful person, and it sounds as if you are lucky to have her! It is very interesting for me to learn more about you and your family! You also are a great writer and I am impressed by your English!
- I can honestly say that I had NO difficulty reading your paper. I have done this before, where I conversed with students learning English. They were from a lot of different countries, but you amazed me. I never stopped at one sentence just to get an idea of what your message was!!
- I have corrected some grammatical mistakes. Overall, I was very impressed and proud of your English fluency. You did a fantastic job, since I had no trouble understanding your message.
- You use punctuation very well, and have a good vocabulary!

Keep the overall focus on meaning, not on correction

Students can work to mitigate the importance of their partners' errors when providing feedback, both in how much time they spend working on language and in how they contextualise the feedback.

Examples

- I would recommend inserting more commas. This is a mistake a lot of people make.
- A lot of times, even English writers will use the wrong verb agreement because there is more than one noun in the sentence.

Do not expect to know how to explain everything

Language teachers often have to look up explanations and resources to help teach some of the more complicated constructs of the language they are teaching. Students should know that, while they are not expected to be an expert on teaching their native language, they can be of assistance by looking up resources online or by asking their own teacher to help with their partners' particular questions.

Be aware of regional and national dialects

Depending on the country of origin of the partners in a telecollaborative exchange, students might be exposed in their online writing to a different dialect or different set of orthographic conventions than they are used to in their textbook learning. In Europe, for example, many students learn British English, and their American partners might not be as familiar with some of the British spelling and vocabulary as their 'non-native' partners are. Students can jointly examine these layers of language as potential areas to explore, not to 'correct'.

Realise that context often influences language choices

Telecollaborative partners can be invaluable in helping one another obtain a more complex view of the pragmatics of language use by pointing out differences in language register, in the contexts of use, and in multiple connotations of words or expressions.

Conclusion

As instructors and researchers continue to explore a language-based focus in telecollaboration, many issues are likely to arise. From a sociocultural perspective, questions of cultural contexts, learner preferences and socioinstitutional constraints can be explored. Cognitivist research will help shed light on questions about task types and long- and short-term linguistic gains that might take place online. Applied linguists can examine which specific aspects of grammar lend themselves best for peer feedback in telecollaborative exchanges. In the English language, for example, Ferris (2002) has outlined important areas such as verb tense and aspect issues, the use of articles and other determiners, noun endings, errors in word form and word order. The same kind of mapping would be needed for a variety of other languages in order to prepare for successful bilingual exchanges. Finally, language education research can focus on a range of pedagogical issues such as the balance between autonomy and reciprocity (Appel & Mullen, 2000), the teacher's role as facilitator (Belz & Müller-Hartmann, 2003; Ware & Kramsch, 2005) and effective ways to support foreign language students in providing feedback (Ferris, 2002).

In short, the turn in telecollaborative projects to a language-based focus adds another layer of context to already complex issues in L2 learning inquiry, as researchers examine issues surrounding feedback, language instruction and language acquisition. Despite the lack of unified directives from research, however, instructors can confidently turn to their own pedagogical contexts armed with a sufficient amount of information to begin exploring how a language-focused approach can work in their particular contexts. We have provided here a set of recommendations to help guide instructional decisions pertaining to the instructional context, the participants' needs and goals, the purposes of feedback, activities for structuring interaction and strategies students can use as they maintain communicative flow with an integrated focus on language.

References

Appel, C. and Mullen, T. (2000) Pedagogical considerations for a web-based tandem language learning environment. *Computers and Education* 34, 291–308.

Belz, J. (2003) Linguistic perspectives on the development of intercultural competence in telecollaboration. *Language Learning and Technology* 7 (2), 68–117.

Belz, J. and Mueller-Hartmann, A. (2003) Teachers as intercultural learners: Negotiating German–American telecollaboration along the institutional fault-line. *Modern Language Journal* 87 (1), 71–89.

Berg, E.C. (1999) The effects of trained peer response on ESL students' revision types and writing quality. *Journal of Second Language Writing* 8, 215–241.

Breen, J. and Candlin, D. (1980) The essentials of a communicative curriculum in language teaching. *Applied Linguistics* 1 (2), 89–112.

Brown, H.D. (1994) *Principles of Language Learning and Teaching* (3rd edn). Englewood Cliffs, NJ: Prentice-Hall.

Canale, M. (1983) From communicative competence to communicative language pedagogy. In J.C. Richards and R.W. Schmidt (eds) *Language and Communication* (pp. 2–27). London: Longman.

Canale, M. and Swain, M. (1980) Theoretical bases of communicative approaches to second language teaching and testing. *Applied Linguistics* 1, 1–47.

Chandler, J. (2003) The efficacy of various kinds of error correction for improvement of the accuracy and fluency of L2 student writing. *Journal of Second Language Writing* 12, 267–296.

Chomsky, N. (1964) *Current Issues in Linguistic Theory*. The Hague: Mouton.

Chomsky, N. (1965) *Aspects of a Theory of Syntax*. Cambridge, MA: MIT Press.

Connor, U. and Asenavage, K. (1994) Peer response groups in ESL writing classes: How much impact on revision? *Journal of Second Language Writing* 3 (3), 257–276.

Ferris, D. (2002) *Treatment of Error in Second Language Writing*. Ann Arbor: University of Michigan Press.

Ferris, D. and Roberts, B. (2001) Error feedback in L2 writing classes: How explicit does it need to be? *Journal of Second Language Writing* 10, 161–184.

Furstenberg, G., Levet, S., English, K. and Maillet, K. (2001) Giving a virtual voice to the silent language of culture: The CULTURA project. *Language Learning and Technology* 5 (1), 55–102.

Horowitz, D. (1986) Process not product: Less than meets the eye. *TESOL Quarterly* 20, 141–144.

Hyland, F. (1998) The impact of teacher written feedback on individual writers. *Journal of Second Language Writing* 7 (3), 255–286.

Hyland, F. and Hyland, K. (2001) Sugaring the pill: Praise and criticism in written feedback. *Journal of Second Language Writing* 10 (3), 185–212.

Hymes, D. (1972) On communicative competence. In J.B. Pride and J. Holmes (eds) *Sociolinguistics* (pp. 269–293). New York: Penguin.

Keh, C. (1990) Feedback in the writing process: A model and methods for implementation. *ELT Journal* 44 (4), 294–305.

Kern, R. (1995) Restructuring classroom interaction with networked computers: Effects on quality and quantity of language production. *Modern Language Journal* 79 (4), 457–476.

Kern, R. (1996) Computer-mediated communication: Using e-mail exchanges to explore personal histories in two cultures. In M. Warschauer (ed.) *Telecollaboration in Foreign Language Learning* (pp. 105–120). Honolulu, HI: University of Hawaii Press.

Kern, R. (2000) *Literacy and Language Teaching*. Oxford: Oxford University Press.

Kötter, M. (2003) Negotiation of meaning and codeswitching in on-line tandems. *Language Learning and Technology* 7 (2), 145–172.

Krashen, S. (1984) *Writing, Research, Theory, and Application*. Oxford: Pergamon Press.

Larsen-Freeman, D. (2003) *Teaching Language: From Grammar to Grammaring*. Boston: Heinle.

Lee, L. (2004) Learners' perspectives on networked collaborative interaction with native speakers of Spanish in the U.S. *Language Learning and Technology* 8 (1), 83–100.

Leki, I. (1991) The preference of ESL students for error correction in college level writing classes. *Foreign Language Annals 24* (3), 203–218.

Levy, M. and Kennedy, C. (2004) A task-cycling pedagogy using stimulated reflection and audio-conferencing in foreign language learning. *Language Learning and Technology* 8 (2), 50–69.

Liu, J. and Sadler, R. (2003) The effect and affect of peer review in electronic versus traditional modes on L2 writing. *Journal of English for Academic Purposes* 2, 193–227.

Mendonca, C.O. and Johnson, K.E. (1994) Peer review negotiations: Revision activities in ESL writing instruction. *TESOL Quarterly* 23 (4), 745–768.

O'Dowd, R. (2003) Understanding the 'other side': Intercultural learning in a Spanish–English e-mail exchange. *Language Learning and Technology* 7 (2), 118–144.

O'Rourke, B. (2005) Form-focused interaction in on-line tandem learning. *CALICO Journal* 22 (3), 433–466.

Paulus, T. (1999) The effect of peer and teacher feedback on student writing. *Journal of Second Language Writing* 8, 265–289.

Pellettieri, J. (2000) Negotiation in cyberspace: The role of chatting in the development of grammatical competence in the virtual foreign language classroom. In M. Warschauer and R. Kern (eds) *Network-based Language Teaching: Concepts and Practice* (pp. 59–86). Cambridge: Cambridge University Press.

Reid, J. (1998) 'Eye' learners and 'ear' learners: Identifying the language needs of international students and U.S. resident writers. In P. Byrd and J.M. Reid (eds) *Grammar in the Composition Classroom: Essays on Teaching ESL for College-bound Students* (pp. 3–17). Boston: Heinle and Heinle.

Robb, T. (2004) Moodle: A virtual learning environment for the rest of us. *TESL-EJ* 8 (2), 1–8.

Ros i Sole, C. and Truman, M. (2005) Feedback in distance language learning: Current practices and new directions. In B. Holmberg, M. Shelley and C. White (eds) *Distance Education and Languages: Evolution and Change* (pp. 72–91). Buffalo: Multilingual Matters.

Schwienhorst, K. (2000) Virtual reality and learner autonomy in second language acquisition. Unpublished manuscript, Trinity College, Dublin.

Segalowitz, N. and Lightbown, P.M. (1999) Psycholinguistic approaches to SLA. *Annual Review of Applied Linguistics* 19, 43–63.

Sotillo, S.M. (2000) Discourse functions and syntactic complexity in synchronous and asynchronous communication. *Language Learning and Technology* 4 (1), 82–119.

Stanley, J. (1992) Coaching student writers to be effective peer evaluators. *Journal of Second Language Writing* 1 (3), 217–233.

Swan, M. (1985a) A critical look at the communicative approach (1). *ELT Journal* 39 (1), 2–12.

Swan, M. (1985b) A critical look at the communicative approach (2). *ELT Journal* 39 (2), 76–87.

Thorne, S. (2003) Artifacts and cultures-of-use in intercultural communication. *Language Learning and Technology* 7 (2), 38–67.

Truscott, J. (1996) The case against grammar correction in L2 writing classes. *Language Learning* 46, 327–369.

Ur, P. (1996) The communicative approach revisited. *GRETA. Revista para Profesores de Inglés* 4 (2), 5–7.

Villamil, O.S. and Guerrero, M.C.M. (1996) Peer revision in the L2 classroom: Social-cognitive activities, mediating strategies, and aspects of social behaviour. *Journal of Second Language Writing* 5 (1), 51–75.

Villamil, O.S. and Guerrero, M.C.M. (2006) Sociocultural theory: A framework for understanding the social-cognitive dimensions of peer feedback. In K. Hyland and F. Hyland (eds) *Feedback in Second Language Writing: Contexts and Issues* (pp. 23–41). New York: Cambridge University Press.

Ware, P. (2005) 'Missed communication' in on-line communication: Tensions in fostering successful on-line interactions. *Language Learning and Technology* 9 (2), 64–89.

Ware, P. and Kramsch, C. (2005) Toward an intercultural stance: Teaching German and English through telecollaboration. *Modern Language Journal* 89 (2), 190–205.

Warschauer, M. (1996) Comparing face-to-face and electronic communication in the second language classroom. *CALICO Journal* 13 (2/3), 7–26.

White, L., Spada, S., Lightbown, P.M., and Ranta, L. (1991) Input enhancement and L2 question formation. *Applied Linguistics* 12 (4), 416–432.

Zhang, S. (1995) Reexamining the affective advantage of peer feedback in the ESL writing class. *Journal of Second Language Writing* 4, 209–222.

Chapter 7

The Development of Intercultural Communicative Competence in Telecollaborative Partnerships

JULIE A. BELZ

Introduction

The hallmark of telecollaboration is the use of Internet communication tools (e.g. e-mail, chat, blogs, videoconferencing) to link linguistically and culturally disparate groups of language learners and teachers in institutionalised settings for the purposes of (bilingual) social interaction and project-based intercultural collaboration (Appel, 1999; Belz & Thorne, 2006; Carney, 2006; Fischer, 1998; Little & Brammerts, 1996; Tella, 1991; Warschauer, 1996; Warschauer & Kern, 2000). The anticipated goals of such learning arrangements are foreign language (L2) linguistic development and intercultural (communicative) competence (Byram, 1997; Zarate, 2003), i.e. the ability to situate and interpret L2 texts, artefacts, events, behaviours, storylines and interactions within contextually appropriate frames of reference. Intercultural competence further entails the ability to view the self through the eyes of the other, an act of psychological de-centring which may lead to a critical reassessment of one's taken-for-granted world (Byram, 1989, 2003).

A clear example of what it means to interpret L2 texts within culturally appropriate frames of reference can be seen in Maori writer Patricia Grace's (1987) short story *Butterflies* as discussed in Cazden (2001: 154). In this fictionalised account of a very young Maori girl's experiences at school with her *Pakeha* or white teacher, she is asked to write a story. Her story reads as follows: 'I killed all the butterflies ... This is me and this is all the butterflies' (Grace, 1987: 61). When the girl arrives home from school, her grandparents, who are hoeing around the cabbages and picking beans in the garden, ask her what her teacher said about her story. The young girl replies that her teacher said that butterflies are very beautiful creatures that fly in the sun and visit all the pretty flowers. According to the girl's teacher,

127

'you don't kill butterflies' (p. 61). When the girl's grandparents hear this report, they stand silently in their cabbage patch for a very long time. Finally, the grandfather says: 'because you see . . . your teacher, she buy [sic] all her cabbages from the supermarket and that's why' (p. 61). The teacher in this story negatively evaluates the killing of the butterflies and, consequently, the girl because she interprets the girl's behaviour, as reported in her story, within her own *Pakeha* frames of reference; she does not consider that 'killing all the butterflies' may mark the girl as helpful and even industrious within Maori frames of reference. If the teacher in this story had told the girl 'you must be a great help to your grandparents' instead of 'you don't kill butterflies', then she would have displayed a measure of intercultural competence.

The underlying rationale for telecollaboration with respect to the development of L2 linguistic competence is the familiar notion within foreign language education circles that exposure to L2 'input' will facilitate L2 development or change over time; nevertheless, relatively few studies report on the development of particular linguistic features in telecollaboration (e.g. Belz & Vyatkina, 2005; Dussias, 2006). The added dimension of social interaction with native-speaking *age peers* has been shown to broaden the range of available discourse options in comparison to traditional L2 classrooms, to alter and increase the (number of) epistemic roles that learners may assume, and to create conditions under which learners desire to present and maintain positive face, which, in turn, may result in enhanced L2 performance (Belz & Kinginger, 2003; Kinginger, 2000, 2004; Thorne, 2003). The rationale for the second goal, the development of intercultural competence, is rooted in the daily demands of our multilingual and globalised world, in the widely held belief that language and culture are inextricably bound together such that language is semiotic of culture, and in the humanistic assumption that intercultural understanding is of moral and ethical value (Corbett, 2003; Doyé, 1999; Garrison & Anderson, 2003; Nieto, 1999). In this latter vein, telecollaboration provides prolonged, cost-effective access to persons from other cultures for those learners who may have little opportunity to engage in intercultural communication and for whom residence abroad is not an option.

In a typical telecollaborative partnership, for example, Russian-speaking learners of English in Moscow might use e-mail and chat in order to interact with English-speaking learners of Russian in the USA on a variety of topics such as educational systems, discrimination, gender roles and the role of religion in everyday life (Bauer *et al.*, 2006). Over the course of the partnership, keypals collaborate electronically using their native language (L1) and their L2 on a series of successively more complex projects under the guidance of competent teachers. To illustrate, learners on each end of an exchange might view a contemporary American film in English and a Russian film in Russian in order to examine how family life is variously constructed at both the linguistic and conceptual levels in the cultures under study as represented in the chosen films (Kinginger *et al.*, 1999). The instructional objectives in such a partnership are thus both linguistic and intercultural.

An alternative configuration is represented by the *Connect Program*, a new educational initiative funded, in part, by the *Ford Foundation*, which utilises web-based videoconferencing in order to connect small groups of college students in the USA and predominantly Muslim countries in the Middle East to 'collaboratively explore the relationship between the US and the Arab [and] Muslim World with the aim of improving intercultural awareness and understanding' (Soliya, 2007). A special emphasis of the *Connect Program* is an exploration of the profound role that the media play in shaping young adults' perceptions of other peoples and cultures. Participants have access to a wealth of online sources, including raw news and interview footage from *Al Jazeera, Reuters* and the *British Broadcasting Company*, in addition to academic and policy documents and lectures from relevant experts. These materials serve as prompts for synchronous and asynchronous discussions among participants and as resources for the production of project-culminating joint articles. Because the intercultural interactions supported by the *Connect Program* take place in English, the targeted instructional objectives are strictly intercultural in nature.

In the next section of this chapter, Byram's (1997) model of intercultural competence is examined in detail. The five principles of the model are introduced, concrete curricular objectives for each principle are discussed and learner behaviours that evidence the attainment of the stated curricular objectives are outlined. The third section is devoted to the pedagogy of telecollaboration (see also Avots, 1991; Belz, 2005a; Cononelos & Oliva, 1993; Kern, 1996; Thorne, 2006; Warschauer, 1995). A discussion of three activities that have been implemented in various telecollaborative partnerships and that have been shown to foster the development of intercultural competence is presented. In the fourth section, excerpts from previously conducted telecollaborative partnerships are analysed in order to give instructors an idea of what the (nascent) development of intercultural competence might look like in the electronic interactions and reflections of their students (see also Belz, 2003; Müller-Hartmann, 2006). The chapter concludes with a discussion of the extent to which intercultural communicative competence may be developed in classroom-based instruction and pedagogical suggestions for future explorations.

What Is Intercultural (Communicative) Competence?

The framework for intercultural (communicative) competence adopted here and in much of the recently published work on telecollaboration is that of Michael Byram as described in his 1997 book *Teaching and Assessing Intercultural Communicative Competence*. Byram, who bases his model on the work of van Ek (1986), sets up a dichotomy between the *tourist* and the *sojourner*. The tourist is a traveller to foreign lands who sets out to experience foreign peoples, cultures and artefacts with the hope that these encounters with otherness will enrich his or her current way of life, but not fundamentally alter it. The sojourner, on the other hand, 'produces effects on a society which challenge its unquestioned and unconscious beliefs, behaviours and meanings, and whose own beliefs, behaviours and meanings are in turn challenged and expected to change'. Byram (1997: 3) argues that it is the qualities of the sojourner that constitute intercultural competence, and that this, in turn, is an integral and definitive part of what it means to learn a foreign language:

> [Foreign language learning] is centrally concerned with communication in a foreign language. The significance of this is not only the practical question of linguistic competence for communication, central though that is, but also the relationship between the language and the cultural practices and beliefs of a group ... the acquisition of a foreign language is ... the relativisation of what seems to the learner to be the natural language of their own identities, and the realisation that these are cultural, and socially constructed.

Thus, the focus of Byram (1997) is on the ways in which foreign language education can contribute to the development of the qualities of the sojourner in the foreign language learner and how those qualities can be assessed in institutional settings.

Byram's framework consists of the following four aspects: (1) *abstract principles* that contribute to the processes of *decentring* (e.g. Berger & Luckmann, 1966; Byram, 1989; Kohlberg *et al.*, 1983), i.e. the ability to relate to and understand the other and to relativise one's own beliefs, practices, values and meanings when faced with those of the other; (2) *curricular objectives* for the institutionalised instruction of intercultural competence; (3) concrete examples of *learner behaviours* that might 'count as' evidence of the development of intercultural competence (Byram, 1997: 57); and

(4) *methods of assessment* for the development of intercultural competence in the institutionalised setting. It should be emphasised that Byram does not envision the teaching of intercultural competence as the simple conveyance of a fixed set of facts about dominant social groups in the foreign culture; instead, he places equal emphasis on equipping learners with the means to access, analyse, compare and evaluate whatever cultural artefacts, practices, values, beliefs or meanings they might encounter (e.g. elite as well as marginalised segments of societies). In effect, Byram stresses *method* as well as *essence* and *object* in the instruction of intercultural competence.

The model consists of five distinct but interdependent principles. These are: (1) *attitudes*, (2) *knowledge*, (3) *skills of discovery and interaction* and (4) *skills of interpreting and relating*. The interplay of the first four principles ideally should lead to the fifth, namely, *critical cultural awareness* or an *evaluative orientation* (Byram, 1997: 43) toward the examination of difference, where learners' evaluative points of reference are made explicit and where the new evaluative orientation toward difference fosters a readiness for political engagement (p. 44). The choice of the word *skills* to designate components of intercultural competence is unfortunate, however, because it carries with it the negative connotation that these components might be 'learnt by a simple technology and transferred unproblematically' from one context to another (Ivanic, 1998: 168), when, in point of fact, intercultural interpretation, relation, discovery and interaction are complex human activities that shape and are shaped by an intimate interface of macro- and microsociological factors, including both history and power (Belz, 2002; Belz & Müller-Hartmann, 2003; Kern, 2000: 249-56; Ware & Kramsch, 2005). In the following paragraphs, each principle of intercultural competence is examined more fully.

Attitudes

Byram states that attitudes of *curiosity* and *openness* are both necessary preconditions as well as outcomes of intercultural learning, as the success of intercultural communication depends on establishing and maintaining good social relationships. The intercultural speaker, i.e. the speaker who is interculturally competent, must exhibit a 'readiness to suspend disbelief and judgment with respect to others' meanings, beliefs and behaviours' and a 'willingness to suspend belief in one's own meanings and behaviors, and to analyse them from the viewpoint of the others with whom one is engaging' (Byram, 1997: 34; see also Kramsch, 1998). For example, English-speaking American learners in an exchange with Arabic-speaking Qatari learners must suspend their belief in the meanings that they might attribute to Islamic dress within their own dominant cultural frames of reference and learn, instead, to interpret its value and significance within Qatari frames of reference. From the first perspective, Islamic dress might be interpreted as a sign of oppression and backwardness, while from the second perspective it signifies modesty, dignity, self-respect, freedom from sexual objectification and a desire to be evaluated on the basis of one's behaviour rather than one's appearance (Esposito, 2002: 96–98).

Concrete curricular objectives for the principle of attitudes include developing in the learner: (1) a willingness to seek out interaction with the other in a relationship of equality; (2) a genuine interest in the other's point of view on phenomena in one's own culture and in the other's culture; (3) a readiness to interrogate the value systems and assumptions behind one's own cultural practices; and (4) a readiness to examine one's own affective reactions to the experience of otherness and to cope with these reactions. In general, the interest of the intercultural speaker in the other is distinct from the interests of those whose interaction with the other is motivated by economic profit or by a fascination with the 'exotic'.

Byram's (1997) conceptualisation of the intercultural speaker with respect to *attitudes* seems reminiscent of linguistic anthropologist Michael Agar's (1994: 22–26) discussion of 'number 1 types'. Agar (1994: 23) writes:

> There are two ways of looking at differences between you and somebody else. One way is to figure out that the differences are the tip of the iceberg, the signal that two different *systems* are at work. Another way is to notice all the things that the other person lacks when compared to you, the so-called *deficit theory* approach. Number-one types – American or any other – use the deficit theory. They're the best, anything else is less than the best, and anyone who would call into question who they are when they're already the best is a fool or a masochist or even, as they used to say in America before *perestroika*, a Communist. (italics in the original)

At the risk of suggesting a 'deficit' definition, the intercultural speaker is *not* a 'number-one type' with respect to his or her attitudes about foreign cultures and peoples.

Relational knowledge

Byram (1997: 35) states that individuals bring both *declarative* and *procedural* knowledge to the fore in interactions with members of other cultures. *Declarative knowledge* is factual in nature and refers to information about social groups and their cultures in one's own country and in the foreign country (e.g. many Amish live in Pennsylvania; some African–Americans speak Ebonics). *Procedural knowledge* encompasses information about the appropriate processes of interaction at both the individual and societal levels. All knowledge, however, is relational because it is contingent upon one's own socialisation processes; in other words, meaning is relative to context. A concise and eloquent illustration of the relational nature of knowledge is provided in the single-sentence poem *Hijab Scene #2* by Muslim-American poet and academician Mohja Kahf in her collection *E-mails from Scheherazad:*

> 'You people have such restrictive dress for women,' she said, hobbling away in three-inch heels and panty hose to finish out another pink-collar temp pool day. (Kahf, 2003: 42)

In this example, the speaker's 'knowledge' that the *hijab* or headscarf constitutes a restrictive form of dress is juxtaposed with the veiled addressee's 'knowledge' that it is three-inch heels and panty hose that constitute restrictive forms of dress. Both pieces of 'knowledge', however, are contingent upon and relative to the socialisation processes (e.g. schooling, family and community belief systems, regular and selective media portrayals) to which the speaker and the addressee in the poem have been exposed and in which they have participated.

The intercultural speaker is aware of the contingent nature of knowledge and this awareness may afford appropriate intercultural interaction. In Byram's model, the learner not only 'gathers facts' about the foreign culture, but is able to put this information into dialogue with information about his or her own country in similar topical domains. So, for example, an American learner of German would not only learn about the restriction of Jewish civil liberties in early 20th-century Germany in a German course, but he or she would be able to put that information into dialogue with the restriction of Japanese–American civil liberties in the USA in the 1940s as portrayed, for example, in the juvenile novels *Damals war es Friedrich* (Richter, 2001) and *Farewell to Manzanar* (Houston & Houston, 1983), respectively. It should be emphasised that this type of factual juxtaposition and the subsequent learning that may result from it requires extensive factual knowledge of *one's own culture* as well as that of the other; instructors should not necessarily assume that learners possess the requisite factual knowledge of their own cultures.

Important curricular objectives for this component of intercultural competence include knowledge of: (1) social institutions and their impact on daily life; social and class distinctions and their markers; the processes of social interaction; (2) historical and contemporary relationships between the two countries in question including major events and people; stories about these relationships from both sides and from diverse groups within each country; (3) the national memories of each country, including icons, symbols, trends, myths, landmarks, artefacts of popular culture, regional distinctions, their markers and their meanings; and (4) the types of misunderstandings that may occur between members of the two countries in question and the origins of these misunderstandings such as culturally-contingent interpretations of psychological constructs like *patriotism* and *democracy* or social behaviour such as *public displays of affection* or *flying the national flag*.

   In Byram's (1997: 90) vision of intercultural competence, it is not sufficient for an intercultural speaker to rattle off a list of facts and figures about the foreign culture or even their own culture, a type of learning that he designates as 'shallow'; instead, intercultural competence (in the domain of knowledge) should be identified with 'underlying understanding, metacognition, and the ability to reflect on one's own thinking and respond to experience'. This type of learning is known as 'deep learning' (Entwistle cited in Gipps, 1994: 24) and cannot be assessed in terms of psychometric objective tests, the hallmark of which is the multiple-choice question. Deep learning of intercultural knowledge may be assessed through: (1) comparative essay writing; (2) the ability to identify sources of intercultural misunderstanding in interaction; or (3) critical commentaries on intercultural phenomena (e.g. collegiate school spirit in the USA versus professional soccer fanaticism in Germany) *and* intracultural inconsistencies (e.g. the separation of church and state as articulated in the US constitution and the common practice of incorporating elements of the Christian holiday of Christmas into the art and music curricula of US public schools).

Skills of discovery and interaction

   Byram (1997: 38) defines the *skills of discovery* as 'the ability to recognise significant phenomena in a foreign environment and to elicit their meanings and connotations, and their relationship to other phenomena'. Unlike the *skills of interpreting and relating*, which draw on the learner's existing knowledge, the *skills of discovery* are needed in situations where individuals have little prior knowledge of the foreign culture or when interlocutors are unable to explain what is obvious for them in their 'taken-for-granted reality' (Byram, 1997: 99).

One important mode of discovery is social interaction. Byram (1997: 61) characterises the *skills of interaction* as the 'ability to operate knowledge, attitudes and skills under the constraints of real time communication ... ' In telecollaboration, the following of Byram's (1997: 61–63) many curricular objectives appear to be the most relevant for the *skills of discovery and interaction*: (1) the ability to employ a variety of questioning techniques in order to elicit from members of the foreign culture the 'allusions, connotations and presuppositions' inherent in any kind of text, including official documents, films, TV shows, press releases, service encounters and newspaper articles; (2) the ability to identify and interpret the underlying cultural ideology of contemporary and historical foreign texts and to relate the inherent ideology to similar or dissimilar ideologies in the learner's own culture; and (3) the ability to use various conventions of communicative practice in both the learner's and the other's culture in order to establish and maintain functional social relationships with members of the foreign culture over time.

The attainment of this latter objective is exemplified by Mrs. Andrea Curtin, a white American character in *Tears of the Giraffe* (McCall Smith, 2000), the second instalment in a best-selling mystery series that chronicles the life and times of Precious Ramotswe, the traditionally built proprietor of the only ladies' detective agency in Botswana. In the scene in question, Mma Ramotswe is about to close her office for a well deserved lunch one hot and dusty afternoon, when Mrs. Curtin, a white woman in khaki pants, arrives unannounced outside her agency in a large car. Despite her untimely appearance, Mrs. Curtin is able to establish a positive social relationship with Mma Ramotswe via her appropriate use of communicative conventions, which secures her admittance into the inner offices of the agency:

> The woman took her hand, correctly, Mma Ramotswe noticed, in the proper Botswana way, placing her left hand on her right forearm as a mark of respect. Most white people shook hands very rudely, snatching just one hand and leaving their other hand free to perform all sorts of mischief. This woman had at least learned something about how to behave. (McCall Smith, 2000: 24)

Above all, the *skills of discovery* are linked linguistically to the ability to pose and to respond to 'deep learning' questions, but also to intercultural understandings of phatic communion, politeness phenomena, face work (e.g. Scollon & Scollon, 2001), and the ability to access appropriate data sources, when necessary, through the social institutions of the foreign culture.

Skills of interpreting and relating

Byram (1997: 52) defines the *skills of interpreting and relating* as the 'ability to interpret a document or event from another culture, to explain it and relate it to documents from one's own'. Unlike the *skills of discovery and interaction*, the *skills of interpreting and relation* may draw on pre-existing knowledge gained through formal or other types of education and they do not necessarily involve real-time interaction with an interlocutor. It is important to note that the outcome of the application of these skills is not necessarily a 'balance of opposites, or a moderate pluralism of opinions'; instead, relating phenomena in one culture to those in another may result in 'paradoxical, irreducible confrontation that may change one in the process' (Kramsch, 1993: 231). Curricular objectives (Byram, 1997: 61) for this component of the model include: (1) identification of socioculturally contingent (as opposed to absolute) perspectives; (2) the identification of intercultural misunderstanding and dysfunction; and (3) the ability to mediate between inconsistent or conflicting interpretations of phenomena. In a telecollaborative partnership one might assess these skills by asking learners to comment on and analyse in retrospect contentious, questionable or unclear points in their previous telecollaborative interactions. This assessment methodology assumes that learners have been examining telecollaborative 'langua-cultural ruptures' (Belz & Müller-Hartmann, 2003: 85) under the guidance of their instructor over the course of their partnership.

Discussion of Byram's (1997) model

Byram is one of very few scholars, as Bredella (2000: 146) notes, who extensively operationalises the notion of intercultural competence in instructed foreign language learning. This detailed explication is no doubt valuable for curriculum planners, teacher educators, teachers and learners alike because it enables the establishment of concrete instructional objectives, which some language educators find to be indispensable for syllabus design and learner assessment (see Ferris & Hedgcock, 2005: 89). This same level of specificity, however, lays bare several aspects of the model that require further critical reflection.

First, the initial dichotomisation of the language learner into the tourist and the sojourner might downplay the important fact that not all language learners are in the privileged position of travellers to foreign lands. Much second language learning takes place under conditions of occupation, invasion, colonisation, slavery, economic and social marginalisation, and, more recently, cultural imperialism via telecommunications technologies, without the privilege of volitional travel. As language learning is eminently context-dependent, as Byram (1997) repeatedly notes, these configurations will influence the development of intercultural competence, the methods by which it is assessed, and, indeed, its societal and individual valuation. For example, an Arabic-speaking Palestinian who travels daily to Israel for work may have a very different understanding of both the meaning and function of intercultural communicative competence with respect to Hebrew than a Russian-speaking Jewish immigrant to the same country (see, for example, Ben-Rafael *et al.*, 2006). In the first case, a measure of intercultural competence in Hebrew may be a matter of economic survival; in the second case, intercultural competence may serve as a means of social assimilation and acceptance. In other words, the relatively comfortable and positive tones of tourism may not be associated with all situations in which intercultural competence is fostered or required. Thus, teachers will need to be aware that students will react differently to intercultural competence as an instructional objective.

In my own German–American partnerships over the years, bilingual native speakers of English on the US side (e.g. heritage learners of German, English–Spanish bilinguals) have not consistently invested in the classroom-based development of intercultural competence in the same way as monolingual native speakers of English, perhaps because they had already developed some of these skills by virtue of their life experiences and were not in need of 'learning' them in the institutionalised setting. They may wish, instead, to focus solely on linguistic instructional objectives.

Second, Byram (1997: 20, 32, 36, 39–40) appears to equate the concept of 'culture' with that of 'nation'. Such a position does not adequately recognise or value nation-internal diversity (e.g. Germans of Turkish extraction or Frenchmen of North-African origin) or the existence of ideologically or ethnically bound groups that span national borders (e.g. the Muslim *ummah* or community) or who have no national borders (the Sinti-Roma people; the Kurds). O'Dowd (2003: 126–128) discusses the possible consequences of a lack of recognition of nation-internal differences in telecollaborative partnerships. Juan, a learner in an exchange between Spain and England, presents León (not Spain) as his 'nation' in his very first e-mail to his partner, Alice, and further explains that 'the Spanish identity' is 'an invention'. Alice, however, appears to ignore or not adequately value Juan's differentiation of León and Spain and, as a result, the partnership does not function well for the remainder of the semester.

Third, the language-based distinction between *intercultural competence* and *intercultural communicative competence* is a problematic one because it downplays again internal diversity among members of the same speech community. For instance, the ability to switch registers and dialects within one's own speech community is, in my opinion, a matter of *communicative* competence which requires linguistic talents not less than those of bi- or multilingual codeswitchers. The development of inter-cultural competence is, in essence, cognitive development as it requires a 'shift in perspective' (Byram, 1997: 108) and a 'leap in insight' (p. 105).

Fourth, the establishment of an assessable threshold of intercultural competence (Byram, 1997: 43, 76–78) is, to my mind, a blow to the validity of cultural relativity because the notion of a threshold assumes a standard or reference point that is inevitably value-laden and culture-specific. If the assessment of a threshold is to take place in the context of a particular institution, as Byram suggests, then the point of reference will typically be formulated in terms of the dominant cultural values and again downplay the presence and importance of institution-internal diversity.

Finally, the suggestion that international human rights agendas should form the 'moral orientation' by means of which learners evaluate varying belief systems is questionable because, as Byram (1997: 46) rightly notes, international human rights doctrines have been developed within chiefly Western ideological frameworks, and, therefore, implicitly value these belief systems over non-Western traditions.

How Do I Teach Intercultural Communicative Competence?

Telecollaborative pedagogy is commonly characterised as ethno-graphic, dialogic and critical. Learners in telecollaboration can be viewed as *ethnographers* because they are engaged in the ethnographic processes of observing, participating, describing, analysing and interpreting the language behaviours of their keypals in relevant and authentic situations (Carel, 2001; Holliday, 1996; O'Dowd, 2006; Robinson-Stuart & Nocon, 1996). Telecollaboration is *dialogic* because the utterances produced and examined in the course of an exchange arise out of interactions with multiple others (Morgan & Cain, 2000). The plurality of the responses provided by these multiple others highlights the fact that meanings are not universal and unitary but rather local, diverse, and frequently the site of struggle and conflict (Schneider & von der Emde, 2006). Finally, telecollaboration is *critical* in the sense that learners are not passive receptacles of received knowledge (i.e. a facts-and-figures approach to culture learning), but rather active participants in a dynamic process of knowledge construction based on the juxtaposition of various texts (e.g. e-mails from numerous keypals) in the particular context of the given learning exchange.

In many telecollaborative partnerships learners engage in a series of carefully negotiated and successively more complex teacher-guided tasks and/or projects that typically involve the following three kinds of activities: (1) personal relationship building; (2) the exploration of linguistic and cultural rich points; and (3) product-oriented intercultural collaboration.

Personal relationship building

One of the biggest draws of telecollaboration for secondary and university-level learners is the opportunity to communicate one-on-one with a native-speaking age peer for a prolonged period of time. Such interaction usually involves personal introductions, the disclosure of biographical information, various types of identity display in visual and/or textual forms and the exchange of information regarding personal or work-related experiences, all of which may lead to the establishment of personal relationships. Valued personal relationships have been found to be facilitative of rich telecollaborative encounters (Belz, 2002; O'Dowd, 2003).

A common means of personal introduction in telecollaboration is the construction of websites. Individual students prepare a personal website containing a 'web-biography' in order to introduce themselves to their foreign keypals. Participants may also work in groups to construct additional websites that introduce aspects of their university experiences such as living arrangements or degree requirements to their foreign partners. At the outset of the web project, teachers should practice vocabulary and idioms that will enable learners to share personal information. Typically, American students require assistance with vocabulary used to convey information about high school activities and educational/social experiences particular to the US context (e.g. 'I was a member of the swim team/played varsity basketball/was the president of the Spanish club'; 'I did an internship at Lockheed Martin Corporation/ joined the ROTC'; 'I got a scholarship for my undergraduate studies/ pledged a fraternity').

Vocabulary work goes hand-in-hand with the acquisition of declarative knowledge about both the local and target cultures. As learners prepare to introduce themselves to their keypals in the foreign language, they will not only need the words and phrases to express their own experiences and identities, but also declarative knowledge about the specificity and/or universality of those experiences in order to get their meanings across to their partners, to answer eventual questions about them, and to ask informed questions about their partners' experiences. As Kern (2000: 232) points out, he had to 'consistently remind [his American] students to think about how to represent [themselves and their experiences] to a group of French peers who did not necessarily share a good deal of cultural common ground with them'. To illustrate, an American learner who does not know that European universities, by and large, do not charge tuition will not necessarily realise that she may have to note the prohibitive tuition costs at US universities in order for her keypal to appreciate the significance of her disclosure that she received a scholarship. In the case of a European–American exchange, declarative knowledge about university life might include information about the absence of sports teams, cheerleaders, the Greek system and tuition at the majority of European institutions, compulsory military and/or social service for young people in some European countries, the concept of the 'college town', the relative size and format of university courses, the nature of student–professor interactions, and the technological outfitting of institutions.

When constructing 'web-biographies', learners will need to prepare multiple drafts of their texts and receive extensive feedback from their instructors on the cultural situatedness of their experiences as well as on the target language vocabulary and grammar used to convey that information. Teachers will also need to lead students in reflective examination of the images that they choose to include in their websites and how these images contribute to the identities that they construct and present to their keypals. For example, what type of identity will American learners construct for themselves in the eyes of their keypals if they choose a picture of a cowboy, or the American flag, or Mickey Mouse as the primary image on their website? Will a given image be recognisable to their foreign partners? Will it have the same meaning for the foreign keypals as it does for the American students? Could it potentially (and perhaps unwittingly) cast them in a negative light in the eyes of their keypals? One relevant example comes from a partnership I conducted between the USA and Germany in 2000. The American students chose a large photograph of their football mascot, the Nittany Lion, as the main image on their introductory website. Many were surprised and some were clearly upset when their German partners asked them why they have a picture of a child's stuffed bear on their homepage. Learning to manage affective responses in intercultural interactions is an important aspect of intercultural competence.

In an effort to address the issue of managing affective responses to unexpected or unfamiliar keypal behaviour or disclosures, teachers might share excerpts from previous keypal correspondence with their students, if available, prior to students' first electronically mediated intercultural interactions. Learners might need to become sensitised not only to the types of questions their keypals might ask but also to the varying conversational styles that exist in different cultures (e.g. taboo topics, directness versus indirectness, politeness, positive and negative face, methods of topic management). The following three examples are excerpts from e-mail correspondence written by Germans (translated into English), which I have used to prepare American college students in rural Pennsylvania for the types of interactions that they may have with their German keypals:

(1) You guys asked me whether I experienced any prejudice in Louisiana. At the beginning [of my stay there] I honestly didn't pay any attention to it. But one day I was driving with an American friend of mine and we got lost. We found ourselves in a small town called Pitkin. As we were approaching the town, we saw a sign that really shocked me. It read: 'Blacks are not welcome here!' We were actually going to stop in the town to ask directions. But we didn't do it because my friend Cora was black.

(2) We have a couple of questions. Is it really against the law to let a child run around naked on a public beach? Or is it just a moral thing to you, rooted in your Puritanical history? Somebody told us that if you are topless on the beach that people come up to you and ask you to cover yourself up ... Were you allowed to bring your friends (male or female) to your room, just to hang around when you were a teenager? Or did your parents consider your room only as bedroom? In Germany it's normal to bring friends into your bedroom even if they are boys. When I (Anna) was in Rhode Island, I wasn't even allowed to bring my boyfriends into my bedroom. We had to hang out in the family room.

(3) It occurred to us that there's a big difference between American and German families. In Germany, it's common in most families to talk about sex and birth control. In addition, many 16-year-olds are allowed to spend the night with their boyfriend or girlfriend. Why do you think that it's different in the US? Maybe it has something to do with religion?

In addition to preparing students for the potential discussion of issues that they might find to be taboo, exposure to such excerpts serves a number of other functions as well. First, they provide learners with an advance opportunity to 'try out' their affective responses to such questions in a relatively low stakes environment (i.e. discussion with their instructor rather than their keypals). Second, they provide them with a taste of an outsider's perspective on aspects of their own culture. Third, they can discover in advance and prepare for the eventuality that their partners have more information about their culture than they have about their partners' culture. Fourth, learners gain insight ahead of time into the ways in which local behaviours might be interpreted and valued by members of another culture. Finally, exposure to the content of previous telecollaborative interactions allows students to compare their own lived experiences with the experiences recounted by foreign partners; this, in turn, may encourage them to begin to relativise their own taken-for-granted reality prior to the onset of telecollaborative interaction.

Once learners have exchanged initial messages with their keypals, teachers should organise a non-telecollaborative class session (i.e. no correspondence with partners during the session) in which they introduce their foreign keypals to their classmates at the home location. This activity will not only give students a chance to practise vocabulary and idioms relating to personal introductions (and to check with an instructor if they have understood the partners' e-mails), but it will also give them the opportunity to become familiar with a broader range of foreign keypals, to look for differences and similarities between the life experiences of the keypals and the ways in which they introduce themselves, and to make comparisons between their own lives and those of their partners. In order to prepare for this session, learners can fill out a worksheet containing the following prompts: (1) My partner(s) is (are) called . . . ; (2) She/he (they) is (are) from . . . ; (3) In the first e-mail my partner(s) . . . ; (4) I was surprised because . . . ; (5) In my response to my partner's/partners' first e-mail . . . ; and (6) In my opinion . . .

Teachers might want to bring in a map of the partners' country and mark each keypal's hometown as they are introduced by the members of the local group. Students are also typically interested in the perceived 'foreignness' of their partners' names and may not be able to tell if they are men or women based on their names alone. As the telecollaborative partnership progresses, teachers should consistently schedule non-telecollaborative sessions in which learners at the home location share and discuss with their classmates excerpts from their on-going tele-collaborative correspondence.

Personal relationship building in telecollaboration is supported, first and foremost, by regular correspondence between keypals. Participants should be required to send a specified number of messages to their partners each week. Teachers should schedule their courses in technology classrooms containing individual terminals for each learner as much as possible and these sessions should be devoted to message composition in order to facilitate regular correspondence with keypals. Furthermore, class periods on each end of the partnership (e.g. in the USA and Europe) should overlap in real time at least once a week so that learners may participate in synchronous interactions if they choose to do so. Collaborating instructors may also find simultaneous sessions to be of use for 'housekeeping' and organisational purposes.

Personal relationship building is also facilitated when partners ask each other many questions. Therefore, teachers should ensure that learners know how to pose appropriate questions from both linguistic and sociocultural perspectives. In general, there are three types of questions: (1) rhetorical; (2) confirmation-seeking; and (3) information-seeking. The latter type is further divided into *either/or*, *yes/no*, *what/how/where/when* (e.g. what is the capital of Maine?), opinion (e.g. what do you think about the presidential election?) and *why*-questions. While rhetorical questions do not typically require an answer and information-confirming questions are designed to confirm or disconfirm the questioner's perceptions, information-seeking questions are used when the questioner wants to elicit knowledge from the hearer.

The subcategories of the information-seeking question differ with respect to the ways in which they position the respondent as an intercultural informant. For example, *why*-questions allow respondents a relatively wide berth for the presentation of their own point of view, whereas *either/or*-questions offer much less space for personal expression because they compel the respondent to select from among proffered alternatives. Thus, frequent use of *why*-questions may position the hearer as a languacultural expert, whereas a preponderance of *either/or*-questions may position her as 'an arbiter of the questioner's perceptions' (Belz, 2005b: 14). For example, Anke, a German learner in a 2000 German–American partnership uses an *either/or*-question with her American partner, Eric, when discussing a previous experience that she had as an exchange student in Canada. In contradistinction to her own parents' practices in Germany, her host parents in Canada did not allow her Canadian boyfriend to sleep over. Anke, in search of relational knowledge, asks Eric about his own parents' rules with respect to mixed gender sleepovers: 'Are your parents cool with these kinds of things or scared?' Belz (2005b: 21) explains that the phrasing of this question 'may preclude intercultural discussion of this topic because [the German partners] rule out and simultaneously devalue alternative possibilities, such as Eric's parents disallowing not only mixed-sex "sleepovers", but dating in general'.

Chronological patterning of question types over the course of a telecollaborative partnership is also an important point. On the whole, learners should not begin their partnerships with a high frequency of rhetorical or confirmation-checking questions because the latter generally entail assumptions and partners in intercultural exchanges should be in the process of suspending their beliefs and judgements about their keypals' culture. Instead, *what/how/when/where*-questions lend themselves better to the elicitation of personal information, while *why*-questions help to clarify and elaborate on shared information. *What/how*-questions and, in particular, opinion and *why*-questions should cluster during those segments of partnerships where learners are exploring culturally situated texts such as newspaper articles, short stories, contemporary films, and interesting e-mails and chat excerpts.

Finally, it should be stressed that *answering* questions is equally important for the establishment of personal relationships in telecollaboration. A general finding in the literature to date is that successful telecollaborative partnerships are characterised by consistent responses to posed questions. In sum, teachers should show learners how to ask questions; they should model appropriate questions for them; they should encourage learners to ask more opinion, *what/how* and *why*-questions than *yes/no* or *either/or*-questions; and they should peruse telecollaborative discourse to make sure that learners are both asking and answering questions.

The exploration of linguistic and cultural rich points

Agar (1994) coins the term *languaculture* to index the reflexivity between language and culture. In other words, language is shaped by culture and culture, in turn, is shaped by language use:

> Language, in all its varieties, in all the ways it appears in everyday life, builds a world of meanings. When you run into different meanings, when you become aware of your own and work to build a bridge to the others, 'culture' is what you're up to. Language fills the spaces between us with sound; culture forges the human connection through them. Culture is in language, and language is loaded with culture ... whenever you hear the word *language* or the word *culture*, you might wonder about the missing half ...

'Languaculture' is a reminder, I hope, of the necessary connection between its two parts ... (Agar, 1994: 28, 60)

Rich points are pieces of discourse that indicate that two *languacultures* or conceptual systems have come into contact. Agar (1994: 99–100) explains the concept in the following way: 'When two languacultures come into contact, *yours* and *theirs*, the most interesting problems, the ones that attract your attention, are the vertical cliffs. These cliffs are difficult because ... the problematic bit of language is puttied thickly into far-reaching networks of association and many situations of use' (italics in the original).

One example of a rich point is *los toros* or bullfighting. O'Dowd (2003: 128) explains that for some 'bullfighting is a cruel sport where animals are toyed with, tortured and then slaughtered in the name of culture and tradition, while for others, *los toros* represents tradition and bravery and is seen as a fair combat between man and beast'. Other examples of rich points include abortion (a woman's right to choose versus the murder of an innocent child), hunting (a space for (parent–child) bonding versus animal murder) and female clergy (gender equity versus the violation of tradition/divine law). An excellent example of a linguistic rich point is provided by educational linguist James Gee (2005) in his discussion of 'Indian' and 'non-Indian' viewpoints on the appropriate behaviours of students and teachers in the classroom:

> Although many 'non-Indians' find it proper to ask questions of someone who is instructing them, 'Indians' regard questions in such a situation as being inattentive, rude, insolent ... The person who has taken the role of 'student' shows attentiveness by avoiding eye contact and by being silent. The teaching situation, then, as a witnessed monolog, lacks the dialogical features that characterise some Western instruction. (Gee, 2005: 25)

When members of one languaculture encounter a rich point in a second languaculture, lack of understanding is often the result. This inability to understand the rich point typically is not based on deficient lexical knowledge, but rather on insufficient factual knowledge of the specific network of culturally relative associations and meanings in which the rich point makes sense to members of the second languaculture. In short, a rich point is a reflex of culture-specific ideas, beliefs or constructs as manifested in language or other types of communicative patterns.

The exploration of linguistic and cultural rich points is a key activity in telecollaborative exchanges. One way in which learners can explore rich points is through the use of cultural surveys. Such surveys generally consist of two versions (one in L1 and one in L2) of a list of 10–20 teacher-formulated questions, which are designed to throw various rich points between the two participating groups into sharp relief. The surveys should be posted online so that learners may respond to them easily and conveniently. In addition, all answers to the given questions should be available online. If the responses to each question are displayed in a table where the left-hand column represents answers from Group A and the right-hand column represents answers from Group B, then learners may look for similarities and differences both within and across groups. In partnerships where linguistic competence constitutes an instructional goal, learners should answer the survey in their L1 in order to provide their keypals with an accurate model of the target language (e.g. Version A in German is answered by native speakers of German in German, while Version B in English is answered by native speakers of English in English in a German–American exchange). Learners will then read their netpals' answers in L2, and, in a subsequent exercise, they can use their L2 in order to summarise or reflect on their partners' or classmates' responses in preparation for online intercultural discussion of survey results.

Nader Morkus (personal communication, 2006) designed a cultural survey for an exchange between students at the *University of South Florida* in the USA and the *Arab Academy for Science, Technology, and Maritime Transport* in Alexandria, Egypt. Questions included: (1) Is it absolutely necessary for you to obtain your family's approval of the person you want to marry? Explain; (2) What do you think about wearing shorts to class?; (3) Do you think women should have the right to have an abortion? Explain; (4) Do you think it is ok for one to marry one's cousin? Explain; (5) Do you think elderly people should be sent to nursing homes or live with their families? Explain; and (6) What do you think about people who have sex before marriage? Representative responses to the final question are given in Table 7.1. Because this partnership did not focus on the development of linguistic competence, all responses were provided in English, the *lingua franca* of the exchange.

Reading the responses to the surveys will provide learners with factual knowledge about the beliefs, practices, meanings and values of their keypals as well as their fellow classmates on the home side. While the availability of such local knowledge is generally motivating to learners, teachers should caution them to check apparent tendencies in the data with more macro-level demographic statistics. Opinion polls such as *Gallup*, *Zogby* and the *Pew Charitable Trust* and national surveys such as those

Table 7.1 Egyptian and American responses to a cultural survey

What do you think about people who have sex before marriage?

Egyptian responses	American responses
I don't think it's right … you're losing part of yourself when you do so and afterwards you regret it.	Nothing wrong with it.
This is something totally forbidden and unacceptable. We were brought up learning that girls should not be touched by anyone unless it's her husband … It makes girls more precious.	I tend to think they are smart. I consider sexual compatibility to be an important part of a happy marriage … The choice of a marriage partner is very important and should be made with as much information … as possible.
According to our religion (Islam), it's considered a sin to have pre-marriage sex. But socially speaking, I think people who have pre-marriage sex are spoiling the whole idea of 'marriage'. Sex is a way to get to know your life partner more intimately and is not to be taken as casually as it is nowadays.	It's probably a good idea. When else are they going to have sex? After the marriage? There is an old saying … Put a penny in a jar for every time you have sex before you are married. Take two pennies out for every time you have sex after you are married. By the time you die/separate, you will still have pennies in the jar.
They are like the bottle of water that u finish and throw in the garbage: 'CHEAP'	I think they should be able to do whatever they want as long as it is safe and a consensual, educated decision.
They're either not raised well, or they have psychological problems, and most of these problems come from their parents.	I believe in staying pure before marriage in the sense that your husband or wife should be the first ones to be with you in such an intimate sense since they are the ones that will cherish you for the rest of your lives.
Well for me as a Christian guy I believe it's a sin.	No big deal.

Table 7.1 (*Continued*)

What do you think about people who have sex before marriage?

Egyptian responses	American responses
It's a personal freedom, as long as both sides agree, but it's against religion and it's against ethics, I think.	If they are in love then I think it's a beautiful part of life. I don't approve of people who engage in casual sex. But sex with someone you love is an act of love. Something like that should never be repressed.
I disapprove with anyone that has sex before marriage because if you get pregnant you would be throwing your life away, and I think that it's not something that people should rush into with some random person, it is more special when you are married to that person.	I think around 50–60% of Americans today are having sex before marriage. It's a pretty common thing, so I don't think badly on people who do it. Truthfully, I will probably have sex before marriage. I am not very religious.

maintained by the *US Census Bureau* are good sources. For example, students should be encouraged to check statements like '50–60% of Americans today are having sex before marriage' against available databases thereby facilitating the development of skills of discovery. Examination of differences in response between the two groups can provide learners with relational knowledge. For example, all Egyptians sampled here (Muslims and Christians alike) disapprove of sex before marriage, while only a minority of Americans shares the same opinion. Investigations of group-internal diversity facilitate the development of skills of relating by encouraging the ability to mediate between inconsistent or conflicting interpretations of phenomena. For example, how can one relate and/or reconcile the contradictory American responses such as 'I believe in staying pure before marriage' and '[sex before marriage] is probably a good idea'? Finally, skills of interpretation are fostered by discussing potential relationships between given responses and sociocultural factors.

Another common activity for the investigation of cultural rich points is the reading and electronic discussion of parallel texts, linguistically different renditions of the same theme or topic. While any type of text can be used, contemporary films and juvenile literature are common choices (Burwitz-Melzer, 2001; Kinginger *et al.*, 1999; Müller-Hartmann, 2000). My partner instructor, Andreas Müller-Hartmann, and I have frequently used the children's novel *Ben liebt Anna* by award-winning German author Peter Härtling and the juvenile novel *If You Come Softly* by African–American novelist Jacquelyn Woodson as the first set of parallel texts in our exchanges. Both books deal with first love and intercultural relationships but the stories, of course, are written in different languages and are the products of different cultures. The learners' task in reading these parallel novels is not only the discovery of rich points, but the comparison of culturally contingent beliefs, practices, values and constructs. Once these are elucidated and examined during class-internal discussions, learners should summarise their findings and formulate discussion points for Internet-mediated intercultural examination with their keypals. Teachers can prepare worksheets on which important rich points and/or cultural differences are highlighted to aid learners in their preparation for intercultural exchanges based on the parallel texts. In this segment of an exchange it is also important for teachers to ensure that learners know how to express opinions and make comparisons and that they are familiar with literary vocabulary (e.g. plot, character, setting). A sample worksheet with some of the relevant details filled in is given in Figure 7.1.

Depending on the length of a given telecollaborative partnership, participants may not have time to read parallel novels. Shorter texts may serve the same purpose. For example, students can read simple articles from the field of comparative education to explore varying educational systems (see Noack, 1999, for a German–American comparison). Students could peruse the websites of their own and partner institutions in order to gather declarative knowledge, prepare questions for their keypals concerning differences or unclear aspects, and to critically examine the ways in which the institutions present themselves to the rest of the world. Foreign language travel brochures or tourist guidebooks are often rich and jarringly surprising sources of information about a foreign culture's perception of one's own culture. Students can read excerpts from these documents and compare the foreign portrayal of their culture with domestic or personal portrayals. For example, in preparation for a German–American telecollaborative exchange I ask students to bring in images that they would use for the cover of a German-language travel brochure for German tourists to the USA. Typical images include the Statue of Liberty, the Golden Gate Bridge and the Grand Canyon. Students were shocked to learn that the actual image on the cover of an authentic German tour book for German travellers to the USA was that of a truck driver inside the cab of a semi. The juxtaposition of these varying icons for US culture can serve as a first step toward processes of decentring that should be encouraged to unfold over the course of telecollaboration. Finally, students could view documentaries or Hollywood films about secondary school and/or university life (*American High*, *Mona Lisa Smile*, *Animal House*, *Drumline*) and then follow-up with keypals during electronic interactions on the relative gap between the filmic portrayal of these institutions and their own lived experiences.

Product-oriented intercultural collaboration

In the final segment of many telecollaborative partnerships, learners work together in transatlantic (or transpacific, etc.) groups in order to produce a bilingual website in which they explore a theme or construct that arises in the course of their semester-long intercultural explorations. It is crucial in the Internet-mediated collaborative execution of such projects that clear product guidelines are given by instructors. These include formal, content and linguistic criteria as well as specifications for features of electronic literacy (Warschauer, 1999) such as images, video clips and hyperlinks for the expansion and elaboration of the stated

Task: Compare and contrast the main characters in *Ben liebt Anna* by Peter Härtling and in *If You Come Softly* by Jacqueline Woodson.

Who is an outsider? From what perspective? For what reason?

Feature	Ben	Anna	Ellie	Miah
Age	9	9	15	15
Place of birth	Germany	Poland	USA	USA
Native language				
Other languages				African-American Vernacular English
Citizenship	Gemany	Poland	USA	USA
Religion	Christian	Christian	Jew	Christian
Race/Ethnicity	white/German	white/German descent	white	African-American
Family Life				
Parents' Occupation	civil engineer / physician's assistant	unemployed coal miner / housewife	doctor / housewife	film director / author
Living situation				
Socioeconomic Status				

In my opinion _____ is an outsider with respect to _____, because...

Figure 7.1 Prediscussion worksheet for parallel texts

argument. An example of an assessment rubric for the final product in a German–American exchange in which both linguistic and intercultural competences are targeted is given in Appendix 1. In addition, partici-pants must be given adequate time to complete a final project. Bilingual websites require at least a month for topic negotiation, task delegation, research, collection of images, graphics, clips and links, essay drafting, instructor and peer feedback, revisions, web design and web publication. The misalignment of academic calendars may represent an added pressure during collaborative group work at the end of telecollaborative partnerships. In most European–US exchanges, learners are completing final projects during the end of the US semester but near the middle of the European semester. As a result, the American learners may be under pressure to complete larger projects in other courses as well. Understanding and successfully negotiating the various institutional affordances and constraints at play in any given exchange is also an aspect of intercultural competence not to be overlooked or underestimated.

In partnerships that I have conducted over the years, final projects have dealt with the following topics: German and American perspectives on censorship; filmic and TV portrayals of middle class family life; reality and appearance in particular texts; cross-cultural perspectives on racism; images of success in German and American films; a comparison of German and American mothers; family relationships in contemporary films; patriotism and national identity; cross-cultural perspectives on sexuality; and cross-cultural explorations of friendship and beauty.

How do I know if my students are developing intercultural communicative competence?

The most obvious way in which to ascertain whether or not learners are developing intercultural competence is to examine the content of their keypal correspondence. This is not as simplistic as it seems however because one must be careful to avoid equating positive comments about the other as unequivocal signs of intercultural competence. If an American learner tells her Spanish partner that siestas are 'so cool', this comment alone does not mean that the American has developed intercultural competence. Similarly, a participant in a telecollaborative partnership is not necessarily an intercultural speaker because she has told a researcher in a post-project interview that she 'really liked her partner and learned so much from him'. Furthermore, teachers and learners must resist the pull to equate the adoption of the other's point of view with the attainment of intercultural competence. Becoming an intercultural speaker does not mean agreeing with your partner's point of view or convincing your partner of the validity of your own point of view.

In order to better understand how the content of an electronic interaction might index intercultural competence, consider Example (4) below, an excerpt from a synchronous chat that took place on 16 November 2004, between American Carolyn and German Emma (both names are pseudonyms). In this example, Carolyn and Emma are discussing a cultural rich point that they discovered in their reading and subsequent discussion of Härtling (1997), namely, public nudity. There is a scene in the novel where the two 9-year-old protagonists, Ben and Anna, swim together naked in a lake during an outing with Ben's family. Ben's mother is aware of the swim and she seems to take this behaviour in stride. Invariably, the German and American students have different opinions with regard to the social/moral acceptability of this behaviour. In a classroom exercise in which the learners compare the published English translation of this well known novel, they discover that the main characters swim in their clothes; in effect, the keypals discover that the English version of the text has been censored. One reason why discussions surrounding this text are so rich is because the operation of the skills of relating and interpreting required to execute the comparison of the German and English versions of the text lead some of the American students to a 'paradoxical, irreducible confrontation' (Kramsch, 1993: 231). They understand that censorship is the 'suppression or attempted suppression of something regarded as objectionable'; nevertheless, they are unwilling or unable to see the deletion of this scene in the English translation as an act of censorship. In the excerpt below, Emma is questioning Carolyn about the deletion:

(4)

Emma:	Warum glaubt ihr sind Ben und Anna in der englischen	1
	Übersetzung nicht nackt? *(Why do you think that Ben and Anna*	2
	are not naked in the English translation?)	3
Carolyn:	It seems really weird for people to do that, not something you'd	4
	usually talk about in a children's book	5
Emma:	Wir hatten schon in der zweiten Klasse Aufklärungsunterricht!	6
	(We had sex education in second grade!)	7
Carolyn:	Ja, ich hatte in der dritte Klasse Aufklaerungsunterricht, aber es	8
	war nicht etwas, dass wir probieren sollten … nur machen	9
	Erwachsene das. *(Yes, I had sex education in third grade, but it was*	10
	not something that we should try … only adults do it.)	11
Emma:	They didn't tell us to try it either.	12
Carolyn:	Wenn ich es lese, sehe ich etwas sexuelles … wie ihr gesagt	13
	habt, ist es einen anderen Kultur. *(When I read it, I see something*	14
	sexual … like you said it is a different culture.)	15
Emma:	But they are nine years old. They don't think about sex when	16
	they are naked!	17
Emma:	So do you have problems that they hugged each other when	18
	they were swimming naked?	19
Carolyn:	Yeah, pretty much … it seems inappropriate in an American	20
	context.	21

Emma: But they hugged each other like fish do! And what is less sexual   22
than fish?   23
Carolyn: Good point, but it still seems weird to me ... aber ich glaube   24
meine groesste Problem ist, dass sie einander umarmen (... *but*   25
I believe that my biggest problem is that they hug one another).   26
Emma: But they are friends. Friends hug each other. And a bathing suit   27
is not much cloth, is it? ...   28

In this excerpt, Emma displays her ability to operate the skills of discovery and relating with regard to Carolyn's opinion via the various questioning techniques and counter-arguments she employs. She opens in Lines 1–3 with a *why*-question designed to elicit Carolyn's opinion about the deletion. When Carolyn states in Lines 4–5 that nudity is not something that one typically finds in a children's book, Emma counters that she had sex education in the school in second grade. Carolyn holds her ground in Lines 8–11 stating that she also had sex ed in school at an early age, but she further refines her position by noting the difference between theory and praxis. By swimming naked, Härtling's protagonists cross the line between theory and praxis, which Carolyn finds unacceptable. Emma however counters by stating that her sex education courses were also theory-oriented. Carolyn takes a different tact in Lines 14–15 by stating that she sees something more than innocent skinny-dipping in the scene in question; instead, she believes the children's behaviour to be sexual in nature and this is why she thinks the English version was changed. Emma forces Carolyn to refine her position further in Lines 18–19 when she asks her if it is the hugging that leads Carolyn to believe that the scene is sexual. Carolyn confirms this interpretation in Lines 20–21 and Emma immediately counters by suggesting that the hug was asexual and fishlike. In Line 24 Carolyn admits that Emma has a good point but she still maintains her position that a naked hug in the water between a boy and a girl to be sexual in nature and therefore subject to censorship. In Line 27 Emma further interrogates Carolyn's position by suggesting that it's normal for friends to hug and that the nudity really doesn't make a difference because there's not much difference between wearing a bathing suit and being naked anyway.

Carolyn, for her part, displays intercultural competence because she is able to suspend her belief that public nudity is an absolute wrong. This is seen in Lines 13–15 when she states that the incident in question occurs 'in another culture'. It's important to note that Carolyn maintains her position that the scene conveys something sexual, but she is able to relativise her interpretation to her own particular frames of reference. She again relativises her viewpoint in Line 20 when she labels Ben and Anna's behaviour as inappropriate in an American context. Of note, too, is the fact that she mitigates this assertion through the use of the verb 'seems' and the adverb 'pretty much'. Finally, Carolyn displays a degree of intercultural competence because she demonstrates an ability to reflect on her own thinking processes with regard to the issue at hand. This reflective process is seen when she says 'I think my biggest problem is … ' Though in different ways, both Carolyn and Emma demonstrate in this excerpt that they are at least beginning to acquire the means by which to access, analyse, compare and evaluate artefacts, practices, values, beliefs and meanings in other cultures and in their own taken-for-granted realities.

In addition to the content of keypal interactions, teachers can look to the presence (or absence) of specific linguistic features in the transcripts of telecollaborative interactions as signposts of intercultural competence. Questions, addressed in detail in the previous section, are the only linguistic feature that Byram (1997: 62) mentions as an index of the operation of skills of discovery. Additional linguistic features such as appraisal may function as markers of intercultural development.

Martin (2000: 144) defines appraisal as 'the semantic resources [interlocutors use] to negotiate emotions, judgments, and valuations, alongside resources for amplifying and engaging with these evaluations'. The appraisal system is divided into several subsystems, the most important of which for our purposes are attitude and graduation. Attitude refers to the linguistic resources speakers use to convey emotional responses, construe moral evaluations of human behaviour, and express the aesthetic quality of natural phenomena and the products of human behaviour, while the subsystem of graduation comprises those linguistic resources that speakers use in order to raise or lower the intensity of a wide range of semantic categories. Because intercultural competence entails modifying or re-evaluating one's evaluations of other societies, cultures and individuals as well as re-analysing one's evaluations of the self and one's own culture, the subsystem of attitude provides a concrete linguistic procedure for revealing how speakers engage in such re-evaluation in the empirical details of their talk. Several examples of the linguistic resources used to convey attitude and graduation in telecollaborative interactions are given in (5)–(9) below:

(5) negative affect: 'We *don't like* it when you don't answer our emails.'

(6) positive affect: 'I am *glad* you liked our homepage!'

(7) negative judgement: 'We cannot believe you actually like the movie American Beauty.'

(8) positive judgement: 'Your English is very *impressive*.'

(9) negative appreciation: 'We are *not* very *impressed* with your work!'

(10) positive appreciation: 'Well, back to *Ben liebt Anna*, really *cute*, but thinking back I have never experienced anything like this in my childhood.'

For the assessment of all aspects of intercultural competence, Byram (1997: 104–105) suggests criterion-referenced performance in particular situations as opposed to norm-referenced exhibition of facts; qualitative progression in contrast to quantitative display; and leaps in insight (p. 105) as compared to incremental increases in knowledge. Furthermore, progress is defined in terms of frequency of occurrence of particular 'intercultural behaviours' rather than as an all-or-nothing phenomenon. This is an important point because it encourages teachers not to look for definitive evidence of intercultural competence in a single piece of data such as Carolyn and Emma's discussion of public nudity given in Example (4) above, but rather to look for patterns of changes over time.

Byram (1997: 108) suggests that the key factor to consider in assessing the *attitudes* component of intercultural competence is 'the existence or absence of a perspective shift'. One potential way to track such a perspective shift would be to look for a decrease in the use of negative judgement over the course of a partnership. Another linguistic indicator of intercultural competence might be a tempering of one's emotional response to keypals' statements (e.g. no longer becoming upset when keypals mistake the Nittany Lion for a bear because you now realise that American football is a local rather than universal pastime and that sports' teams are not an integral part of most European universities). A third marker might be a gradual softening of the way in which one positions herself with respect to the 'absolute' truth of utterances (e.g. France is the best! → France is one of the best countries in the world. → Like most things, France has both positive and negative qualities.)

A final point concerns the scope of application of intercultural competence. For example, can an individual be considered to be an intercultural speaker if she exhibits a readiness to suspend disbelief and judgement with respect to the meanings, beliefs and behaviours of one group, but not with regard to a second group? I have noticed over the years that learners in my German–American exchanges have begun to express measures of intercultural competence with respect to one another, but that they still hold rather absolute and unrelativised views of other groups. A clear example comes in the form of responses to one of the questions on the cultural survey: Would you marry someone from another culture? The same learners who begin to understand the significance of football for Americans in general, who begin to relativise their evaluations of public nudity and who start to question their whole hearted belief in the positive virtues of patriotism, state that they would marry anyone but a Muslim because of the way that they treat their women, a perception which may have been nursed along, in part, by the powerful media influences that the *Connect Program* seeks to interrogate. Kern (2000: 256) wisely reminds us that 'intolerance must be acknowledged as a cultural fact and explored through discussion that frames opposing perspectives critically'. Critical framing, however, involves the metalingual component of 'stepping back and looking at the 'then and there' of communication' (Kern, 2000: 133). 'Through critical framing,' the New London Group (1996) explains, 'learners can gain the necessary personal and theoretical distance from what they have learned, constructively critique it, account for its cultural location, creatively extend and apply it, and eventually innovate on their own, within old communities and in new ones.'

Conclusion

Proponents as well as opponents of intercultural competence in foreign language education have suggested that the classroom is an insufficiently rich learning environment with regard to opportunities for apprenticeship into the diverse and complex forms of linguistic behaviour that both index and constitute intercultural competence (e.g. House, 1997: 17). Some scholars even have claimed that intercultural competence is 'unattainable through any kind of teaching' (Harden, 2000: 120) and that it can only be developed and put into practice in the context of first-hand experiences in 'real life'. Harden (2000: 120), for example, makes the following statement:

> . . . it is hard to imagine how [intercultural competence] could be put into practice other than by life, by first hand experience and it is doubtful if such issues make sense within the narrow confines of institutionalised language-learning. The central question here seems to be one that lies beyond the realm of classroom and textbook as it deals with the formation of experience and the construction of identity.

House (1997: 18) appears to support this viewpoint when she states: 'Es ist ja auch nicht das Ziel von Unterricht, dem Alltagsleben und der Alltagskultur Konkurrenz zu machen' (It is also not the goal of instruction to compete with daily life and daily culture). Byram (1997: 64–69), however, maintains that intercultural competence can and should be developed in three configurations: (a) in the classroom; (b) via field work outside the classroom; and (3) by means of independent learning. The classroom, Byram (1997: 66–67) points out, provides opportunities for the teaching of relational knowledge and the skills of interpreting and relating documents or events. 'What the classroom cannot usually offer', Byram (1997: 68) continues, 'is the opportunity to develop the skills of interaction in real time.'

In a more recent review of language and culture learning, Byram and Feng (2004: 152) note that advances in communication technologies have begun to address any perceived deficiencies in classroom-based culture learning by enabling intercultural interaction in real time on a broad scale. Just as psychologist Sherry Turkle (1997) has shown that 'life on the screen' can be as real and as intense as off-screen life, leading to online romance and even marriage, and as communication theorist Joseph Walther (1996) has argued that mediated relationships may be *hyperpersonal*, i.e. better and more consuming, than unmediated relationships, the research on telecollaboration indicates that intercultural competence can develop in institutionalised settings under the careful guidance of languacultural experts or teachers. Learners who have not yet begun to decentre are generally unable to interpret foreign peoples and cultures from any other point of view but their own. This state of affairs is seen in the opening lines of Mrs. Curtin's explanation of what a white woman is doing in Mma Ramotswe's detective agency:

> I came to Africa twelve years ago. I was forty-three and Africa meant nothing to me. I suppose I had the usual ideas about [Africa] – a hotchpotch of images of big game and savannah and Kilimanjaro rising out of the clouds. I also thought of famines and civil wars and potbellied, half-naked children staring at the camera, sunk in hopelessness. (McCall Smith, 2000: 27)

In this excerpt, Mrs. Curtin clearly lacks declarative knowledge of Africa; her evaluations of Africa are shaped by her own culturally contingent frames of reference and they smack of a 'number 1 type' theory of otherness. But as time goes on, Mrs. Curtin begins to display the qualities of the sojourner:

We had found a country where the people treated one another well, with respect, and where there were values other than grab, grab, grab which prevails back home. I felt humbled, in a way. Everything in my own country seemed so shoddy and superficial when held up against what I saw in Africa. People suffered here, and many of them had very little, but they had this wonderful feeling for others. When I first heard African people calling others – complete strangers – their brother or their sister, it sounded odd to my ears. But after a while I knew exactly what it meant and I started to think the same way ... I was learning lessons. I had come to Africa and I was learning lessons. (McCall Smith, 2000: 29–30)

Through travel to Africa, Mrs. Curtin's own cultural values and beliefs began to be challenged. Her first encounters with otherness 'sounded odd' to her ears, but because she exhibited a readiness to interrogate the value systems behind her own cultural practices and to investigate those behind others, her meanings began to change. Mrs. Curtin was learning lessons.

Appendix A Final Product assessment rubric

Kriterien	super	sehr gut	gut	befried-igend	nicht befried-igend	Kommentar
Formale Kriterien						
Länge des Essays						
Titel des Essays						
Strategischer Gebrauch beider Sprachen						Beispiele:
Inhaltliche Kriterien:						
Deutlicher Vergleich verschiedener Texte/Figuren/Themen						Beispiele:
Unterschiedliche kulturelle Perspektiven						Beispiele:
Kreativität						
Sprachliche Kriterien:						
Wortfolge: Das Verb im Hauptsatz Das Verb im Nebensatz						
Nebensätze/unterordnende Konjunktionen						Gebrauchte Konjunktionen hier auflisten:

Relativsätze	Ein Beispiel hier angeben:
Idiomatische Phrasen	Beispiele:
Die Auflistung/das Hinzufügen der Argumente (erstens, zweitens, drittens, außerdem, weiter, usw)	Beispiele:
Hyperlinkstruktur	
Links • zusätzliche, relevante Informationen • Vertiefung des Arguments durch Links • Auseinandersetzung mit anderen Perspektiven durch Links	
Images	
Extra Punkte	
Gebrauch des Passivs	Beispiel:
Sound	
Clips	
Infinitivsätze	Beispiel:

References

Agar, M. (1994) Language Shock: Understanding the Culture of Conversation. New York: William Morrow.

Appel, M.-C. (1999) Tandem Language Learning by E-mail: Some Basic Principles and a Case Study. Centre for Language and Communication Studies Occasional Paper 54. Dublin: Trinity College Dublin.

Arnold, N. and Ducate, L. (2006) Future foreign language teachers' social and cognitive collaboration in an on-line environment. Language Learning & Technology 10, 42–66.

Avots, J. (1991) Linking the foreign language classroom to the world. In J. Philips (ed.) Building Bridges and Making Connections. Northeast Conference on the Teaching of Foreign Languages, Middlebury, VT.

Bauer, B., deBenedette, L., Furstenberg, G., Levet, S. and Waryn, S. (2006) The Cultura Project. In J.A. Belz and S.L. Thorne (eds) Internet-mediated Intercultural Foreign Language Education. Boston, MA: Heinle and Heinle.

Belz, J.A. (2001) Institutional and individual dimensions of transatlantic group work in network-based language teaching. ReCALL 13 (2), 213–231.

Belz, J.A. (2002) Social dimensions of telecollaborative foreign language study. Language Learning & Technology 6, 60–81. On WWW at http://llt.msu.edu/vol6num1/belz/.

Belz, J.A. (2005a) Telecollaborative foreign language study: A personal overview of praxis and research. In D. Hiple and I. Thompson (eds) Selected Papers from the 2004 NFLRC Symposium on Distance Education, Distributed Learning, and Language Instruction. Honolulu: National Foreign Language Resource Center. On WWW at http://www.nflrc.hawaii.edu/networks/nw44/belz.htm.

Belz, J.A. (2005b) Intercultural questioning, discovery, and tension in Internet-mediated language learning partnerships. Language and Intercultural Communication 5, 3–39.

Belz, J.A. and Kinginger, C. (2003) Discourse options and the development of pragmatic competence by classroom learners of German: The case of address forms. Language Learning 53 (4), 591–647.

Belz, J.A. and Thorne, S.L. (eds) (2006) Internet-Mediated Intercultural Foreign Language Education. Boston, MA: Heinle and Heinle.

Belz, J.A. and Müller-Hartmann, A. (2003) Teachers as intercultural learners: Negotiating German-American telecollaboration along the institutional fault line. The Modern Language Journal 87, 71–89.

Belz, J.A. and Vyatkina, N. (2005) Learner corpus analysis and the development of L2 pragmatic competence in networked intercultural language study: The case of German modal particles. Canadian Modern Language Review/Revue canadienne des langues vivantes 62, 17–48.

Ben-Rafael, E., Shohamy, E., Amara, M.H. and Trumper-Hecht, N. (2006) Linguistic landscape as symbolic construction of the public space: The case of Israel. International Journal of Multilingualism 3 (1), 7–30.

Berger, P.L. and Luckmann, T. (1966) The Social Construction of Reality. Harmondsworth: Penguin.

Bredella, L. (2000) The significance of intercultural understanding in the foreign language classroom. In T. Harden and A. Witte (eds) The Notion of

Intercultural Understanding in the Context of German as a Foreign Language (pp. 145–166). Bern: Peter Lang.

Burwitz-Melzer, E. (2001) Teaching intercultural communicative competence through literature. In M. Byram, A. Nichols and D. Stevens (eds) Developing Intercultural Competence in Practice. Multilingual Matters, Clevedon.

Byram, M. (1989) Intercultural education and foreign language teaching. World Studies Journal 7 (2), 4–7.

Byram, M. (1997) Teaching and Assessing Intercultural Communicative Competence. Clevedon, UK: Multilingual Matters.

Byram, M. (ed.) (2003) Intercultural Competence. Council of Europe, Strasbourg.

Byram, M. and Morgan, C. (1994) Teaching-and-Learning Language-and-Culture. Clevedon: Multilingual Matters.

Byram, M., and Feng, A. (2004) Culture and language learning: Teaching, research and scholarship. Language Teaching 37, 149–168.

Carel, S. (2001) Students as virtual ethnographers: Exploring the language culture connections. In M. Byram, A. Nichols and D. Stevens (eds) Developing Intercultural Competence in Practice. Clevedon: Multilingual Matters.

Carney, N. (2006) Telecollaboration for intercultural learning: An overview of projects involving Japan. The JALT CALL Journal 2, 37–52.

Cazden, C. (2001) Classroom Discourse: The Language of Teaching and Learning (2nd edn). Portsmouth, NH: Heinemann.

Cononelos, T. and Oliva, M. (1993) Using computer networks to enhance foreign language/culture education. Foreign Language Annals 26, 527–534.

Corbett, J. (2003) An Intercultural Approach to English Language Teaching. Clevedon, UK: Multilingual Matters.

Doyé, P. (1999) The Intercultural Dimension: Foreign Language Education in the Primary School. Berlin: Cornelsen.

Dussias, P. (2006) Morphological development in Spanish–American telecollaboration. In J.A. Belz and S.L. Thorne (eds) Internet-mediated Intercultural Foreign Language Education (pp. 121–146). Boston, MA: Heinle & Heinle.

Esposito, J.L. (2002) What Everyone Needs to Know about Islam. Oxford: Oxford University Press.

Ferris, D. and Hedgcock, J. (2005) Teaching ESL Composition: Purpose, Process, and Practice (2nd edn). Mahwah, NJ: Lawrence Erlbaum.

Fischer, G. (1998) E-mail in Foreign Language Teaching: Toward the Creation of Virtual Classrooms. Tübingen: Stauffenberg Verlag.

Furstenberg, G. (2003) Reading between the cultural lines. In P. Patrikis (ed.) Reading Between the Lines: Perspectives on Foreign Language Literacy. New Haven, CT: Yale University Press.

Furstenberg, G., Levet, S., English, K. and Mallet, K. (2001) Giving a virtual voice to the silent language of culture: The Cultura project. Language Learning & Technology 5, 55–102. On WWW at http://llt.msu.edu/vol5num1/fursten berg/default.html

Garrison, R. and Anderson, T. (2003) E-Learning in the 21st Century. London: Routledge.

Gee, J. (2005) An Introduction to Discourse Analysis: Theory and Method (2nd edn). London: Routledge.

Gipps, C. (1994) Beyond Testing: Toward a Theory of Educational Assessment. London: Falmer Press.

Part 3: Issues and Questions in Online Intercultural Exchange

Grace, P. (1987) Electric City and Other Stories. Auckland, NZ: Penguin.
Harden, T. (2000) The limits of understanding. In T. Harden and A. Witte (eds) The Notion of Intercultural Understanding in the Context of German as a Foreign Language (pp. 103–123). Bern: Peter Lang.
Harden, T. and Witte, A. (2000) The Notion of Intercultural Understanding in the Context of German as a Foreign Language. Bern: Peter Lang.
Härtling, P. (1997) Ben liebt Anna [Ben Loves Anna] (2nd edn). Weinheim, Germany: Beltz Verlag.
Holliday, A. (1996) Developing a sociological imagination: Expanding ethnography in international English language education. Applied Linguistics 17, 234–255.
House, J. (1997) Zum Erwerb interkulturelles Kompetenz im Unterricht des Deutschen als Fremdsprache [On the acquisition of intercultural competence in the teaching of German as a foreign language]. Zeitschrift fuer interkulturellen Fremdsprachenunterricht 1 (3), 21pp. On WWW at http://www.spz.tu-darmstadt.de/projekt_ejournal/jg-01-3/beitrag/house.htm.
Houston, J. and Houston, J.D. (1983) Farewell to Manzanar. New York: Laurel-Leaf Books.
Ivanic, R. (1998) Writing and Identity: The Discoursal Construction of Identity in Academic Writing. Amsterdam: John Benjamins.
Kahf, M. (2003) E-mails from Scheherazad. Gainesville, FL: University Press of Florida.
Kern, R. (1996) Computer-mediated communication: Using e-mail exchanges to explore personal histories in two cultures. In M. Warschauer (ed.) Telecollaboration in Foreign Language Learning. Honolulu: University of Hawaii Second Language Teaching and Curriculum Center.
Kern, R. (2000) Literacy and Language Teaching. Oxford: Oxford University Press.
Kinginger, C. (2000) Learning the pragmatics of solidarity in the networked foreign language classroom. In J.K. Hall (ed.) Second and Foreign Language Learning through Classroom Interaction. Mahwah, NJ: Erlbaum.
Kinginger, C. (2004) Communicative foreign language teaching through tele-collaboration. In O. St. John, K. van Esch and E. Schalkwijk (eds) New Insights into Foreign Language Learning and Teaching. Frankfurt: Peter Lang.
Kinginger, C., Gouvrès-Hayward, A. and Simpson, V. (1999) A tele-collaborative course on French-American intercultural communication. The French Review 72, 853–866.
Kohlberg, L., Levine, C. and Hewer, A. (1983) Moral Stages: A Current Formulation and Response to Critics. Basel, Switzerland: Karger.
Kötter, M. (2002) Tandem Learning on the Internet: Learner Interactions in On-line Virtual Environments. Frankfurt: Peter Lang.
Kramsch, C. (1993) Context and Culture in Language Teaching. Oxford: Oxford University Press.
Kramsch, C. (1998) The privilege of the intercultural speaker. In M. Byram and M. Fleming (eds) Language Learning in Intercultural Perspective: Approaches through Drama and Ethnography. New York: Cambridge University Press.
Little, D. and Brammerts, H. (eds) (1996) A Guide to Language Learning in Tandem via the Internet. Centre for Language and Communication Studies,

Occasional Paper 46, Trinity College, Dublin. [Accessed on-line via ERIC ED399789.]

Martin, J. (2000) Beyond exchange: Appraisal systems in English. In S. Hunston and G. Thompson (eds) Evaluation in Text (pp. 142–175). Oxford, England: Oxford University Press.

McCall Smith, A. (2000) Tears of the Giraffe. New York: Random House.

Morgan, C. and Cain, A. (2000) Foreign Language and Culture Learning from a Dialogic Perspective. Clevedon, UK: Multilingual Matters.

Müller-Hartmann, A. (2000) The role of tasks in promoting intercultural learning in electronic learning networks. Language Learning & Technology 4, 129–147. On WWW at http://llt.msu.edu/vol4num2/muller/.

Müller-Hartmann, A. (2006) Learning how to teach intercultural communicative competence via telecollaboration: A model for language teacher education. In J.A. Belz and S.L. Thorne (eds) Internet-mediated Intercultural Foreign Language Education. Boston, MA: Heinle and Heinle.

New London Group (1996) A pedagogy of multiliteracies: Designing social futures. Harvard Educational Review 66 (1). On WWW at http://wwwstatic. kern.org/filer/blogWrite44ManilaWebsite/paul/articles/A_Pedagogy_of_ Multiliteracies_Designing_Social_Futures.htm#11.

Nieto, S. (1999) The Light in Their Eyes: Creating Multicultural Learning Communities. New York: Teachers College Press.

Noack, E. (1999) Comparing U.S. and German education. Like apples and sauerkraut. Phi Delta Kappan 80 (10), 773–776.

O'Dowd, R. (2003) Understanding the 'other side': Intercultural learning in a Spanish–English e-mail exchange. Language Learning & Technology 7, 118–144. On WWW at http://llt.msu.edu/vol7num2/odowd/default.html.

O'Dowd, R. (2006) The use of videoconferencing and email as mediators of intercultural student ethnography. In J.A. Belz and S.L. Thorne (eds) Internet-Mediated Intercultural Foreign Language Education (pp. 86–120). Boston, MA: Heinle and Heinle.

Richter, H.P. (2001) Damals war es Friedrich (46th edn). München: dtv.

Robinson-Stuart, G. and Nocon, H. (1996) Second culture acquisition: Ethnography in the foreign language classroom. The Modern Language Journal 80, 431–449.

Schneider, J. and von der Emde, S. (2006) Conflicts in cyberspace: From communication breakdown to intercultural dialogue in on-line collaborations. In J.A. Belz and S.L. Thorne (eds) Internet-mediated Intercultural Foreign Language Education. Boston, MA: Heinle and Heinle.

Scollon, R. and Scollon, S.W. (2001) Intercultural Communication: A Discourse Approach. Oxford: Blackwell.

Soliya (2007) The Connect Program. On WWW at http://www.soliya.net/ ?mid=0.

Tella, S. (1991) Introducing International Communications Networks and Electronic Mail into Foreign Language Classrooms: A Case Study in Finnish Senior Secondary Schools. Helsinki: Yliopistopaino.

Thorne, S.L. (2003) Artifacts and cultures-of-use in intercultural communication. Language Learning & Technology 7, 38–67. On WWW at http://llt.msu.edu/ vol7num2/thorne/.

Thorne, S.L. (2006) Pedagogical and praxiological lessons from Internet-mediated intercultural foreign language education research. In J.A. Belz and S.L. Thorne (eds) Internet-mediated Intercultural Foreign Language Education. Boston, MA: Heinle and Heinle.

Turkle, S. (1997) Life on the Screen: Identity in the Age of the Internet. New York: Touchstone.

Walther, J. (1996) Computer-mediated communication: Impersonal, interpersonal, and hyperpersonal interaction. Communication Research 23, 3–43.

Ware, P. and Kramsch, C. (2005) Toward in intercultural stance: Teaching German and English through telecollaboration. The Modern Language Journal 89, 190–205.

Warschauer, M. (ed.) (1995) Virtual Connections. Honolulu: University of Hawaii Second Language Teaching and Curriculum Center.

Warschauer, M. (ed.) (1996) Telecollaboration in Foreign Language Learning. Honolulu: University of Hawaii Second Language Teaching and Curriculum Center.

Warschauer, M. (1999) Electronic Literacies: Language, Culture, and Power in On-line Education. Mahwah, NJ: Erlbaum.

Warschauer, M. (2003) Demystifying the digital divide. Scientific American 289, 42–47.

Warschauer, M. and Kern, R. (eds) (2000) Network-Based Language Teaching: Concepts and Practice. New York: Cambridge University Press.

Zarate, G. (2003) Identities and plurilingualism: Pre-conditions for recognition of intercultural competences. In M. Byram (ed.) Intercultural Competence. Council of Europe, Strasbourg.

Chapter 8

Teacher Role in Telecollaboration: Setting up and Managing Exchanges

ANDREAS MÜLLER-HARTMANN

Introduction: Historical Perspective – The Teacher's Role(s) in Telecollaboration

> ... two teachers in distant schools were matched to form a 'twinned' or 'sister-class' partnership according to their own common teaching interests and the grade level of their students. [...] Partner classes engaged in two kinds of exchanges: monthly cultural packages [...] and joint projects, which may be best described as identical long-distance team-teaching units. (Cummins & Sayers 1995: 124–140)

> [...] it is important to stress that the use of new techniques and instruments in the context of interscholastic exchanges was not conceived as a way to 'teacher-proof' the curriculum. Just as these new approaches and correspondence networks benefit students [...] they can also forge links among instructors, vitally supporting teachers during the demanding professional-development process of learning to use new techniques and classroom technologies. (Sayers, 1994: 81)

This is a description of the intercultural exchange projects that Célestin Freinet began to set up in the Modern School Movement in the 1920s, eventually comprising team-teaching partnerships among 10,000 schools worldwide. The idea of team-teaching in 'twinned' or 'sister-class' projects already highlighted the role of the teacher as an organiser, but also as a learner and as a 'teacher-as-researcher', as teachers experimented with and changed new teaching approaches through observation in their classrooms and in cooperation with their partner teachers (Cummins & Sayers, 1995: 126, 137). Consequently, the teacher[1] and his various roles were considered decisive for the success of those projects. Since then, the idea of correspondence projects has been clearly established in the foreign language classroom (see Edelhoff & Liebau, 1988; Wicke, 1995), having achieved new prominence with the advent of asynchronous and synchronous communication tools in the 1990s, such as e-mail, chat, Moo, MUDs and videoconferencing (Blood, 2000; Warschauer, 1995, 1996, 1997, 1999; Warschauer & Kern, 2000). Today, a second generation of communication tools, such as wikis, web-, audio- and videoblogs, as well as pod- and vodcasts open still new opportunities for intercultural exchanges (see Almeida, 2003). Throughout all of these innovations, the role of the teacher has been paramount for the success of intercultural learning via telecollaboration, although research has only recently attached the appropriate importance to this aspect of telecollaborative projects. After examining the historical development of the teacher role in telecollaboration, a methodological approach of dealing with telecollaborative projects will be outlined. Examples from various projects in primary, secondary and teacher education contexts will then give an insight into the role teachers must fulfil. Methodological suggestions, in terms of initiating and developing intercultural telecollaborative negotiation, will be made.

The new technology Freinet used was not the computer, but the printing press. Nevertheless, the assumption of the teacher's role in this exchange of letters and packages was very similar to the context of computer technology and the development of telecollaborative projects in the 1990s, which Warschauer (1995: 53) described as 'electronic team-teaching'. He continues, 'In team-teaching partnerships, classes in different places work together not only to share information but to complete certain tasks or projects.'

The new technology did not replace the teacher, but put him in the midst of designing the new learning environment, allowing him to develop professionally, conjointly with his partner teacher(s) abroad, in the process of these intercultural projects. While the teacher's role in technology-rich learning environments was originally ignored by some researchers (e.g. Rüschoff & Wolff, 1999) due to the euphoria of what the learners could do autonomously with the new media, other researchers, in the early 1990s, realised the important pedagogical role teachers had to fulfil. Ten years ago, Tella (1996: 13) called on teachers to '... be courageous enough to step aside from the "sage on the stage" to the "guide on the side"'. At that time, the term facilitator was used to describe the pedagogical role of the teacher in collaborative projects managing, 'the interaction, usually in the background, by relating individual comments, by suggesting a different interpretation of an idea, or by clarifying a position and so forth' (Ahern, 1997: 230; also see Eck *et al*., 1995: 113; Tella, 1991: 21). While this focused the teacher's work on setting up, supporting, guiding and monitoring the interaction among learners, the concept of the facilitator generally ignored the local institutional constraints and affordances (see Belz & Müller-Hartmann, 2003).

In 1995 Berge included the role of the facilitator in the four general role categories he defined for online tutors, which are also applicable to the teacher's role; the pedagogical, social, managerial and technical role (also see Legutke *et al.*, 2006). The decisive role is the *pedagogical* role. In it, the teacher sets and sequences tasks, initiating and supporting the process of intercultural learning, as well as promoting 'responsible and critical authorship' (Legutke *et al.*, 2006). In his *social* role the teacher creates a supportive and pleasant learning atmosphere and supports collaborative learning among learners in participating groups, trying to establish group cohesiveness. By taking care of the logistics, in terms of time and place, the teacher fulfils his *managerial* role, ensuring that deadlines are met, negotiating institutional constraints in the process. Learners' technical competence is often higher than that of the teacher, but he still has a *technical* responsibility, in terms of introducing tools to the less knowledgeable learners, familiarising participants with both system and software. As Legutke *et al.* (2006) points out, 'It goes without saying that the traditional roles of the teacher to act as *language instructor* providing language resources and monitoring language use do not cease to be relevant. On the contrary, teachers have to be able to deal with the imponderability and complexity that the expanded space of action entails.'

While Berge's list was an important step in realising the multifaceted demands on teachers in technology-rich environments, cross-cultural differences in various institutional settings play significant roles when considering restrictions or enhancements in the fulfilment of these teacher roles. Diversification of research in the field of international telecollaboration clarified the issues involved. The initial euphoria about the potential of telecollaborative projects for the development of intercultural communicative competence (ICC) – often rendered in descriptive studies of successful telecollaborative projects – gave way to further qualitative research studies of local classrooms. Issues teachers faced, when organising and monitoring the projects, were examined. These included institutional constraints, for example, diverging timetables, limited computer access for one partner, different assessment procedures, the danger of intercultural misunderstandings or the question of an intensive versus a more laidback approach to monitoring (Belz & Müller-Hartmann, 2003; Müller-Hartmann, 1999; O'Dowd, 2006; O'Dowd & Ritter, 2006; Ware, 2005).

Recent overviews of research on the use of technology in the foreign language classroom show that, finally, the centrality of the teacher's role in these exchanges has been understood. Referring to the *Cultura* project (see Chapter 4 in this volume), Kern *et al.* (2004: 249) remark on the teacher's work in telecollaboration: 'This marks a key pedagogical change: The teacher shifts out of the "omniscient informant" role and focuses on structuring, juxtaposing, interpreting, and reflecting on intercultural experiences'. Freinet's realisation that no technical innovation will lead to a teacher-proof curriculum, has come full circle. Today the pedagogical and methodological role of the teacher is being focused on: 'These factors signal the important role of the teacher, who is familiar with both cultures and who can set appropriate goals and tasks, monitor communication, and assist in negotiating communicative difficulties' (Kern, 2006: 198–199). In his research on intercultural miscommunication O'Dowd (2006: 139) becomes even more specific. Teachers 'also need to explicitly develop learners' knowledge and skills and cultural awareness by providing factual information, by modelling the analysis of texts from the partner class, by helping learners to create their own correspondence and also by encouraging them to focus on the meanings which the target culture attributes to behaviour as opposed to simply focusing on the behaviour itself'.

While helping learners to discover intercultural meaning, monitoring the collaborative process between the two partner groups becomes decisive. Collaboration needs careful monitoring to make sure that the workload is evenly distributed. Teachers, for example, need to ensure that groups take turns when working on collaborative tasks. Who makes the first suggestion for a solution? Is there a way of allowing both participating groups to initiate the first step in task completion, instead of the same group always reacting? When collaborating with a partner teacher, the teacher needs to consider his partner's class sessions by providing the right input through his learners' work for his colleague's next session. Careful monitoring of developing products and an understanding of the way the colleague works is necessary. While misunderstandings are often helpful for initiating processes of intercultural learning (see Belz, 2002; Belz & Müller-Hartmann 2002), the teacher has a social responsibility to avoid unnecessary friction among partners. Sensitive monitoring of local and interinstitutional group work processes will help to ensure that learners are able to establish positive working, and possibly even personal, relationships.

A Methodological Approach – Task-based Language Learning

As the question of the methodology of telecollaborative projects has increasingly become more relevant in research projects, I would like to suggest a methodological approach that will help teachers deal with such complex learning environments. Task-based language learning (TBLL), another field in foreign language teaching and learning that has seen a decisive development during the past 10 years (see Ellis, 2000, 2003; Nunan, 2004, Willis, 1996), helps to ground teachers' approaches and decisions in the complex environment of an intercultural exchange. TBLL stresses the meaningful use of language without neglecting an appropriate focus on form. When engaged in tasks, learners work purposefully towards a specific goal. Tasks thus have a clear outcome; learners can do them individually or in groups, with a focus on competition or collaboration. Nunan (2004) has provided an approach to planning and structuring TBLL. His task components include *goals, input, procedures, task types or activities, setting, teacher* and *learner roles* (Figure 8.1).

Nunan (2004: 20) differentiates between real-world tasks and pedagogical tasks. Real-world tasks are tasks that learners would encounter, in exactly the same form, outside the classroom, such as negotiating an issue with a partner. Pedagogical tasks, on the other hand, are 'designed not to provide learners with an opportunity to rehearse some out-of-class performance, but to activate their emerging language skills'. This can be done through 'role-plays, simulations, problem-solving tasks and information exchange tasks' (Nunan, 2004: 20). Intercultural exchanges,

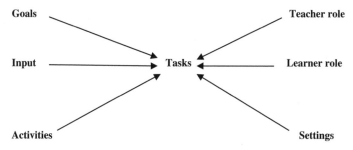

Figure 8.1
Based on Nunan (2004: 40–75)

thus, clearly fulfil the main task criteria, as learners discuss an issue in the foreign language that is meaningful to them, for example, the question of how much pocket-money they get in both contexts or how they finance their mobile phone use. In so doing, the exchange has a clear purpose or objective, i.e. finding out about each others' cultural context while using the foreign language. There usually is a clear outcome or product, such as a survey, a common text, web page or pictures that young learners draw with their partners. Consequently, most tasks in telecollaborative projects are real-world tasks, as learners negotiate issues with other learners outside their classrooms.

On the methodological side of sequencing tasks, Willis (1996) has developed the concept of the task cycle, differentiating between pre-task, task cycle and language focus, which allows teachers to select and sequence tasks in the right order. Willis' task cycle also includes the necessary focus on form, which is dealt with in Chapter 6. In Willis' framework the pre-task phase is meant to prepare the learners for what will come, cognitively, emotionally and from a language point of view, opening a field of awareness. In the task cycle learners do the actual task, and then plan to report their results to the class, which can be done in oral or written form. The presentation of products completes the task cycle. Language focus is a third phase, which has students analyse language, for example, in form of a corpus analysis of e-mail texts (see Eck *et al.*, 1995).'The teacher conducts practice of new words, phrases and patterns occurring in the data, either during or after the analysis' (Willis, 1996: 38). The language focus does not have to follow the task cycle; it can be part of the task cycle when language support becomes necessary and students need to focus on certain structural forms, such as the forming of questions when they do surveys or interviews in the course of their projects.

As pointed out above, telecollaborative projects connect foreign language learners with native speakers or other speakers of the language, having them work on tasks that should be connected to the learners' experiences. Real-world tasks thus structure the collaboration, and their sequence is very much related to Willis' general framework of TBLL. Her sequence of pre-task and task cycle finds its corresponding structure in the three general phases of a telecollaborative project, the contact phase, the one of establishing dialogue and the critical reflection (see Figure 8.2). Before the pre-task(s) of establishing contact can be set, the teacher needs to find possible partners to cooperate with. The best choice is always somebody the teacher knows, either through his own stays abroad or through school partnerships. Knowledge of the partner, as well as his

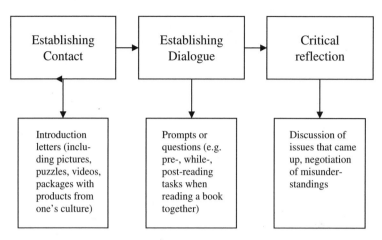

Figure 8.2 General phases of a telecollaborative project

institutional context, will allow the teacher to negotiate the organisational frame and the tasks of the project more easily, as he is able to understand the affordances and constraints his partner is working with. Having an insight into each others' professional context, such as the expectations of the curriculum, possible content matter as well as assessment procedures, helps teachers to judge the reactions of the partner more objectively, thus facilitating their methodological and pedagogical cooperation, while allowing them to avoid cultural misunderstandings on the teacher level.

If a teacher does not have any personal connections abroad, he can use a number of websites (see Table 8.1) to find appropriate partners.

Establishing contact

We will only focus on the most pertinent issues concerning the teacher's role. In Willis' framework the pre-task phase is meant to prepare the learners for what will come. The same is true for the establishing-contact or getting-to-know phase in a telecollaborative project when learners establish contact for the first time (see Figure 8.2). It is the basis for initiating dialogical learning. In order to work together, learners must initially get to know each other and learn about each others' backgrounds, personalities and feelings. These exchanges lay the basis for what will come, allowing learners to become more involved with each other in the following phases in which content will be

Table 8.1 Websites for locating partners for intercultural exchanges

ePALS Classroom Exchange – one of the largest international networks for collaborative school partnerships http://www.epals.com/search/
Kidlink – a platform used by over 100,000 children in over 100 countries to find partners and communicate with young learners across the world http://www.kidlink.org/
Windows of the world – partner linking service http://www.britishcouncil.org/wotw/
Book raps – a book rap is a book discussion conducted via electronic mail http://rite.ed.qut.edu.au/old_oz-teachernet/projects/book-rap/index1.html
European Picture Book Projects – picture books as the basis for intercultural exchanges http://www.ncrcl.ac.uk/eset/
Travel Buddy Projects – international projects especially for young learners http://rite.ed.qut.edu.au/oz-teachernet
MICALL – pedagogy and practice-based methodology for network-based language teaching and learning, including projects for learners in primary and secondary school http://www.micall.net/
IEARN – international network, offering many interdisciplinary projects, often in the field of peace education http://www.iearn.org/
Isabel Perez website on English as a second or foreign language – an extensive compendium of project ideas http://www.isabelperez.com/

negotiated. Simple introduction letters are a good start, but they should be task-oriented and go beyond the simplistic forms of, 'I have got two cats, three guinea-pigs and two sisters'. The teacher will need to set tasks in this phase that generate more specific information and allow for further reactions. If, for example, the aim of the project is to do short surveys about the extent teenagers earn money, the task could be to introduce oneself, adding information about weekend routines. The following letter of an American student (Grade 9) introducing himself to his German partners shows the possibilities that are being generated for survey tasks.

Well this past weekend was fun for me, I had a party at my House on friday, that was fun I had all of my friends there. On saturday I worked from 4:30 until 12:30, and I made $60 in tips. I'm a busser at a pretty nice restaurant. Then on sunday I did my homework, and then I went to a new mall that just opened up by us, that was fun. It is one of the biggest malls in Michigan right now. I think there are over 200 stores in there. Steve

Establishing dialogue

The next phase can build on texts that initiate a dialogue, which the teacher has to support through carefully designed task sequences (see Figure 8.2). With regard to Steve's mail, the next step would be to help learners find interesting aspects in the letter, which could form the basis for an ensuing dialogue about cultural similarities and differences. Such a discovery task (e.g. what is the most interesting, funny or strange information you have received from your partners?) takes learners seriously in their roles as communicators, albeit with the teacher's task support. In a second task, learners can compare their weekend activities, doing surveys in their local classrooms and exchanging the data with their partners. All of these are real-world tasks, as they relate directly to the learners' experience. The exchange of collected data will provoke further questions and discussions, often leading to cultural misunderstandings in the process. When American students, for example, described the custom of Thanksgiving to their partners, the survey the German partners did of their American partners' explanations produced very diverse results:

This week we have Thanksgiving, it is a time when we celebrate the pilgrims landing on Plymouth rock.

Tomorrow, the United States is celebrating the holiday Thanksgiving. We celebrate this because this is when America was first discovered by Columbus is 1492. On this date, we eat lots of turkey, potatoes, ham cranberries, bread, and many other foods.

We are celebrating Thanksgiving in the United States on Thursday. The holiday originated with the Pilgrims who came to this country who depended on the Native Americans to teach them how to grow food and prepare it. So it is basically the coming together of two different cultures and nationalities. Years later the white people would infect the Native Americans with their disease which wiped out millions of lives. But we do not celebrate that part.

Triggered by a simple description/explanation task, the results were fraught with potential intercultural confrontation. How could the German teacher and his class signal to their partners that the explanations were contradictory, not only when comparing the American students' answers, but also in comparison to the English textbook knowledge the German learners had?

Critical reflection

In this third phase of critical reflection (see Figure 8.2) the teacher has to design tasks that negotiate these intercultural fault lines (Kramsch, 1993: 205–232), with respect to their partners, as well as with respect to his students' own culture. As Kramsch (1993: 206) explains, teachers need to develop the capacity 'to recognize the rupture points in the logic of the explanations brought forth by their students in order to bring cross-cultural aspects of communication to the fore'. In the Thanksgiving example above, a possible follow-up task could be to compare their partners' explanations to the German learners' own knowledge and/or factual information in their English textbooks. Learners should then discuss, in groups, how they would inform their partners about the discrepancies, before a whole-class discussion decides on the final procedure. Learners, then, have the possibility of developing ICC. One approach might be to simply present the discrepancies to their partners, and ask them to solve the problem. This would allow partners to save face and come up with a solution. At the same time, though, the German learners need to realise that they, too, have gaps in terms of their national historical knowledge. Having learners define a similar festivity in their culture (in Germany this could be the 'Erntedankfest', an approximate equivalent to Thanksgiving) will allow learners to realise their own shortcomings, thus preventing the development of stereotypes, i.e. the partners not being knowledgeable about their own history.

While Willis' task cycle mirrors the phases of a collaborative project, it should also be noted that each phase in the project can develop its own task cycle(s), depending on the complexity of the project and which direction it takes. Teachers need to be flexible, as discussion points might lead to new fields or more misunderstandings might evolve, which necessitate further task support to solve the issues (see also the following section).

As this chapter is about the role of the teacher, and the demands of the role(s) are intricately interwoven with the more autonomous roles of learners in telecollaborative projects, we will mainly focus on teacher and learner roles in their interrelationship with task design (see Nunan's framework in Figure 8.1). The way teachers cooperate in setting tasks for their learners is decisive for the development of ICC. In the following two parts we will differentiate between young learners (6–12 years of age) and older learners (13–18+ years of age), as learners' language proficiency decides on the kinds of tasks that are suitable as well as the degree of teacher support and monitoring to achieve ICC.

At the same time the examples will show that demands on the teacher are very high when initiating and developing ICC while organising and monitoring such projects. Teacher pre- and in-service education needs to develop the experiential knowledge base that will allow teachers to develop such competences. Thus, the final part focuses on teacher education.

Context for Young Learners

Teacher and learner roles

When organising intercultural telecollaborative projects for younger learners a number of aspects that characterise young learners' learning processes need to be kept in mind. While the goal of ICC is the same, language input for young learners needs to be more carefully chosen and scaffolded. Young learners are not only less advanced on a linguistic level, but also on a cognitive level, which makes it particularly important to choose appropriate content matter.

A telecollaborative project for young learners might develop from the following request, posted on the St. Olaf list:

Aloha,

We are a kindergarten class in Koloa on the island of Kauai in the state of Hawaii and our country is the United States of America. We are studying the seasons and since it's usually warm and sunny here in Hawaii, the color of our leaves don't change so we don't know what Fall leaves look like. We hope that you can help us by sending us some Fall leaves and in return we would send you some shells from our beautiful beaches. Please let us know if you can help by contacting our librarian, Jennifer Cramer. Her e-mail address is jenny@aloha.net

The above project is truly collaborative, as both sides contribute from their specific cultural context. It supports the interdisciplinary approach, i.e.

content and language-integrated learning (CLIL), which plays an important role in most primary foreign language classrooms. Topic choice, here, clearly supports dealing with other subjects as well, such as art, biology or geography. Generally, subject matter should have a real-world connection, hence dealing with topics of young learners' experience, such as family, friends, hobbies, pets, school and the local environment. At the same time, the CLIL approach also supports a multimodal approach to learning, which enhances young learners' preference for the visual, haptic and kinaesthetic. Buddy projects offer great opportunities in this respect, as learners do not only send e-mails, but they actually send a stuffed animal to their partners (see Travel Buddy site above), receive one themselves and take the animal around in their local context. The animal thus 'experiences' different contexts, which are then represented through photos and texts on a common website.

As the attention span of young learners is short, texts and tasks need to be less complex and more game-like, especially with very young learners (see examples on the MICALL site). In the previous example, the project could consist of an exchange of short introduction letters, the exchange of the desired products and a thank-you note. On the local classroom level, this project can then be extended in some subjects, such as an exhibition of the received shells in biology.

While older learners are able to work more independently, younger learners need a lot more structure and support from the teacher. While the teacher needs to mediate projects with older learners as well (see examples below), in learning contexts with younger learners he is obviously not a 'guide on the side', but he is much more prominent, openly and intensively organising, structuring, supporting and monitoring.

The task cycle

As Milton and Garbi (2000: 1) point out, we should 'not overtax young learners' cognitive abilities and skills'. This demands careful scaffolding in terms of keyboard skills, for example, or linguistic skills. When planning such a project, language support in the task cycle becomes a decisive issue. In the MICALL project young learners created their own short homepages on the learning platform (see previous section). By integrating pictures and links into their homepages, learners were able to express their ideas and identities in a multimodal way. While low language proficiency is often a hindrance to genuine communication in telecollaboration, learners are generally able to grasp technical tools intuitively if they are designed appropriately. After the German teacher had shown, i.e. modelled to her 5th graders (they had had half a year of

English) how to set up a homepage on the MICALL platform, she told them that they would start constructing their pages in the next lesson. When the teacher checked the platform later in the afternoon, a number of homepages were already up; learners had grasped the design concept easily, and being highly motivated about presenting themselves online, they had not waited until the next lesson (private correspondence).

On the linguistic side, though, language support is necessary, as young learners are rarely able to write sufficiently in the foreign language. Scaffolds are decisive in providing structure for introductory letters. They simultaneously offer learners enough freedom to use all the language at their disposal and to create individual texts they can identify with. The following is a possible frame for an introduction letter:

Dear partner/.............................,
I will introduce myself to you in this letter.
I am................. twelve/thirteen years old.
.....................a boy/girl.
.....................a twelve-year-old girl.
My surname is............................. and my first name is.......................
People call me..
I have..............two brothers.....................three sisters.
I don't have any brothers or sisters; I am an only child.
I live.................. with my father/stepfather
.... .with my mother/stepmother
.... with my parents
with...........
.... in a boarding school (or another place where you live
    when you cannot live with your parents).
My parents are divorced.
I like.................. football /...................../.......................
I love................. music.
I am fond of singing /...................../.......................
I am in the.......... sixth form of......................... (name of school/
    Germany), I'm in class 6 ...
I think I am easy-going / moody / nice / terrible / difficult / boring /
    spontaneous / calm / cool / quiet / lively.
I like people who...
I don't like people who...
[. . .]   I am looking forward to hearing from you.
Bye for now. (I must go now/ that's all for now/ Bye/)
                                (Based on Schlieger, 2001: 19)

This frame was used in a telecollaborative project between 12-year-old Inuit (Alaska) and German learners. For the German learners, the reading of *Julie and the Wolves* by Jean Craighead George (1972), a book about Inuit culture, presented further preparation for the project. The dialogue phase followed an exchange of introductory letters. The following example of an Inuit child's mail describes her local environment, her hobbies and interests (Schlieger, 2001).

Sabrina

My name is Jessica Younker, I am 11 years old, I am a girl. In Barrow Polar Bears eat people, and we all live in fear every time we go outside.
How are you? I only have two pets, their names are tiger and triger. My birthday is in October, when is your birthday? I play in little dribblers, our team name is Huskies, we never lost a game. Do you play on any teams or play anything? I played on a soccer last year before I played on basketball. Our team name was acrtic foxes. jessica younker.

This mail is full of cultural information for the German learners. On the basis of a discovery task, they listed similarities and differences of all the mails they received. Both classes liked sports, and while some were similar, such as basketball, others were new to the German learners. This triggered questions, creating a dialogic situation. The polar bear description sparked learners' imagination, in terms of stereotypical notions of the Arctic. The mail, though, subverted this stereotype to an extent, as German learners realised that even though polar bears are around and dangerous, they are also a normal part of life for Inuit children in Barrow, Alaska.

Context for Older Learners

Teacher and learner roles

With older learners the teacher increasingly steps back from centre stage, and learners become more prominent in organising their own learning process. The teacher's tasks remain the same, in terms of organising the exchange logistically, developing and sequencing tasks. As learners' level of language proficiency is evolving, they do not need that much explicit language scaffolding any more, in order to communicate with their partners. As synchronous and asynchronous communication can be handled more easily now by the learners, demands on the teacher focus more on supporting collaborative work processes, both on local and on inter-institutional levels. One important facet of collaboration is learners' identities, which become more prominent now, as learners are able to discuss a wider range of topics and issues. As classes are usually too large for each student to have access to a computer in the computer lab, the formation of pairs or groups are the logical solution (see next section). This group formation on the local level finds its counterpart on the inter-institutional level. It is valuable for the development of group identity and, thus, supports the collaborative working process. An example for this is to have learners decide on a common group identity, for example, by way of a group name or a specific icon on the learning platform that is being used.

This involves more intensive monitoring, as learners produce longer texts and engage more deeply in negotiations with the potential of more intercultural misunderstandings. As learners' language proficiency is increasing, word play becomes an issue in learner texts. While this is a positive sign of learners' creative potential, in terms of meaningful language use, it also entails intercultural pitfalls, especially when irony becomes evident.

The task cycle

While younger learners could prepare themselves for the intercultural encounter by looking up on the map to see where the Inuit live (see previous project), older learners require more intensive preparation. O'Dowd has made a number of suggestions about how to prepare learners linguistically, as well as on the pragmatic level (see his site at http://www3.unileon.es/personal/wwdfmrod/collab/). In terms of the contact phase, the early formation of group identities is helpful once learners have exchanged their first introductory letters. In one project between two 10th-grade classes (Germany and Canada), learners discussed their various hobbies and backgrounds, and they came up with group names, such as 'Graceful Dancers' (a group of girls who did ballet), 'The Metal Maniacs' and 'The Computer Freaks', but also 'The Earthtones'. The members of the latter had different ethnic backgrounds and decided to celebrate their diversity by way of their name.

This important phase is decisive in allowing learners to discover their partners' likes and dislikes, as well as their private and educational context. The last aspect becomes especially important with regard to a final group product that is assessed by both teachers. As collaboration needs to be organised according to clear deadlines, which the teacher has to monitor, time pressure is usually an issue in the final phase of collaboration, in which learners are emotionally involved. At that stage a positive and supportive learning atmosphere should have been established within the group, in order for the group members to be able to navigate time and task pressure. The establishing-contact phase lays the basis for this.

In the following example (a German–American project), the teacher made the mistake of connecting the introduction with a controversial task learners were not ready for. The German learners introduced themselves, and, in the same mail, they had asked their partners to list the stereotypes that existed about Germans in the USA. The partners complied in their introduction letters, as can be seen in the following example.

> Hello, my name is Jennifer Brendon. I am very intrigued that your class is interested in our culture. I am a fifteen-year-old-girl ... My height measures out to five feet and six inches, which I am very proud of.
>
> Some stereotypes of the German race include drinking a lot of beer, eating sauerkraut and brats (YUCK), didn't like the Jewish race, and big, burly women who don't shave.
>
> I hope I have not offended any of you. I think conversing with students from different countries is a really great idea.
>
> Jennifer
> (American student)

> Hi Jennifer,
> How are you? I hope you are fine. My name is Thorsten Markmann ...
> I were impressed about your dislikes and likes, but your thoughts about typical Germans are wrong. Maybe in south of Germany are a few people, who eat sauerkraut and drink a lot of beer, but here in Hessen, the most people hate sauerkraut and doesn't drink much beer and the most girls are not big and burly. The most are smaller than you are and they shave themselves. I hope I doesn't offend you with my aggressive opinion ...
>
> Yours Thorsten
> (German student)

Here, the teacher jumped right from the dialogue phase into the critical reflection phase (see Figure 8.2) without allowing learners to become familiar with each other and develop relationships. Even though these two learners manage the interaction by using their ICC skills (showing openness and curiosity towards the partners, correct start and end of mails, attempts to allow partner to save face), one can easily see that this could have ended disastrously. Thorsten created new stereotypes (generalising about the South of Germany) and the teachers needed to do quite a bit of follow-up work to handle the situation. Even though such intercultural fault lines are often helpful for learning about each other, teachers should not push this issue in early tasks, as many learner texts contain potential for ICC anyway (see the e-mail by Steve on page 175) and conflicts emerge easily enough. The teacher's responsibility, thus, is not only to initiate ICC through setting appropriate tasks, but also to assume responsibility on the affective level, to help learners establish a positive and trustworthy relationship. Stereotypes emerge and are hardened quickly.

This leads us to the third context, teacher education. Teachers primarily must develop the competences that allow them to design and handle such learning environments.

Teacher Education

Teacher and learner roles

In a German university seminar (see Chapter 7 for a description of the project) student teachers voiced their expectations and concerns about the telecollaborative project they were about to embark on.

> I wanted to learn how to manage and organise a whole class of 28 pupils doing an e-mail project and not losing control of what is going on. (Beatrice)

> I wondered before the course how the new media could change lessons in school, how they effect the communication and in what way they finally change our role as a teacher. (Norbert)

> The computer can shut down before you can save your e-mail, the server won't let you in, etc. It's also hard to keep an eye on all students while they are online (...). I came to the conclusion that this project is definitely worth facing these 'fears' because benefits seem to be much higher. (Tanja)

As can be gleaned from the quotes, the complexity of telecollaboration creates a lot of insecurity among student teachers. They realise that the teacher role puts a lot of demands on them. They primarily fear the pitfalls of technology. In addition to that, they feel that the teacher role they have become accustomed to, will need to change. Working online it will be difficult to control learners, and they have not realised, yet, that instead of controlling every step, they need to monitor the emerging independence of their learners.

By going through such a project at the university level, i.e. by becoming learners themselves, student teachers can develop the necessary knowledge base, as the training course provides a secure space for such experiences (see also Müller-Hartmann, 2006 for a detailed account of this approach). Student teachers do not have to deal with the institutional constraints the same project at the school level would involve. Institutional constraints have an impact on the university project as well, but they are mostly navigated by the instructor, who can explain problems and help the novices to develop an understanding of why the partners acted in certain ways. After having experienced the potential and problems of telecollaborative projects and the processes of intercultural learning such projects entail, student teachers begin to develop an experiential knowledge base. In a second step, they need to reflect about the project to realise the processes involved, 'slowly becoming teachers again', as one student formulated in her portfolio (see Müller-Hartmann, 2006: 80).

The task cycle

After having completed a telecollaborative project, student teachers reflect on their experience on the basis of the magnifying glass approach. At first they individually make a mind map about their experience and then choose one (critical) incident they put under the magnifying glass by drawing it (they receive a large piece of paper with the frame of a magnifying glass on it). Language use is not allowed. The (anonymous) drawings of the student teachers form the basis of a group discussion where students randomly pick one or two drawings to describe what they think what kind of experience is visualised or compare them. This leads to an intensive discussion of the experiences the student teachers consider especially pertinent.Before student teachers embarked on the project, they were asked to design a list of dos and don'ts for a telecollaborative project in an 8th-grade class. This allows them to activate their existing knowledge about such projects. After the first reflection this list will be rewritten, using the knowledge gained from their experiences. Applying Nunan's general structure of TBLL (see Figure 8.1), they revise their lists and connect their telecollaborative experience with the methodological approach of TBLL, establishing a network that attributes the revised dos and don'ts to all six aspects of Nunan's concept.

Apart from reading published knowledge about telecollaborative projects and ICC (e.g. Byram, 1997; Donath, 1996), a third and final reflective step is the analysis of learner texts from their future professional field, the foreign language classroom. In the following example, student teachers (Jutta, Manu(ela), Christian; in italics) monitor the chat environment in an English (7th grade: Hannah, Ali(ce), Tim) – German (8th grade: Max, Leonard) project about Louis Sachar's award-winning young adult novel *Holes* (1998). When two brackets appear in succession in the chat, (e.g. [Tim&Jony] > [juttawe]) they indicate that the first person is 'whispering' to the second. In this case the other chatters do not see what is being written. This important function helps moderators to communicate with individual learners while helping them, without interrupting the discussion thread. Moderators can also communicate with each other (see second session).

The analysis task would be: What is the teacher's role in this exchange and what role do tasks play?

First chat session: Establishing contact

14:42:31 [hannah & ali] Hello, Hannah isn't here, it's just alice.

14:42:34 [Max & Leonar] servus.

14:42:52 [Max & Leonar] ahhh ... good morning.

14:43:16 [juttawe] Sorry, I thought your name was Ali 🐢

14:43:56 [Max & Leonar] from where exacly in england do you come from.

14:53:43 [juttawe] Was there a hole in Stanleys life before he came to Camp Green Lake and was it still there when he left? What do you think?

14:54:45 [Tim & Jony] > [juttawe] yes there was but it healed whilst at camp green lake.

14:54:48 [Max & Leonar] because he's self-confident the first time in his life.

14:54:54 [hannah & ali] there was a hole in stanleys life because he didnt have enough money and he was unhappy about himself.

15:02:41 [juttawe] We liked the part best where Zero and Stanley became friends.

15:02:49 [Max & Leonar] that they both know somebody who likes them and for who they feel rsponsible.

15:02:59 [hannah & ali] The fact that Stanley and Zero combined their strength and cleverness together to survive.

15:03:49 [juttawe] All of your answers are really great!!! 🐷

15:04:08 [Manu] Think about your own best friends. What do you particularly like about your friends?

15:04:58 [hannah & ali] I like my friends because they are kind and understanding. Well, mostly.

15:05:20 [Manu] What exactly do you mean with understanding?

During this session (here just an excerpt) the two student teachers were still very dominant, asking questions of the learners instead of letting the chat develop and allowing the learners to get to know each other. Reflecting upon this phase, Jutta was quite frustrated for being so dominant, and she decided to change her approach in the next session. A third student teacher (Christian) joined the following session.

Second chat session: Establishing dialogue

14:41:31 *[ChristianH]* > *[juttawe]* Will you organise this a little?

14:41:43 [Max & Leonar] how's the wheather in cornwall?

14:41:57 [hannah & ali] Rainy, but sometimes sunny.

14:42:01 *[juttawe]* > *[ChristianH]* sure, just relax ☺

14:45:55 [hannah & ali] I hate football I mean.

14:46:06 [Tim & Jony] Footballs really good isnt it but I like Rugby.

14:46:27 *[ChristianH]* How can anybody hate football?

14:46:54 [hannah & ali] Rounders takes too ling to explain.

14:47:10 [hannah & ali] long, I mean.

14:47:34 *[juttawe]* Ok, that's no problem.

14:47:35 *[ChristianH]* Hey Hanny, take your time to explain!

14:47:38 [Tim & Jony] Nobody can not like football.

14:47:43 [Max & Leonar] Let's talk about bootcamps now . . .

14:48:34 *[juttawe]* What do you know about boot camps?

14:48:54 [hannah & ali] What's a boot camp???

14:49:38 [Tim & Jony] People are took to boot camps and get punished for what ever they did that was bad.

14:49:38 [Max & Leonar] children are send there because they got criminal or som problems with their parents.

14:49:42 *[ChristianH]* Bootcamps are some kind of millitary camps, right?

14:49:48 [Max & Leonar] it's really hard there.

14:50:18 *[juttawe]* Are there camps like that in your country?

14:50:39 [Tim & Jony] The bad thing is mainly some sort of crime.

14:50:45 [Max & Leonar] nope.

14:50:51 [hannah & ali] Rounders involves hitting a ball with a bat and running round the outside of four posts before the feilding team get you out by hitting a post with the ball or catching it.
14:51:19 [*ChristianH*] Thanx, Hanna.
14:51:31 [hannah & ali] I don't think we have boot camps, though I'm not sure.
14:51:48 [Max & Leonar] do youn mean baseb.
14:51:52 [*juttawe*] What do you imagine it to be like in a boot camp?
14:51:58 [Tim & Jony] Do you have bootcamps in your country.
14:52:18 [hannah & ali] Do you mean what???
14:52:27 [Max & Leonar] i think it's called feuerball in german.
14:55:05 [hannah & ali] Alternitives? Prison, capital punishment (In America and other countries), juvinile detention centres ...

In this part of the chat, different discussion threads develop. While there is a discussion going on about bootcamps (a central issue in the young adult novel), there is also a discussion about sport in the two countries. It takes a while for Hannah and Alice to provide the explanation of 'Rounders', a game that is not known in Germany, but which adds further cultural information to the exchange.Meanwhile, the two student teachers have gained from their first session. While Christian is still a bit insecure about how to fill the moderator's role, Jutta is now more relaxed and lets the learners develop the chat. Consequently, it is Max and Leonard this time (at 14:47:43) who pose the first question about the actual topic of this chat, the novel *Holes* and bootcamps. The learners are also quite capable of opening their chat by initiating a conversation about a very typical topic, the weather.

While in this example student teachers learned how learners negotiated tasks by monitoring a real-time chat discussion, the analysis and reflection of these texts are decisive, as can be seen in Jutta's change of behaviour from the first to the second chat session. The stored chat data thus offer the possibility of analysing one's approach as well as designing solutions to problems that were encountered in the process so as to handle future sessions more competently and to design tasks differently for the learners to avoid conflicts.

Conclusion

We have seen that the demands on teachers are very complex in telecollaborative learning environments. Teacher education plays a decisive role in helping teachers to develop the necessary knowledge base to tackle the requirements of initiating, supporting and monitoring truly collaborative exchanges. By experiencing these projects in the relatively safe environment, for example, of a university seminar, teachers have the opportunity to become intercultural speakers themselves (see Kramsch & Ware, 2005; Müller-Hartmann, 2006). Without this competence of ICC it will be very difficult for them to help learners develop ICC. While these projects are demanding, they also offer great potential. Collaborative projects almost automatically call for a task-based approach, otherwise learners will be unable to negotiate issues that are meaningful to them. Allowing learners the necessary freedom to work on their tasks, the teachers will realise how their own role changes, freeing them to spend more time and energy on supporting and monitoring their learners' collaborative learning process.

To sum up, teachers should keep in mind the following key elements when organising intercultural collaborative projects:

- Be flexible in your aims when negotiating the project with your partner – s/he might have to deal with very different context requirements, such as access to technology or assessment procedures.
- Look for appropriate parallel texts for discussions that represent cultures involved in the exchange – focusing just on one culture easily leads to the wrong notion of cultural experts and nonexperts and is bound to create problems of an intercultural nature.
- Choose technical tools that fit the project aim and the learners' needs and make sure they are available in the participating classrooms.
- Consider the learners' age, their language proficiency level and their technological background (skills, experience, habits) when designing project aim and tasks.
- Set up basic rules with your learners, such as the number of exchanges per week, the length of texts, deadlines for submitting task results to the partners or the teacher(s) etc.
- Set up similar rules with your partner teacher(s) and stick to them – if you have problems making a deadline, inform your partner as soon as possible.
- Set up a clear timeframe for the project, stick to the phases (see Figure 8.2) outlined here and do not forget to evaluate project results with your learners and the partners.
- Have students reflect periodically about the stage of the project and the relation to their partners.
- Integrate self- and peer-assessment into the project, for example in terms of students' participation in team work.

- Before you start the project use examples of former projects to show learners appropriate language use, how to avoid intercultural conflicts and how to solve them if they occur.
- Analyse and reflect on incoming mails with your class to solve communication problems that might occur in some of the groups.
- Encourage colleagues in your school to work together with you on a project or to join you for some sessions to get an idea of what intercultural telecollaboration is like.

Last but not least, after having found the right partner – which can take two to three attempts, failures included – teachers will support and help each other when negotiating the pitfalls of intercultural fault lines and they will also share the workload, something which Freinet already intended in the exchanges he organised. The final quotes are proof that team-teaching actually can take place.

I did receive Thomas' email this morning. I know this is upsetting to you. I think this kind of student action is not uncommon. This is why it is important to have a good strong teacher relationship as we do. We can support each other when kids act like kids. *smile* (American teacher, private correspondence)

I think the whole episode was a learning experience for my students [. . .] Thanks for your patience and also for caring so much about what my students say. (Canadian teacher, private correspondence)

On the private level a lot has happened as well. We have known each other for two years. [. . .] We have never talked on the phone and we understand each other well. We deal with each other in a warm, friendly and very reliable way, in a word the optimal partner. (German teacher, private correspondence)

Note
1. For easier reading the masculine form is chosen in this article, always including male and female teachers, if not otherwise noted.

References
Ahern, T.C. (1998) Groups, tasks, and CMC: Designing for optimal participation. In Z.L. Berge and M.B. Collins (eds) *Wired Together: The On-line Classroom in K-12. Volume I: Perspectives and Instructional Design* (pp. 221–232). Cresskill, NJ: Hampton Press.
Almeida d'Éca, T. (2003) The use of chat in EFL/ESL. *TESL-EJ* 7 (1). On WWW at http://www-writing.berkeley.edu/TESL-EJ/ej25/int.html.

Belz, J.A. (2002) Social dimensions of telecollaborative foreign language study. *Language Learning and Technology* 6 (1), 60–81. On WWW at http://llt.msu. edu/vol6num1/belz/.

Belz, J.A. and Müller-Hartmann, A. (2002) Deutsch–amerikanische Telekolla-boration im Fremdsprachenunterricht: Lernende im Kreuzfeuer der institu-tionellen Zwänge. *Unterrichtspraxis* 35 (1), 72–82.

Belz, J.A. and Müller-Hartmann, A. (2003) Teachers as intercultural learners: Negotiating German–American telecollaboration along the institutional fault-line. *The Modern Language Journal* 87 (1), 71–89.

Berge, Z.L. (1995) Facilitating computer conferencing: Recommendations from the field. *Educational Technology* 36 (1), 22–29.

Blood, R. (2000) Weblogs: A history and perspective. On WWW at http://www. rebeccablood.net/essays/weblog_history.html. Accessed 9.12.06.

Byram, M. (1997) *Teaching and Assessing Intercultural Communicative Competence*. Clevedon: Multilingual Matters.

Cummins, J. and Sayers, D. (1995) *Brave New Schools. Challenging Cultural Illiteracy through Global Learning Networks*. New York: St. Martin's Press.

Donath, R. (1996) *E-Mail-Projekte im Englischunterricht*. Stuttgart: Klett.

Eck, A., Legenhausen, L. and Wolff, D. (1995) *Telekommunikation und Fremd-sprachenunterricht: Informationen, Projekte, Ergebnisse*. Bochum: AKS.

Edelhoff, C. and Liebau, E. (eds) (1988) *Über die Grenze. Praktisches Lernen im fremdsprachlichen Unterricht*. Weinheim: Beltz.

Ellis, R. (2000) Task-based research and language pedagogy. *Language Teaching Research* 4, 3.

Ellis, R. (2003) *Task-based Language Learning and Teaching*. Oxford: Oxford University Press.

George, J.C. (1972) *Julie and the Wolves*. New York: Harper Collins.

Kern, R. (2006) Perspectives on technology in learning and teaching languages. *TESOL Quarterly* 40 (1), 183–210.

Kern, R., Ware, P. and Warschauer, M. (2004) Crossing frontiers: New directions in on-line pedagogy and research. *Annual Review of Applied Linguistics* 24, 243–260.

Kramsch, C. (1993) *Context and Culture*. Oxford: Oxford University Press.

Kramsch, C. and Ware, P.D. (2004) Intercultural competence on-line? What language teachers need to know. In M. Bigelow and C. Walker (eds) *Creating Teacher Community: Selected Papers from the Third International Conference on Language Teacher Education* (pp. 27–50). Minneapolis, MN: Center for Advanced Research on Language Acquisition.

Legutke, M.K., Müller-Hartmann, A. and Schocker-v. Ditfurth, M. (2006) Preparing teachers for technology-supported English language teaching. In J. Cummins and C. Davison (eds) *Kluwer Handbook on English Language Teaching* (Kluwer International Handbooks of Education) (pp. 1125–1138). Dordrecht: Kluwer.

Milton, J. and Garbi, A. (2000) VIRLAN: Collaborative foreign language learning on the internet for primary age children: Problems and a solution. *Educational Technology & Society* 3 (3). On WWW at http://www.ifets.info/journals/3_3/ d04.html.

Müller-Hartmann, A. (1999) Die Integration der neuen Medien in den schulischen Fremdsprachenunterricht: Interkulturelles Lernen und die Folgen in E-mail-Projekten. *Fremdsprachen Lehren und Lernen* 28, 58–79.

Müller-Hartmann, A. (2000) Wenn sich die Lehrenden nicht verstehen – wie sollen sich da die Lernenden verstehen? Fragen nach der Rolle der Lehrenden in global vernetzten Klassenräumen. In L. Bredella, H. Christ and M.K. Legutke (eds) *Fremdverstehen zwischen Theorie und Praxis.-Arbeiten aus dem Graduiertenkolleg, Didaktik des Fremdverstehens* (pp. 275–301). Tübingen: Narr.

Müller-Hartmann, A. (2000) The role of tasks in promoting intercultural learning in electronic learning networks. *Language Learning & Technology* 4 (2), 129–147. On WWW at http://llt.msu.edu/vol4num2/muller/default.html.

Müller-Hartmann, A. (2006) Learning how to teach intercultural communicative competence via telecollaboration: A model for EFL teacher education. In J. Belz and S. Thorne (eds) *Internet-mediated Intercultural Foreign Language Education* (pp. 63–84). Boston, MA: Heinle & Heinle.

Nunan, D. (2004) *Designing Tasks for the Communicative Classroom*. Cambridge: Cambridge University Press.

O'Dowd, R. (2006) *Telecollaboration and the Development of Intercultural Communicative Competence*. München: Langenscheidt.

O'Dowd, R. and Ritter, M. (2006). Understanding and working with 'failed communication' in telecollaborative exchanges. *CALICO* 23 (3), 623–642.

Rüschoff, B. and Wolff, D. (1999) *Fremdsprachenlernen in der Wissensgesellschaft*. Ismaning: Hueber.

Sachar, L. (1998) *Holes*. New York: Random House.

Sayers, D. (1994) Interscholastic correspondence exchanges in Célestin Freinet's modern school movement: Practical and theoretical implications for computer-mediated student writing networks. In: Sivell, J. (ed.) *Freinet Pedagogy. Theory and Practice* (pp. 65–102). Lewiston: Edwin Mellen Press.

Schlieger, H. (2001) Fächerübergreifendes Unterrichtsprojekt *Inuit Culture. Der Fremdsprachliche Unterricht Englisch* 35 (6), 16–21.

Tella, S. (1991) *Introducing International Communications Networks and Electronic Mail into Foreign Language Classrooms*. Helsinki: Univ. of Helsinki.

Tella, S. (1996) Foreign languages and modern technology: Harmony or hell? In M. Warschauer (ed.) *Telecollaboration in Foreign Language Learning* (pp. 3–17). Honolulu, HI: University of Hawai'i Press.

Ware, P. (2005) 'Missed' communication in on-line communication: Tensions in a German–American telecollaboration. *Language Learning & Technology* 9 (2), 64–89.

Warschauer, M. (1995) *E-Mail for English Teaching. Bringing the Internet and Computer Learning Networks into the Language Classroom*. Alexandria, VA: TESOL.

Warschauer, M. (ed.) (1996) *Telecollaboration in Foreign Language Learning*. Honolulu, HI: University of Hawai'i Press.

Warschauer, M. (1997) Computer-mediated collaborative learning: Theory and practice. *The Modern Language Journal* 81 (4), 470–481.

Warschauer, M. (1999) *Electronic Literacies. Language, Culture, and Power in On-line Education*. Mahwah, NJ: Lawrence Erlbaum.

Warschauer, M. and Kern, R. (eds) (2000) *Network-based Language Teaching: Concepts and Practice*. Cambridge: Cambridge University Press.

Wicke, R.E. (1995) *Kontakte knüpfen*. *Fernstudieneinheit 9* (ed. Goethe-Institut 6 Deutsches Institut für Fernstudienforschung). Berlin: Langenscheidt.

Willis, J. (1996) *A Framework for Task-based Learning*. Harlow: Longman.

Chapter 9

How Can Online Exchanges Be Used with Young Learners?

ISABEL PÉREZ TORRES and MARGARITA VINAGRE

Introduction

Teaching a foreign language to young learners involves a series of conditions that may present specific challenges at some stage, especially if the teaching takes place in a normal secondary school context where the majority of students use a shared first language. One of the typical challenges has to do with providing opportunities for meaningful communication in the foreign language. This is where the use of computer-mediated communication (CMC) activities might help because it can provide authentic contexts for real communication with native speakers (Little *et al.*, 1999) or with other learners of English willing to improve their foreign language.

Offering young students the opportunity to take part in exchange activities has always been an attractive means of motivating them to learn a foreign language. In essence, this is not a new strategy because before the internet era pen pal exchanges involving letter exchanges were carried out, although this often meant having to wait some considerable time for the replies to be received. However, nowadays, the collaborative facilities that the internet offers add a number of incentives that, in the case of young learners, can be especially relevant, such as the factor of immediacy. Moreover, many of these youngsters speak the language of technology quite naturally and can be considered to be 'digital natives' (Prensky, 2001), one of their characteristics being that they are used to communicating through synchronous and asynchronous tools. Young learners use the media as a window to meet other people and a channel to express their opinions. They like sharing experiences and the instant world of the internet is part of their daily routine. As a consequence, telecollaboration seems to be a natural way for youngsters to learn a foreign language.

Furthermore, the internet is considered to be a typical constructivist learning environment (Jonassen, 1994), as it enhances collaboration and interaction through many different web tools and facilities. For instance, the flexibility provided by e-mail allows us to set up exchanges in which students can work in more varied collaborative scenarios than in a typical letter-based correspondence. In this respect, we can observe a stark contrast with regard to previous forms of communication in terms of variety and convenience.

Telecollaboration can take a variety of forms: asynchronous communication through e-mail, bulletin boards, wikis and blogs, or synchronous communication through real-time chats, MOO's or videoconferencing. Although all of these forms of interaction facilitate communication, they have their own technical characteristics and correspond to many different pedagogical aims. For instance, some require an instant online connection (e.g. chats), whilst others could be prepared off-line and then be sent online (e.g. e-mail, blogs). Some might be more orientated towards personal exchanges (e.g. e-mail), whilst others facilitate collaborative projects (e.g. wikis).

As a more general analysis of all these CMC tools is carried out in Chapter 10, this chapter will focus exclusively on asynchronous communication and, more specifically, on e-mail interaction within a secondary school context.

There is a growing body of research that investigates the integration of e-mail into language learning environments and its effectiveness as a tool for promoting foreign language learning (Barson *et al.*, 1993; Müller-Hartmann, 2000, Van Handle & Corl, 1998; Vinagre, 2005). E-mail exchanges are text-based and computer-mediated, both of which define the nature of the communicative interaction. First, the permanence of written texts, as opposed to oral speech, means that the messages can be analysed again and again, thus facilitating reflection and learning awareness. As Schwienhorst (1998: 125) suggests, 'The major advantage of written communication is ... the possibility for each learner to preserve the entire communication ...' and to have 'an enormous sample of his or her own efforts in the target language' for future use. Nevertheless, although electronic mail uses the written medium, it has assumed functions and features usually associated with spoken language as well as formal writing (Davis & Brewer, 1997). Therefore, the development of speaking skills in the foreign language is also facilitated, in addition to reading and writing skills.

Second, e-mail asynchronicity allows participants time to compose their messages and consider their answers, which also encourages critical reflection. As Gonglewsky *et al.* (2001:3) point out: 'Because it is separated from face-to-face contact, the high pressure of such immediate demand for production is lessened, and learners can take their time formulating their thoughts [. . .]. Finally, its impersonality encourages equal opportunity participation (González-Bueno, 1998; Warschauer, 1995)'.

Some of the above-mentioned aspects have proven to be particularly useful with young learners. As Young (2003) mentions, these learners are willing to use a second language due to the lessening of 'psychological barriers' in asynchronous CMC activities. Moreover, young students involved in this type of exchange demonstrate increased critical thinking and problem-solving skills. In Young's opinion, these positive effects may be related to the effects of asynchronous CMC noted by Hron and Friedrich (2003): being able to compose a message 'in peace', the existence of a long-term record for reference and the absence of social cues requiring appropriate timing as in face-to-face communication.

These are some of the reasons why we decided to focus our analysis on e-mail exchanges. Furthermore, we might also mention the fact that e-mail is one of the oldest tools on the internet and, in this respect, extensive research has been carried out within this field, which provides a rich background for further studies within this area.

Computer-mediated Collaborative Learning

Collaborative learning has been the focus of a wide range of studies over the last 20 years. The term 'collaborative learning' refers to a mode of learning in which students work in pairs or small groups towards a common goal. When this goal is to learn a second language, we refer to a partnership between students who are learning each other's mother tongue. These learners meet regularly and work together with the purpose of improving their own communicative competence in the target language and helping their partners achieve the same goal. Kohonen (1992: 33–34) explains with respect to cooperative language learning that:

> [. . .] since all members . . . share a common goal, they are motivated to work together or mutual benefit in order to maximize their own and each other's learning. This creates a positive interdependence among the learners: they perceive that they can reach their goal best when the others in the same learning group also do as well as possible.

Collaborative work places emphasis on 'open[ing] up the minds of members of a collaborative team to each other and to the possibilities that lie beyond the reach of any of the individuals' (Mason, 1970: 112). Within the context of electronic communication, collaborative learning can take place without members being physically in the same location. When applied to language learning, we can see that collaborative learning provides students with an excellent opportunity to improve their competence in the second language in authentic contexts through real communication with speakers of English. Collaborative e-mail exchanges are widely used in schools, colleges and universities across the world because they lend themselves to instruction based on sociocultural principles. The pedagogical framework that supports collaborative language learning can be traced back to Piaget's (1928, 1932) constructivist theory and to Vygotsky's (1962, 1978) sociocultural theory.

Piaget's theory reflects on how cognitive development takes place in individuals. He views the learner's knowledge as adaptive, as we are constantly constructing knowledge. Effectively, we ask questions, develop answers and interact. By doing these things we build up knowledge in the mind. According to this author, the construction of knowledge is individual, but learning is the result of a process that takes place through the interaction of those who are learning. Thus 'a given level of individual development allows participation in certain social interactions which produce new individual states which, in turn, make possible more sophisticated social interactions, and so on' (Laister & Koubek, 2001: 3). A constructivist approach to learning emphasises collaborative group work in authentic activities, work in which the participants bring their own perspectives to bear on the activity. These differences in approach should foster negotiation of meaning and problem-solving through shared understanding.

Vygotsky's (1962; 1978) sociocultural theory stresses the importance of social relationships to the development of learning. The central concept in his theory is 'the zone of proximal development' (ZPD), where learners construct the new language through socially mediated interaction (Brown, 2000: 287). The ZPD can be defined as:

> [...] the distance between the actual development level as determined by independent problem solving and the level of potential development as determined through problem solving under adult guidance or in collaboration with more capable peers. (Vygotsky, 1978: 86)

This approach stresses the crucial importance of collaboration in the learning process. Thus, interactive communication should be facilitated through the use of alternative learner-centred environments, where students can work together and help each other, either in pairs or small groups.

By bringing together Piaget and Vygotsky's theories on the importance of social relationships to the development of learning, it becomes clear that collaborative learning, if it is to be successful, must rely on two aspects: negotiation of meaning and collaboration within pairs or groups in order to promote language learning through problem-solving, performance of tasks, critical thinking and reflection.

The development of the above-mentioned aspects is greatly encouraged by the very nature of CMC (participants usually do not know each other and non-verbal communication is reduced to the use of emoticons and punctuation marks) and by the fact that participants in collaborative e-mail exchanges often belong to different countries and cultures. This specific set-up often calls for negotiation of meaning, critical thinking and reflection, as, in order to make the exchange successful, participants need to create a 'sound social space' (Kreijns *et al.*, 2004: 156). This social space is characterised by 'effective working relationships, strong group cohesiveness, trust, respect and belonging, satisfaction, and a strong sense of community' (Kreijns *et al.*, 2004: 157). Creating this sound social space becomes a prerequisite for the success of computer-supported collaborative learning (CSCL) exchanges, as it enables 'cognitive processes such as elaborating, questioning and defining to take place, all of which are necessary for the social construction of knowledge and competence building' (Kreijns *et al.*, 2004: 156).

E-mail Exchanges in Secondary School Classrooms

From the points outlined above it becomes clear that there are significant linguistic and nonlinguistic reasons to support the use of e-mail exchanges in a secondary school language classroom:

- It motivates students to use the language in real communicative environments.
- It is a good opportunity to practise reading and writing in a contextualised situation.
- It allows reflection and self-correction before and after writing.
- It allows collaborative and constructivist learning.
- It improves language use as the exchange project advances.
- It generates writing materials that can be re-used, not only to learn and reflect upon the language itself, but also to provide authentic texts for other language activities.

In the following sections, we will deal with all the various factors involved in setting up e-mail exchanges with young learners, with a view to providing effective answers to many of the questions that may arise when a teacher initiates an e-mail classroom exchange:

- How should we plan e-mail activities?
- How can we contact other teachers or students?
- Who would be the best e-pals for our students?
- How long should an exchange take?
- How can we use e-mail exchanges to deal with language aspects such as grammar, whilst also addressing issues such as culture?
- How can we handle errors in e-mail exchanges?
- How can we avoid frustration amongst students and teachers?

In order to illustrate our answers to these questions, we shall comment on a number of examples of real e-mail experiences that have been carried out in secondary schools. These should also provide some insights into how teachers can ensure a successful telecollaborative learning exchange.

Typology of E-mail Interaction

The type of interaction that can be established between students through e-mail exchanges depends on many factors: 'the learners' characteristics, their relationship, the nature of the task or the context' (Dillenbourg & Self, 1995). Students' profiles, encompassing aspects such as age, computer skills, language level, etc., are decisive when designing the scenario in which the exchange will take place. Other aspects to be considered are the language aims that we pursue and the non-linguistic objectives that the exchange can help us to achieve, such as group awareness and social interaction skills. Below, we describe a typology of e-mail scenarios and suggest how they can be adapted to specific learning contexts (Pérez Torres, 1999).

Student(s) – student (one-to-one, two-to-one, three-to-one)

Individual exchanges in which one student sends e-mail messages to another student are possibly the most commonplace scenario for this form of collaborative learning. However, this type of exchange also opens up other possibilities, such as interaction between one student, at one end, and one or more students, at the other. The option 'one-to-various' could be implemented in the case of students who are not very familiar with technology, which means that the other members of the group can provide assistance in this respect. This type of exchange is also appropriate for students who are very young or in cases where there are significant differences regarding the language level of the students on each side. In all these cases, by allowing students to share the responsibility of carrying out certain tasks by e-mail, we can encourage equal participation in the exchange experience among group members, thus ensuring satisfactory results from the very beginning. At a later stage, students who work together may become more independent and write their e-mails individually once they have gained confidence and the necessary computer skills.

Group-to-group

A second scenario consists of a group of students interacting with another. The size of the groups can vary according to a series of factors and objectives (number of students in one classroom, group tasks, project features, etc.). Another possibility is to divide large classes into smaller groups that will maintain a group-to-group exchange. This type of scenario is particularly suitable in the case of small classes of no more than six students (a good example of this is what, in the Spanish educational system, is called 'second language groups'), so that the whole class can be involved in a project as a group. As we shall see in the following section, a group-to-group exchange is more appropriate when the task consists of working together on collaborative writing projects and the end product is sizeable and extensive and requires the involvement of all the students in the class.

Teacher-to-student(s)

The key participants in this scenario are the two class teachers, who are native speakers of their respective languages and maintain correspondence with the other teacher's students. This type of interaction is not very common and is recommended only when the interaction takes place in two different languages. Thus, the students use their second language to communicate with the teacher who is a native speaker, which means that the teacher acts as the expert who helps the students in his counterpart's class improve their second language. This type of exchange can coincide with other types of interaction (student-to-student, group-to-group). Correcting or advising students would be the most useful activity the teacher can carry out in this type of scenario.

Native speaker-to-students

This can be considered a variation of the previous type of interaction. It may occur when there is an exchange between a class/group of students and a member of the target culture, which is to say, an adult native speaker who answers the students' questions about the topic of interest. The native speaker could be someone who is considered an expert in the matter or, at the very least, someone who is well informed about the topic. For instance, if your class is doing research on immigration in Britain, then they might try to get into contact with a migrant worker or someone who works for the UK's social services.

Choosing and Finding E-mail Partners

Finding an answer to the question of who will be the best partner for a specific student is one of the key issues when it comes to implementing e-mail exchange for language purposes. A partnership comprises two elements: the teacher and the student, and each will now be examined in the following sections.

The partner teacher

The role of the teacher is especially decisive in the case of young learners. Unlike adult learners, who will have an intrinsic motivation to start and continue with the experience, it is widely agreed that, although young learners might have some intrinsic motivation, they also need to be externally motivated at the initial stage. This encouragement should be continued throughout the rest of the e-mail learning experience. This means that the teacher will need to play an active role throughout the e-mail interaction, effectively fulfilling the following functions:

- Determining the linguistic and nonlinguistic objectives.
- Planning the stages of the exchange.
- Explaining the objectives of the exchange to the students and setting out the general guidelines.
- Supporting students throughout the entire learning process.
- Defining a means of assessing and evaluating the experience so that improvements can be introduced in future exchanges.

Supporting the students is essential and teachers need to provide guidance and scaffolding with regard to the tasks that the students are required to carry out (see Müller-Hartmann, this volume). They must maintain constant and fluent communication with their students and with the teacher based in the other school. Therefore, when it comes to implementing exchanges in a secondary school environment, finding the right teacher for a specific project is as essential as providing adequate support to the students. In this respect, the two teachers involved should be committed to sustaining the project and must be ready to interact with each other at a teacher-to-teacher level when necessary.

One particular aspect on which teachers should agree from the beginning are the rules of netiquette that their students have to follow. This is something that students must take into account in every message they send and should be reminded of, especially during the initial stages of the exchange. There are several lists of rules on the web that could be adopted and adapted. However, it would be better for these rules to be negotiated by the teachers, based on a previous discussion with the students. It is important that the rules should not be too numerous or complicated. They might refer to the form that messages should take or to their content. These guidelines might include the following:

1 Keep your letters short enough for your e-pal to be able to respond to what you say.
2 Make use of the subject box. This helps your e-pal to sort incoming mail.
3 You may use emoticons to express emotions. :-)
4 Don't write exclusively in capital letters. This is interpreted as yelling and it is more difficult to read texts of this kind.
5 Try to maintain a balance between giving and asking for information.
6 After the initial contact, remember to acknowledge what your e-pal has said previously and then include information and questions that will keep the correspondence going.
7 Be prepared to give information about yourself in return for the information that you ask your e-pal to share with you. For example, when you ask your e-pal how he/she feels about something, offer the same information about yourself.
8 Be careful when using humour in your message. Tone of voice is lost in e-mail, so your e-pal may misinterpret your meaning.

Where and how to contact partner teachers

There are plenty of sites where we can search for and contact potential partner teachers. Some of them have been active for several years now and can be safely recommended. Evidently, those that are specific for second language learners are more useful for our teaching and learning purposes. They are normally organised according to age and interests and some are teacher-oriented, so they include descriptions of various project proposals. The following is a list of websites, organised in random order, which may be useful when it comes to contacting partners for secondary school exchanges:

- The Student List Project, http://sl-lists.net/. A number of forums for teachers and students of all levels administered by Thomas N. Robb in a Moodle environment.
- Students of the World, http://www.studentsoftheworld.info/. Another site for students and teachers. It is maintained by the association of the same name. It also includes chats, blogs and clubs.
- Linguistic Funland, http://www.linguistic-funland.com/addapal.html. Both students and teachers can post requests. It is maintained by www.tesol.net.
- Dave Sperling's Forum, for teachers looking for keypals http://www.eslcafe.com/forums/teacher/viewforum.php?f=20.

Apart from these sites, over the last few years a number of e-mail platforms have emerged for young learners that not only allow users to search for partners, but also serve as learning environments where teachers can manage the entire e-mail interaction. Among these, ePALS Classroom Exchange is probably the most popular among teachers who want to set up a classroom exchange with other schools around the world. It is largely used for cross-cultural exchanges, project sharing and language learning (see list of references to web pages at the end of the chapter). Another programme that has become a major portal for teachers, enabling them to contact other schools, is the European eTwinning Programme. This is not restricted to language learning or to e-mail interaction, but includes all types of subjects and projects (see Domínguez Miguela, this volume). A recent and similar portal is Global Gateway, a British portal that aims to serve as a gateway to educational partnerships between schools and colleges across the world.

The procedure to be followed on most of these sites is similar; the teacher has to register and then complete a number of fields with the relevant information about his students and his objectives, which may include the following:

- Description of the group of students: country, number, level, background, first language, etc.
- Description of the target group of students and what kind of collaboration we expect to establish.
- Aims and details of the exchange or project, such as duration, target language, technological aspects, etc.

An accurate description of the students and the project will help us find the right partner, although our aims may vary as the exchange experience proceeds.

The partner class

The second dimension of a partnership consists of the students. Deciding which students should be matched with their corresponding partners will depend on their language level, interests and technological skills, as well as the objectives we aim to achieve in carrying out the exchange. Obviously, we want the students to practise the foreign language they are learning and, in this respect, the key question is whether we should establish an exchange with native speakers or with other second language learners who are also interested in practising within an authentic communicative context. Let us consider the following exchange set-up as an example:

Exchange Set-Up 1: A group of young students whose L1 is Spanish and L2 is English. The group's L2 level is lower intermediate. Our objectives are to improve their writing and reading skills in English, using the vocabulary they know with regard to certain topics (music, sport, school issues, food, holidays, etc.) and learning how others express themselves when discussing the same topics. It is preferable if they write to students of a similar age or within a two-year age band. The following variations on this exchange set-up are also possible:

The first option is to establish an exchange with a group of native English speakers. However, this is only a good choice if they want to learn Spanish as a second language and they also have a lower intermediate level of Spanish. If this is not the case, both groups may experience a sense of frustration and find the experience to be somewhat forced.

A second option is to pair them with a group of non-native students who also want to improve their English as a second language and have a similar level of competence in the L2 (e.g. Dutch students wanting to practice English at a lower intermediate level).

A third possibility is for one of the groups of students involved in the exchange to come from different countries, whilst they actually live in a country where they need to use English on a daily basis. Thus, they are not native English speakers as such, but learners of English as a foreign language. In fact, this third option, combined with a good team of teachers, has proven to be one of the most successful scenarios over the nine years we have organised exchanges with young learners (e.g. a group of students from a Spanish secondary school paired with a group of students from France and Iran, but living in the USA and studying English as an L2 there).

Finally, another possible group might consist of students who want to practise Spanish, but who can express themselves quite correctly in English, even though their L1 may be a different language altogether (e.g. a group of Swedish students wanting to practise Spanish, but who are able to express themselves in English at an intermediate level).

Types of E-mail Activities for Young Learners

The core objective of an online language exchange is to enhance communication in a contextualised setting, one that can even constitute a real context, at least at some point of the interaction. Therefore, communication must be encouraged by means of the activities proposed by teachers or by students, within a given context. These activities can belong to different categories, but all of them will involve the exchange of information, communication and negotiation of meaning, although not always to the same degree. This will depend on the difficulty of the task. The most usual approaches when planning an e-mail interaction with young learners are task-based learning (TBL) and content-based learning (CBL). Both approaches are based on the common premise that the emphasis should be placed more on language meaning and communication than on language form. The objective is to use language in order to enhance fluency rather than accuracy. From the perspective of CBL, the second language is a means 'to convey informational content of interest and relevance to the learner' (Brown, 1994: 220). However, TBL is based on the concept of task, a term that, according to Ellis (1994: 595), 'refers to the idea of some kind of activity designed to engage the learner in using the language communicatively or reflectively in order to arrive at an outcome other than that of learning a specified feature of the L2'. This is mainly what we ask students to do when taking part in e-mail exchanges, namely to focus on content and use the language for a communicative purpose.

Nevertheless, in addition to the preponderance of this communicative approach to language learning, and based on research on SLA, Long (1985; 2000) argues that a task-based approach can also provide 'focus on form' by means of interaction and input, 'two major players in the process of acquisition' encouraging negotiation of meaning (Long, 1991; Long & Crookes, 1992; 1993). The teacher's emphasis on 'form' should occur as an answer to the students' needs and difficulties at a particular stage in the communicative use of language. Relating to this, and based on our direct experience in the classroom, we also believe that e-mail exchanges become more relevant and useful when they are integrated in the curriculum, either connected to vocabulary and content topics or to the grammar and functions that the students are studying at a specific time (e.g. doing a task about freedom of youth in different countries linked to the study of 'can' and 'can't' in the curriculum).

Apart from the learning approach and the linguistic objectives, other contextual variables to be taken into account when we plan e-mail activities with young learners include cultural background and interests. Time issues constitute another important factor. The duration of the exchange should be discussed by the teachers, taking into account school holidays and other relevant events that could interfere with the progress of the activity. Long-term exchanges require considerable input and follow-up, making demands on time that are often unfeasible for extracurricular activities. From our own experience, it is better to start with a short introductory task in order to evaluate how the interaction between students works. This can be followed up by a longer or more complex task, once the students are used to the mechanics of the exchange.

Thus, at an operational level, once we define a particular e-mail setting (student-to-student; group-to-group) and contact a partner class, the next step is to design how the exchange will develop, including the types of activities that will be pursued (many of which will be task-based), scaffolding and evaluation.

Below, we describe a list of common activities that can be carried out as part of the e-mail interaction. Some activities are more appropriate for interaction based on just one language; for example, researching a project together. Other activities are more useful in a language exchange context in which each group uses either their L1 or their L2; for example, discussing personal experiences. By completing these activities, students are able to get involved in real communication with their partners and have the opportunity to use and reflect on their language learning process.

1 Exchanging messages focused on individual personal information. Under this heading we can include students' initial introductions and discussions of personal experiences or topics of personal interest, such as music, hobbies, sport, culture, etc. Students can be asked to carry out different tasks, including the following: asking and answering questions, guessing answers, explaining experiences and plans, proposing and choosing personal alternatives, etc.

2 Exploring topics together in order to acquire knowledge about a chosen theme, in pairs (student-to-student) or in groups (group-to-group). This can be done through specific strategies such as 'treasure hunts or knowledge hunts', either based on the use of web resources or not. In this case, students are required to search for the answer to various questionnaires prepared by the teachers or the other students in order to share information with their e-pals (e.g. Christmas topic: students come from different countries and cultures and explore the

topic using a questionnaire prepared by one of the exchange groups). The final task consists of preparing a web page containing all kinds of information about how people, in general, and the students, in particular, celebrate Christmas in their home country. (See this example at http://www.isabelperez.com/x-mas.htm.)

3   Taking part in game-based activities in which the students have to work together closely in order to negotiate meaning and complete the task. Some examples of this type of task include reconstructing story puzzles, writing chain stories, playing a simulation game, etc. For instance, we might give students the initial and/or the final sentence of a story and ask them to write sentences in turns until they complete a whole story. Simulation games force the students to play roles in order to perform a task, such as one student playing the role of an 'agony aunt' when answering the questions posed by the other student.

4   Carrying out WebQuests or other types of research projects on any topics of interest: cultural, social, scientific, etc. These activities are based on constructivist theories and are normally based on problem-solving, which means that students have to reach a consensus or find a solution or alternative answers. Whatever the case may be, they are required to construct their own knowledge from the resources they use and, perhaps more importantly, from the interaction they have with their partners. These types of activities are recommended for a later stage in the exchange, once personal contact has been established. If necessary, projects may be shortened or divided into minor tasks that can be completed separately. An example of this may be a WebQuest, whose final purpose consists of writing a tale or legend together by combining elements from different cultures, a task that requires the students to carry out some prior research on tales and legends in their own countries and in other cultures, based on an analysis of the similarities and differences. This minor task is one that the students can complete even if they are unable to write the final story, due to linguistic or operational obstacles (e.g. time constraints).

All of the e-mail activities described above are task-based and content-oriented, which means that students interact via e-mail with their counterparts in other cultures with the main objective of using language in order to communicate within a contextualised situation. In many cases they take advantage of the authentic and meaningful context provided by the internet. The end result will be a stronger sense of cultural awareness and cultural enrichment, as well as language improvement, even if the students only focus on form in order to understand the meaning or to be sure that they are not committing too many mistakes. Other activities are explicitly language form-oriented and can be included within the online interaction process, especially in the case of exchanges where students' L1 is the L2 of the other group and vice versa. In exchanges of this kind, students may actually enjoy doing some language exercises with the help of their partners; for example, correcting each other's errors or completing texts in the target language, which are normally prepared by their e-pals. Another useful and reflective activity is to examine the errors that our partners commit in our L1, recognising and establishing the differences between two given languages and how this know-how could be transferred to our use of an L2; that is to say, an analysis of the errors we are most likely to make when using their L1 as an L2, based on an awareness of the mistakes they committed when using our L1 as an L2. For example, a young student using Spanish as an L2 might write '*yo gusto jugar* la guitarra', whereas the correct sentence would be '*me* gusta *tocar* la guitarra'. Based on these errors, the Spanish e-pal can infer that in English he must say 'I like playing the guitar'; that is to say, 'like' is not a reflexive verb in English and the translation of 'tocar' is not 'to touch' but 'to play'. Finally, students can ask L1 speakers questions about language use directly and vice versa. This would be the best scenario for a teacher taking part in a student-to-teacher exchange.

We might make a final observation regarding the use of scaffolding in order to support students in the communicative tasks requested. We believe that, in the case of young learners, scaffolding is particularly necessary in order to enable them to accomplish the goals established at all stages of the e-mail exchange, whilst sustaining their sense of motivation and keeping frustration at bay. Scaffolding implies that the task is accompanied by some kind of contextual support that clarifies meaning and procedures. It may involve the use of questions, prompt lists, glossaries, diagrams, charts, tables, graphs, etc., that the students are required to use in order to complete a particular task. Furthermore, scaffolding is an essential element of any WebQuest (Dodge, 2001; March, 2003). However, students will not only require scaffolding when carrying out large projects. Depending on their age, level, the stage in the process, etc., they may need all kinds of support in order to initiate or continue the interaction.

Finally, the evaluation of the learners' progress needs to be carried out in different ways depending on the objectives of the exchange. Whether the emphasis is placed on linguistic development, cultural awareness, vocabulary acquisition, improvement of writing skills or the development of learner autonomy, is bound to determine the form of evaluation that is applied. Thus, linguistic development can be assessed through mutual error correction and the provision of feedback, whereas cultural awareness might be evaluated through an end-of-year oral presentation. Acquisition of new vocabulary can be assessed by asking the students to keep a record of all new vocabulary that they encounter in a learning diary and to write sentences or stories in which this vocabulary is incorporated. The learning diary itself can be a good instrument to assess the development of cultural awareness and vocabulary acquisition if we ask students to keep a detailed record of these aspects every time they get in touch with their online partners.

Together with the form of assessment or evaluation that we may decide to apply as teachers, it is interesting to provide students with self-evaluation questionnaires, as an important evaluative dimension of this type of project depends on the students' perception of online exchanges as a mode of learning. How learners feel about what they are doing is likely to have an important impact on their involvement in the learning process.

Managing the E-mail Experience

In previous sections we addressed many of the questions posed at the beginning of this chapter. Perhaps the only aspect we have not mentioned so far relates to the technical conditions required in order to set up an e-mail exchange, along with other practical considerations, such as the following:

- Who sends the messages?
- Does the teacher read and check all the messages before the students send them to their e-pals?
- Does the teacher have an input into the content of the messages? etc.

These questions often arise when managing an e-mail exchange experience. First, with regard to technical issues, conditions in schools today have improved considerably compared to former times, which means that most have access to a high-speed connection and, at the very least, a computer room where teachers can supervise students. The other questions in our list will depend on the individuals themselves, with the teacher deciding how best to proceed with each group. We suggest that records be kept of all messages, either in printed form or in virtual format if we are using one of the platforms available online. This is useful not only in terms of checking the interaction that is taking place (including aspects such as communication, language and content), but also in terms of following up and assessing the activity.

With a view to supporting teachers who wish to implement an e-mail exchange in order to enhance language use, we have compiled a recommendation check-list that corresponds to the three stages that any e-mail project must logically include:

Preparatory stage

- Find teacher partners (individual e-pals could be considered, but these are only advisable in very special cases).
- Exchange information with the other teacher on various topics: students' level and characteristics, school details, time schedule, etc.
- Determine the distribution of the students and the scenario to be used (student-to-student(s); group-to-group; teacher-student).
- Plan a project with clear linguistic and nonlinguistic objectives.
- Determine the tasks to be carried out during the activity (exchanging personal information, exploring topics, etc.).
- Determine the outcome of the activity (web page, poster, compilation of messages, etc).
- Establish a series of criteria or questions to help you assess the project.

Implementation stage

- Tell the students about how you have set up the exchange.
- Give them information about the other school and students.
- Revise the e-mail etiquette with them that you are going to follow.
- Establish the time-span of the e-mail exchange.
- Explain the technical procedures required for sending e-mails; describe how the platform you are going to use works, etc.
- Keep a record of the messages and ask the students to do the same.
- Help them to complete the scheduled tasks and follow their progress.
- Give them support and provide the necessary scaffolding throughout the process.
- Revise any language aspects when they arise and when the students ask for clarification.

Final stage

- Prepare some 'follow-up activities' in order to revise what they have done.
- Evaluate the whole process by canvassing the opinion of the other teacher, your students and their e-pals.

• Be prepared to make use of the messages and the output of the e-mail project, as a source of authentic materials to be employed with the same group or with another group of students.

Conclusion

Using the internet as a pedagogical tool has opened up an enormous range of possibilities for language teaching and learning. One of the major advances that has taken place relates to CMC, which can take either a synchronous or asynchronous form. It has been suggested that asynchronous CMC and e-mail, in particular, can facilitate communication and, therefore, encourage language practice. This is especially true with young students, given that asynchronous communication allows them to reflect upon their writing and compose their messages at their own pace. Furthermore, young learners are becoming increasingly familiar with digital communication systems, which provides an excellent basis for an e-mail exchange project in a secondary school language classroom. In this chapter, we began by analysing the benefits of CMC and collaborative learning, going on to address many of the questions that may arise when a teacher implements an e-mail project within a classroom context. It becomes clear that, although young people may be highly motivated to take part in an e-mail project at the initial stage, they require constant support from the teacher throughout the entire process. Thus, it is important to find the appropriate teacher-partner to discuss and plan the exchange in advance, in order to ensure that the entire experience is a successful one. Finally, most of the learning objectives in e-mail exchanges are task-based, with the main focus being placed on effective communication. It is the teacher's role to decide when and how to help the students to focus on linguistic development or to place the emphasis on the development of other aspects, such as cultural awareness, vocabulary acquisition, writing skills and learner autonomy.

References

Barson, J., Frommer, J. and Schwartz, M. (1993) Foreign language learning using e-mail in a task-oriented perspective: Interuniversity experiments in communication and collaboration. *Journal of Science Education and Technology* 2 (2), 565–584.

Brown, H.D. (2000) *Principles of Language Learning and Teaching* (4th edn). New York: Longman.

Davis, B.H. and Brewer, J.P. (1997) *Electronic Discourse: Linguistic Individuals in Virtual Space*. Albany, NY: SUNY Press.

Dillenbourg, P. and Self, J. (1995) Designing human–computer collaborative learning. In C. O'Malley (ed.) *Computer Supported Collaborative Learning* (pp. 245–264). Berlin: Springer-Verlag.

Dodge, B. (2001) FOCUS: Five rules for writing a great WebQuest. *Learning & Leading with Technology* 28 (8), 6–9.

Ellis, R. (1994) *The Study of Second Language Acquisition.* Oxford: Oxford University Press.

Gonglewsky, M., Meloni, C. and Brant, J. (2001) Using e-mail in foreign language teaching: rationale and suggestions. *The Internet TESL Journal* 3(3). On WWW at http://iteslj.org/Techniques/Meloni-Email.html.

González-Bueno, M. (1998) The effects of electronic mail on Spanish L2 discourse. *Language Learning & Technology* 1 (2), 55–70.

Hron, A. and Friedrich, H. (2003) A review of web-based collaborative learning: factors beyond technology. *Journal of Computer Assisted Learning* 19 (1), 70–79.

Jonassen, D.H. (1994) Thinking technology: Toward a constructivist design model. *Educational Technology* 34 (4), 34–37.

Kohonen, V. (1992) Experiential language learning: second language learning as cooperative learner education. In D. Nunan (ed.) *Collaborative Language Learning and Teaching* (pp. 14–39). Cambridge: Cambridge University Press.

Kreijns, K., Kirschner, P., Jochems, W. and Van Buuren, H. (2004) Determining sociability, social space, and social presence in (a) synchronous collaborative groups. *Cyberpsychology & Behaviour* 7 (2), 155–172.

Laister, J. and Koubek, A. (2001) Third generation learning platforms. Requirements and motivation for collaborative learning. On WWW at http://www.eurodl.org/materials/contrib/2001/icl01/laister.htm. Accessed 9.11.06.

Little, D., Ushioda, E., Appel, M.C., Moran, J., O'Rourke, B. and Schwienhorst, K. (1999) *Evaluating tandem learning by e-mail: report on a bilateral project.* CLCS Occasional Paper No. 55. Dublin: Trinity College, Centre for Language and Communication Studies.

Long, M.H. (1985) Input and second language acquisition theory. In S.M. Gass and C.G. Madden (eds) *Input in Second Language Acquisition* (pp. 377–393). Rowley, MA: Newbury House.

Long, M.H. (1991) Focus on form: A design feature in language teaching methodology. In K. de Bot, R. Ginsberg and C. Kramsch (eds) *Foreign Language Research in Cross-Cultural Perspective* (pp. 39–52). Amsterdam. John Benjamin.

Long, M.H. (2000) Focus on form in task-based language teaching. In R. Lambert and E. Shohamy (eds) *Language Policy and Pedagogy* (pp. 179–192). Amsterdam and Philadelphia: John Benjamins.

Long, M.H. and Crookes, G. (1992) Three approaches to task-based language teaching. *TESOL Quarterly* 26 (1), 27–56.

Long, M.H. and Crookes, G. (1993) Units of analysis in syllabus design: The case for Task. In G. Crookes and S.M. Gass (eds) *Tasks in Pedagogical Context. Integrating Theory and Practice* (pp. 9–54). Clevedon: Multilingual Matters.

March, T. (2003) The learning power of WebQuests. *Educational Leadership* 61 (4), 42–47.

Mason, E. (1970) *Collaborative Learning.* London: Ward Lock Educational.

Müller-Hartmann, A. (2000) The role of tasks in promoting intercultural learning in electronic learning networks. *Language Learning and Technology* 4 (2), 129–147. On WWW at http://llt.msu.edu/vol4num2/muller/default.html.

Pérez Torres, I. (1999) E-mail activities with secondary classrooms. In T. Harris and I. Sanz (eds) *ELT: Through the Looking Glass* (pp. 131–134). Granada: GRETA.

Piaget, J. (1928) *Judgement and Reasoning in the Child*. New York: Harcourt Brace.

Piaget, J. (1932) *The Moral Judgement of the Child*. London: Routledge & Keagan.

Prensky, M. (2001) Digital natives, digital immigrants. *On the Horizon*. NCB University Press 9 (5).

Schwienhorst, K. (1998) The 'third place' – virtual reality applications for second language learning. *ReCALL* 10 (1), 118–126.

Van Handle, D.C. and Corl, K.A. (1998) Extending the dialogue: Using electronic mail and the Internet to promote conversation and writing in intermediate level German language courses. *CALICO Journal* 15 (1–3), 129–143.

Vinagre, M. (2005) Fostering language learning by e-mail: an English–Spanish exchange. *Computer Assisted Language Learning* 18 (5), 369–388.

Vygotsky, L.S. (1962) *Thought and Language*. Cambridge, MA: MIT Press.

Vygotsky, L.S. (1978) *Mind and Society*. Cambridge, MA: Harvard University Press.

Warschauer, M. (1995) Comparing face-to-face and electronic discussion in the second language classroom. *CALICO Journal* 13 (2 & 3), 7–26.

Young, S. (2003) Integrating ICT into second language education in a vocational high school. *Journal of Computer Assisted Learning* 19 (4), 447–461.

Web pages referred to in Chapter 9

ePALS classroom exchange: http://www.epals.com/

Global Gateway: http://www.globalgateway.org.uk/

Chapter 10
Choosing the Appropriate Communication Tools for an Online Exchange

MELINDA DOOLY

Introduction

This chapter will look at the way in which information and communication technologies (ICT) can be used to assist telecollaborative language learning, and more importantly, we will deal with the issue of *how* to select the 'right tool for the job'. Integrating ICT tools into an educational environment is not simply a question of 'plugging' in the tool to initiate the learning process. The success of a telecollaborative project does not depend only upon the tool, no matter how much potential the tool may have for educational purposes; the way in which the tool is applied is equally important. As Papert (1987: 22) pointed out two decades ago, 'technocratic thinking' can lead to a false belief in the omnipotence of the tool to bring about learning. Thus, this chapter first considers how the features of internet-based tools can be used to support online collaboration amongst distanced peers and the importance this has for interaction and communication. This will be followed by a look at the tools themselves and how they can be used to support telecollaborative learning.

There are many well founded arguments for the incorporation of network-based tools into the learning environment, especially in the area of language learning. Internet-related learning environments are being lauded for creating new opportunities for innovative teaching approaches due to their potential for 'interactive' opportunities for collaborative language projects that focus on using the language to learn the language (Richards, 2005, Rudd *et al.*, 2006). Network-based learning is also seen as a necessary tool for preparing students to face the challenges and changes in the world marketplace and the many other new technological demands imminent in the near future. This means that educators must adapt and/

213

or find new pedagogical approaches that embrace these changes and challenges. So-called 'traditional classrooms' have been frequently criticised for a lack of personal attention, for being a cause for boredom, and for focusing on outdated knowledge and inappropriate skills for future workplaces. Traditional classrooms have also been criticised for a lack of attention to diverse populations (Diamond, 1997; Gardiner, 1997; Handy, 1998; Roueche, 1998). In search of solutions to these commonly mentioned 'problem' areas researchers have voiced the need for more active learning, learner-centred principles and collaborative learning (Bonk & Kim, 1998; Cove & Love, 1996). More focus on technology, both as necessary skills for students to learn and as an improvement to the educational environment, has also been frequently promoted – inevitably contributing to quite high expectations for technology to transform education.

However, as with any advance in pedagogical methods or pedagogical tools, each teacher should take full stock of their own situation before 'diving in head-first' into a network-based project. As Kling (1984) and Bowers (1988) have pointed out, educational technologies are not 'value-free tools' nor are advocates of new technologies without their own agendas. Articles about technology in education are often written by authors affiliated with technology-oriented departments or technology support centres. For teachers reading this literature, it is easy to get carried away with the 'good news' coming from different areas of education about wonderful experiences and projects being carried out across the world which integrate the learning process in the classroom with online learning opportunities. Arguably, the more technologically experienced the instructor, the more likely that he or she will be better able to handle problems that might create obstacles to the learning process. Most teachers, however, are not specialists in technology and should not be expected to immediately know how to effectively use technology – the lack of equipment, time and training can be deterrents to efficient implementation in the classroom. In such circumstances, finding the most appropriate tool that best fits the necessities of each situated learning environment can be a challenge.

Moreover, like a multivitamin tablet, new technologies and telecollaboration is not a cure-all, nor can telecollaboration be perceived as a one-size-fits-all effort. There are many different tools available for online communication, and this gamut is constantly being revised, improved and incremented. Simply reading the list of available technology for synchronous and asynchronous networking can be daunting for even the most ICT-experienced educator and perhaps even discouraging for teachers who have just begun exploring its possibilities. The list runs from electronic mail, blogs, instant messaging, MOO environments, electronic forums, and portals to online telephony – and of course, this is hardly a complete list and new innovations are coming out daily. What one should bear in mind when confronted with such a cornucopia of possibilities is that all of these are merely tools. Just as chalk at one time was an empowering tool that helped teachers better explain their lessons (it was a technological innovation in its own way), the tools mentioned here should be at the service of the teachers and students and not the other way around. There are advantages and disadvantages to using network-based communication and these must be taken into consideration when planning a telecollaborative project. Being well informed is the first step towards finding the 'best fit' of the technological tool for the intended project.

Provided that we understand the limitations of each technology as well as its capabilities, and more importantly, provided that we understand the people we are trying to educate and the kind of education we are trying to give them, we can use technology in ways that will really help. There is no technological panacea; there are only technological solutions to some educational problems (Simpson, 1985: 91).

Scaffolding at a Distance

The term 'collaborative learning' is used to refer to a learning 'philosophy' aimed at getting students to work together in small groups. However, different from 'group work', collaborative learning requires working together at different tasks, but toward a common goal. Perhaps more importantly, because collaborative learning combines 'group goals' and 'individual accountability' (Slavin, 1989; Totten *et al.*, 1991), *every group member* should learn something that they will share with the rest of the group.

So what does this have to do with the internet? According to Vygotsky (1978), students can perform at higher intellectual levels in collaborative situations than when working individually. Added to this is the notion that group diversity can contribute positively to the learning process because students are faced with different interpretations, explanations or conceptualisations about what they are studying and this forces them to 're-think' their own viewpoints (Bruner, 1986). It is intuitively obvious that integrating network-based learning into the process of collaborative learning can be very beneficial in terms of knowledge and experience as it helps provide optimal circumstances for exchanging and 're-thinking' ideas.

Central to the concept of collaborative learning is the idea of cultural and social 'artefacts' as 'mediators' for human development (Leontiev,

1983; Vygotsky, 1978). Through artefacts, learners acquire, construct and retrieve different kinds of knowledge; however these artefacts play both an operational and interactional role. The 'artefact' as operational role seems fairly straightforward, however it also plays an interactional role by helping the learner incorporate the way knowledge is constructed both at an individual level of understanding and at a collaborative level – sometimes referred to as 'scaffolding'. The social, interpersonal level of learning occurs through the tools chosen for mediating the scaffolding. This concept of a collaborative learning process highlights the importance the tool will have for the success of the learning process.

The process of learning that takes place between the interpersonal and intrapersonal (the level where the knowledge is 'internalised') was described by Vygotsky as the 'zone of proximal development' (ZPD). The ZPD is 'the distance between the actual development level as determined by independent problem solving and the level of potential development as determined through problem solving under adult guidance or in collaboration with more capable peers' (Vygotsky, 1978: 86). However, in recent years the idea of collaboration has been rightfully extended by many educators to include *collaboration amongst equal peers* and not just adults or more capable peers. This emphasises the role of peers as both *active and reflective participants* (Dorish & Belkotti, 1992). In this process, the learners support each other and provide resources that can be used for constructing knowledge.

Of course, for this collaboration to take place, the learner must have an 'understanding of the activities of the others, which provides context for [their] own activity' (Dorish & Belkotti, 1992: 107). In the case of telecollaborative learning, this understanding of the other's activities must be made explicit, through *meta-communicative activities* (Fjuk, 1998) and the success or failure of doing so can have a significant impact on the actual collaborative learning process. As Lund and Smordal (2006) have pointed out, in face-to-face educational settings, even with the integration of technologies into the designed classroom activities, the teacher is always present – whether this is 'upfront' or 'subtle'. The introduction of new technologies does not necessarily 'challenge or transcend the socio-historically established practices of the classroom' (Lund & Smordal, 2006: 2) wherein the teacher maintains principal control of the resources and how they are employed. Institutional (and teacher) practices do not automatically change when new technologies are introduced into the educational environment; which is one of the reasons, as Lund and Smordal argue, that Learning Management Systems tend to imitate face-to-face arrangement of material ('repositories for instructional material and learner management tools', p. 2) rather than focusing on the 'collaborative potential' of online technology. Thus, the way in which teachers negotiate online environments to encourage their students' collaborative learning opportunities will influence the learning process.

In other words, a telecollaborative project is not just a question of getting students to sit down in front of a computer and begin chatting with a school partner in another country or asking them to find information about a country the teacher has arbitrarily chosen. The students of today are going to be working members of the society of tomorrow and that will mean understanding that advances in technology are tools that they can use to organise their work and efforts. By putting emphasis on teamwork through ICT tools, the students will learn to think creatively, to solve problems, to make decisions as a team, and learn to select the relevant tools themselves – thus imitating the circumstances of their future workplace. As workgroup collaboration, knowledge management, learning technologies and processes converge, the need for this type of knowledge will become increasingly more prevalent in the job market. The role of the teacher is to organise the learners' activities in a way that is propitious for distributed collaborative learning and the ICT tool – in its role of artefact for learning – can help lay the cornerstone.

Issues when Choosing Communication Tools

We now turn to some initial issues that emerge during the process of selecting the ICT mode most appropriate for each telecollaborative project. A first – and quite straightforward – question to ask is what is the appropriate 'delivery mode' to be used (see the subsection 'Synchronous or asynchronous collaboration?'). Making decisions about delivery and considering how to integrate ICT into learner-centred classrooms must begin with an honest evaluation of the scope and limitations of the actual learning environment(s) involved in the telecollaboration. The point of departure must be the learners – what they already know, expectations about the learning processes, different learning modalities and so forth – but before looking at some issues in designing a telecollaborative project, we must first consider what a good telecollaborative project entails (subsection 'What makes a good telecollaborative activity?'). A hypothetical telecollaborative project is provided to illustrate ways to integrate ICT modes at different stages in the project (subsection 'Learner-centred or technology-centred: Always at odds?'), followed by a description of a 'needs analysis' design plan for setting up telecollaborative projects ('Needs analysis').

Synchronous or asynchronous collaboration?

Within the overall perspective of teaching, incorporating ICT into collaborative learning is not that different from any other class planning as long as we maintain the initial idea of ICT as simply another tool or resource for enhancing what is really important – the learning process. The planning must revolve around the class needs, not the tool itself. Online collaboration does require a careful design of the 'work flow processes' and this is where the decision of which ICT tool(s) to use comes into play. One of the first decisions to make when designing the project work flow is whether to use synchronous delivery of the materials and input, asynchronous delivery, or both at the same time. This consideration is more pertinent than it may appear at first. Asynchronous collaborative activities, due to the very nature of the distribution of time and space, will develop differently than collaboration in situations where the participants are sharing both time and space (Fjuk, 1988). On the other hand, with synchronous activities, while the participants share the same timeframe for carrying out the activities, the activities must be managed from different spaces. Either way, the nature of collaboration will be different than in face-to-face collaboration, meaning that the tools selected must help replace the communication and interaction which is common in face-to-face situations. Moreover, the tool must optimise the 'Vygotskian' collaboration effectively. But before looking at the tools, first consider the two possible modes of communication.

Synchronous delivery means that students are participating in the activity at the same time, using the same delivery mode. This mode of delivery can be somewhat similar to more traditional classrooms if the internet tools are principally used by the instructor to present information, answer questions or to monitor discussions. Of course, synchronous delivery can also be used for students to interact with each other, which is the main focus of telecollaborative learning. This type of delivery requires having a pre-set time for interaction for the students and enough computer terminals and bandwidth to keep interruptions of the exchanges to a minimum.

Asynchronous delivery means the material and input can be accessed at anytime (day or night), whenever it is most convenient for the individual learner. Whole classes can also use it when the schedules of the partner schools do not coincide. Classes can work together to 'leave' materials for the partners to 'pick up' later. Asynchronous delivery may be the best option for autonomous pair work, for extensive reading or writing activities and for attending to questions, concerns and long debates.

What makes a good telecollaborative activity?

As stated earlier, however, the most relevant aspect to telecollaboration is the design of the activity, not the tool itself. The question many teachers might ask is exactly what makes a good telecollaborative activity? Ideally, in a telecollaborative project, tasks are established that will encourage students to reflect how they came to their solutions of each problem they encountered and provide the students with opportunities to analyse, synthesise and evaluate their ideas together. This means facilitating discussion and interaction so that students are forced to go beyond mere statements of opinion.

A good telecollaborative project will also incorporate tasks that ensure positive interdependence between the participants. Students should know and understand that their interaction in the group is linked to the others in such a way that success can only be achieved by everyone contributing their part. Knowing that their participation is essential for the whole group can be a powerful motivational factor (Kohn, 1986). Furthermore, the telecollaborative project should help the learners develop interpersonal communication. Interpersonal communication should not be confused with good language skills. Effective interpersonal communication means that group members communicate with each other on a regular basis, and are careful to ensure that their communication is clear and relevant (Johnson & Johnson, 2000).

Of course, the autonomy of making contact with the other partners will depend on the ages of the students and the resources of the school. If the students are young, then times and methods of communication between the collaborative groups will probably be decided by the teachers and will be contingent upon class schedules and computer resources. With older or more autonomous students, group collaboration (and subsequently, contact with partners) may be the responsibility of the students them-selves. In this case, interpersonal communication is essential and could even be considered a factor for final assessment.

A good telecollaborative project will be designed to help the students to collaborate. Although this may seem redundant, in fact, it should be a basis of the teaching paradigm. Learning to collaborate means learning to share one's own opinion with others (and providing reasons and evidence for that opinion) while also respecting opinions different from one's own. It also helps each learner to see the importance they have to the overall goal of the group, thus empowering the student as an integral part of a collaborative group, not as an individual.

Finally, a good telecollaborative project will be designed so that the ICT tools and the in-class activities (not online) are all part of a cohesive whole. In other words, the activities carried out in class and the activities carried out online with the partner schools should not be divorced from each other. The students need to see coherency between what they are doing face-to-face and what they are asked to do with their partner school. This means designing activities that have a place in the overall curriculum of the class, not 'added-on' activities.

Learner-centred or technology-centred: Always at odds?

One of the principal roles for the teacher in telecollaboration is to ensure the organisation of online activities that are favourable for distributed collaborative learning. It is very important to ensure that the students, as principal stakeholders in the learning process, feel comfortable with the entire telecollaborative project. Inevitably, this is not always the case and this is often downplayed in the literature written about the use of ICT in education. One thing that is often understated is students' persistent frustrations in web-based collaboration – this can be caused by many different factors such as technical difficulties, lack of effective advice (e.g. Abrahamson, 1998; Brown, 1996; Rahm & Reed, 1998), and anxiety, which can impede the learning process (Darke, 1988).

Effective online collaborative learning projects will take into account the fact that learners vary in the way in which they concentrate on, process and retain information, and will endeavour to integrate different learning modalities by providing a variety of experiences and different activities. These activities should cover a wide range of learning opportunities that use visual, auditory and motor/kinaesthetic processes. Trying to meet the learning styles of each student may seem overwhelming, especially with classes of 20–30 students, but the fact that telecollaboration inevitably involves more than one teacher means that each teacher will bring his or her particular strengths to the learning environment and help meet the needs of different learning styles, modalities and multiple intelligences. One effective approach for partnered teachers is to conceptualise a performance-based collaborative project and then select the tools according to the expected procedures and outcomes, always ensuring that the different learning modalities are covered.

For instance, the combination of e-mails between pairs and group discussion boards or blogs as part of a knowledge building process can be an effective way to begin the project using tools that students are (usually) familiar with. Of course, it is recognised that each class is a world in itself and it may be the case that some students are not familiar with any internet tools, or have only used e-mail and web pages but have never participated in any other online communicative activity. Therefore, when combining different activities and tools, it is a good idea to know which tools the students are familiar with beforehand, and begin with activities that use these formats.

To illustrate this, it is easiest to begin with a general framework of a hypothetical project and then discuss the different tool possibilities. Suppose we have a project in which the students in all the partner schools are asked to read literature that highlights particular 'cultural values' (for instance, the now popular *Chronicles of Narnia* by C.S. Lewis). The students could begin an e-mail correspondence between pairs to discuss their opinions about the role of the 'Saviour' Lion called Aslan. Other activities are then introduced which incorporate new networking tools (e.g. a blog that explains and expands upon the opinions discussed between the distanced partners).

More activities that appeal to different learning styles can gradually be integrated into the sequence of activities, for example, students can search and post texts and images that express their feelings about the way religion or culture is portrayed in the books, add an audioblog, work in distanced teams to create a wiki that highlights the different cultures of the world and how they are portrayed in different world media and literature (beginning with the assigned literature) or go online for a synchronous chat session to debate and try to reach a consensus about any topic related to the project. A class web page – different sections can be created together between distanced group partners – will help illustrate the knowledge gained from the entire process. This can serve not only as the end product but as a means for the students to summarise and assimilate their own knowledge. In other words, the possibilities for incorporating telecollaborative tools are limitless – in the end, the limits (better said, restraints) must be decided by the teacher(s) in accordance to the context, contents and learners.

Needs analysis

A good way to help decide which modes are most useful and efficient for a telecollaborative project is to begin with a needs analysis. A needs analysis can be done through a 'scenario based design' – a detailed description of the ways in which the stakeholders (teachers and students) already use technology in the language learning process. This enables the teacher to better understand the tools students already use (both inside and outside the classroom) and thus provide an analysis for incorporating familiar and new technologies into the teaching and learning activities. This scenario-based design is usually done through a textual description – for example, in the form of a log of each time technology is used during a period of time. The log should include the learner's point of view of each episode, including suggestions for alternative technological resources and ways to focus the use of the technology already in use. It should also include information about what the learners already know (and use outside of the classroom) and what they would like to know more about when dealing with the different technologies. The scenarios can also be used as a file – to help keep track of past design rationale and to reflect on ways to improve activities that did not fully meet the design aims, as well as ways to enhance successful activities.

Following the description of technological use, other questions dealing with the integration of ICT modes should be considered as well.

- Is it convenient to integrate new technology into the course at this time?
- Are the resources available for the classroom? For the students?
- Is it expensive?
- Does the institute have enough capacity to provide the infrastructures? (Technical requirements, computer room, internet connection, ability to handle images, sound, etc.)
- Is there a history of adaptation of technology into the learning process (e.g. overhead projectors, slide projectors, video machines, etc.)?
- What is the students' technological background? (Skills, experience, habits, etc. – this will be made apparent in the log.)
- What do students need to learn to be able to adapt to the new changes? (This will also come out in the log.)
- What is the teacher's technological background (skills, experience, habits, etc.)?
- What does the teacher need to learn to be able to adapt to the new changes?
- How much time will be involved in the preparation? In the implementation?
- Will it make a positive impact on the learning process?

Once a scenario has been written that highlights the tools already in use, other tools can be examined to also include them in the telecollaborative language learning activities being planned. A brief outline of some of the more familiar ICT modes and how they might be used are described in the next section, however this is only intended as a guide. The outline takes into consideration the principal features of the tools and how they are *usually* implemented by most users. This is more important than it may seem at first – research indicates that students' comfort level (related to affectiveness in the learning process) is directly linked to ease of access to resources and *familiarity* with the context, content and resources used in the learning process. (Andrusyszyn *et al.*, 2001; Cragg *et al.*, 1998; 1999; Simonson & Maushak, 2001). This brings us to our overview of some of the ICT modes available for telecollaborative projects.

An Overview of Communication Tools Available

A problem that can emerge when considering a telecollaborative project is a variation of the chicken or egg paradox: which comes first, the tools or the learning/activity paradigm? Some teachers may outline their learning paradigm only to discover that the selected tool is not feasible for the project – due to lack of accessibility, resources, time limitations or a myriad of other reasons (see starting questions in the subsection on 'Learner-centred or technology-centred'). Other teachers may prefer to learn about the tools available and then find ways to adapt them to the existing activity outline. Most projects will be a mix of both approaches; this means that the teacher should first consider how they feel that the learning process can best be carried out in their classroom (even if the activities have not been decided yet) and then choose the ICT tools they (and their students) will feel most comfortable with. This is a key factor to successful telecollaborative learning – technological resources are only powerful and relevant to project work when they increase the efficiency of the tasks – not if they distract, overwhelm or divert the focus of the tasks from the content to the technology itself.

So how does one go about choosing the tools for fostering distanced collaborative learning? As was mentioned before, the field of communication technology is constantly evolving and this means that new tools are cropping up at apparently amazing speed. This chapter only looks at the tools that are more easily accessible, familiar to students and teachers, and can be adopted fairly easily to facilitate communication. Some tools such as calendars, RSS feeders and surveys and polls, while arguably communicative in nature, have been left out because they are not usually considered to be particularly conducive to the use and production of target language (beyond acting as complements to other communicative activities). Of course, a telecollaborative project does not necessarily have to only use one ICT mode, as was pointed out in the hypothetical project elaborated in the previous section. Ideally, telecollaboration will integrate more than one mode into the overall design of the project in order to take advantage of the features of each tool.

E-mail

Most schools now provide students with their own e-mail addresses associated to the school (often in the ICT classes). In language teaching, setting up cross-cultural exchanges and making new friends are common objectives of 'e-pal' or 'keypal' projects. Furthermore, e-mail can also be used to share information and knowledge necessary for completing tasks that are part of a 'broader' collaborative effort (e.g. writing to a group member to find out their after-school activities as part of a cross-cultural web page collage).

The advantage to using e-mail is its easy access and the familiarity students have with it. One of the biggest disadvantages is that it can be too time-consuming for students to do during class time or there might not be computer access in the language classroom. This means that students must be autonomous enough to carry out the tasks on their own and have the necessary skills (typing, language, technical) to keep up with the activities. The need for autonomy and punctuality can be exacerbated by the volume of e-mails that can accumulate in the inbox, although this can be curbed by assigning individual partners or groups for exchange as well as negotiating the amount and length of e-mails to be exchanged. Lack of response from the partners can be discouraging for language learners, so the process should be carefully monitored on both ends.

For more advanced language learners, collaborative work that can be done via e-mail can include peer proofreading (attaching drafts of texts for feedback) or they can even be part of the final assessment – the peer's comments, along with revisions stemming from the comments, are included when the paper is turned in.

Nonetheless, teachers should bear in mind that for the upcoming generation of tech-savvy students, e-mail is often considered 'an old and formal communication means' and many now prefer instant messaging or other synchronous tools (Ki-hong, 2004). The use of e-mail may be more suitable for younger students who have less access to international communities via the internet. The exchanges can be set up by the teachers according to previously assigned partners.

Web pages

Many students are already familiar with web page designing and there are several software programs available for web page creation. Students can create individual web pages to introduce themselves to their partners and that allow their partners to send them comments and add to the web page – templates can be provided if necessary. Groups can also work together to create one web page – a collage of digital images combined with short explanations or expressions can be stimulating for beginner language learners. Teachers should bear in mind, however, that web pages are more static than other tools and the need for online communication is limited unless other activities are built into the process (e.g. students exchange information about what should be included in the web page – see hypothetical project outlined in the subsection 'What makes a good telecollaborative activity?').

For older students, with more advanced language skills, web pages can help generate a significant amount of statistical data about the project participants that can be used in cross-curricular activities (e.g. language and social science projects). For instance, students can conduct surveys or compile information about social and cultural identities of their peers in other countries, which they find in their partners' web pages, and include it in reports. Web pages can also function as autobiographical essays and help students learn more about self-presentation.

A more recent tool that is similar to the web page is the 'social network site' called MySpace. Because of its vast popularity (over 78 million registered accounts) and its influence in 'youth culture', MySpace is worth mentioning as a possible educational tool as well. MySpace provides sites where individuals create profiles and link to others ('friends') within the system. Similar to individual web pages, the profile provides an individual's digital representation of their tastes, fashion and identity; however MySpace offers the possibility of easily creating links to other sites within the system, thus creating affiliations. Moreover, the individual sites have built-in messaging systems (similar to e-mail), bulletin boards (electronic forums) and a blogging service (discussion on possible uses of these tools are in the sections of each format). A teacher interested in keeping the tools in one virtual space might find this convenient. The fact that MySpace allows users to restrict who can see their page and contact them may help educators feel more comfortable about creating a student community in a system of millions of users. Of course, there exists the risk that students who are already engaged in the social network may feel that the teacher is impinging upon and appropriating 'their space'. This is an especially delicate issue for adolescents (the principal users of MySpace) who are in a stage of developing their own identities.

Blogs

Blogs are spaces on the web where you can write and publish (post) about a topic or several topics. Unlike traditional websites, they provide instant 'type-n-click publishing' that can be done anywhere, anytime and from any browser. Ostensibly blogs encourage discussion and interaction from many participants as they allow for comments to be posted. Blogs allow for frequent exposure to the target language (reading other blogs for instance), thus students will be able to hypothesise on the use of the target language (for example when faced with new structures and lexicon from other blog respondents). Students can also experiment with the target language if they write their own blogs.

Like the web page, the amount of telecollaborative learning that takes place will depend more on the design of the activity than the tool itself. If the 'ownership' of the blog lies principally with the teacher, then the activity should be designed in such a way that the students are stimulated to respond to the material posted. Depending on the language level of the students, this can range from open-ended questions about a topic displayed in the blog for more advanced students, to one-word answers in an opinion poll for beginning language learners. When designing activities, it can be useful to return to the 'tried and true' communicative approach tasks that have worked well in the classroom and to think of ways to adapt them. For instance, audioblogs can be used much the same way as the 'telephone' game where each student whispers a sentence to the next one until it works its way down the row. Adapting this idea and getting students to record their own sentences and then having their online partners guess the sentences can be a fun way to practice speaking and listening.

More learner-centred activities can also be designed around blogs. This might include posting a 'case study' and soliciting possible solutions or getting students to plan a situation together (for example a trip). This is, of course, similar to a discussion board, but a blog allows a higher volume of posting material (text, audio and visual) whereas a discussion board reply is usually more limited.

Discussion boards (forums)

Like blogs, online discussion boards or forums can promote discussion and reflection between distanced students who do not meet face-to-face. In cross-cultural situations especially, this diversity can produce new reflections for the students when they are faced with unfamiliar perceptions of 'reality'. The amount of language use and the amount of student autonomy will depend, as always, on the design of the activity rather than the tool. The questions can be posted by the teacher only and these questions can be closed or open-ended, depending on the task at hand. Or students can use discussion boards as part of their 'problem-solving' – asking other students to participate in their knowledge construction.

Usually teachers think of discussion boards as a tool for continuing already introduced topics in order to avoid overwhelming the student with new and unfamiliar lexicon and structure. However, it is possible to use forums that are not designed with language learners in mind. For instance, the students can be asked to participate in forums that highlight their country (e.g. a travel discussion board), thus their expertise in the subject can help balance their limited language proficiency. Students can also be instructed to post information and opinions from assigned websites such as BBC or CNN news sites into a shared electronic forum. For more collaborative type activities, discussion boards can be used for 'writing rounds' – an unfinished story can be constructed by the different contributors to the board – and then edited by different working groups, students can post 'exam questions' on a parallel reading assignment between partner classes, or as a Question and Answer session about each online partners' country.

Of course, the use of the discussion board should correspond to the students' needs and limitation. Too many postings can cause students to become frustrated – students may not have enough time to read postings, especially if the class is large and the topics in class change frequently. This can lead them to skip through (or ignore completely) other students' postings before writing their response.

Instant messaging/chat

Instant messaging (known as IM for short) consists of a window that pops up on a screen with a message that is received as soon as the sender hits the return button. This functionality is available on computers with internet connections, telephones via the SMS (Small Messaging System) protocol or on two-way radios (Nextel). Inevitably, instant messaging is more intrusive than electronic mail because it is 'real time' and therefore interrupts whatever the user is doing when a message is received. However, it also provides for a much higher availability and reliability (barring technical problems) for discussion and interaction between participants. IM was once considered to be 'a teen thing' (Thomas, 2001) and not a serious tool for education. However, as with most networking tools, more and more people are using IM in many different settings, including education. IM has principally been adopted in education settings as a means for complementary dialogue between the students and the teacher, for clarification, further explanation of a lecture point, or to mention deadlines or items in the class agenda.

However, like any other networking format, IM can be used for highly collaborative purposes. Much has been written about the use of 'chat sessions' in language learning (see Müller-Hartmann, this volume). Chat sessions are especially appealing to teachers whose students have sufficient levels of the target language to be able to participate in online discussions with other users of the target language. In many cases, the teachers may save the chat text (transcript) to analyse later with the class (error correction, positive reinforcement of demonstrated proficiency and so on).

IM can also be used as a complementary tool for other online activities. For instance, IM can be employed to remind an online partner that they have not posted their assignment in a blog or to ask for clarification about a point in a collaboratively written text. It can also be used to design, carry out and/or evaluate a collaborative project. The teacher should bear in mind, however, that the use of IM and chat sessions does not only require a fairly good command of the target language (in order to be able to follow the conversation and give a timely response) but also requires typing skills and some knowledge of the accepted communication 'codes' (e.g. capital letters are understood to mean shouting and can imply that the message sender is angry).

Other difficulties inherent to synchronous communication also apply – in order for there to be interaction, both parties must be online at the same time. This can be difficult to arrange when the parties live in different time zones and have different daily schedules. The teacher should also keep in mind the amount of bandwidth necessary for chat sessions and should plan accordingly. Attempts to get 25 pairs of students chatting from the same computer room may slow down (or even collapse) the network system of the school. As alternative approaches, different pairs can be scheduled to 'meet' online at different times throughout the school year, or student can take turns interacting with their partners while the rest of the class can watch (the computer screen can be projected onto a big screen) and give input.

Voice chat

Like text chats, voice chats permit real-time interaction between the students. Voice over the Internet Protocol (VOIP) allows the student to speak to others by using a microphone connected to the computer (it can also be used with a web cam so that the speakers can see each other). As this tool becomes more popular, the audio quality is also improving (as bandwidths are becoming bigger, this helps with the audio quality as well). The VOIP feature is now integrated into several instant messenger tools, just as there are videoconferencing applications integrated into many computers. Some VOIP applications are free (e.g. netmeeting for PCs, iChat for Apple and Macintosh, Skype for both PCs and Macintosh), while other platforms must be contracted and paid. (It goes without saying that the quality and number of features is directly correlated to the price.)

Just as text chat and IM are attractive to teachers interested in getting their students to interact with other users of the target language, VOIP application has a wide appeal to teachers who would like to ensure there is a real purpose to the use of the target language. However, many students may not feel confident enough in their own language proficiency to try to carry out a conversation with someone (especially considering that they more than likely have never met this person). Thus, if a teacher is interested in integrating this tool into the overall project, it might be seen as the culminating activity – once the students have already worked together online on other activities and through other tools.

Another alternative to using this tool is to 'invite' someone into the classroom via VOIP and a web camera (webcam). The image of the 'guest' (or expert) can be projected onto a full-size screen and the students can take turns posing questions. This type of activity can be incorporated into a large-scale collaborative project by having each class interview different 'guests' who have key information to the final output of the project. After the interviews, the students will be responsible for communicating the information gleaned from the 'guests' to their partners, via e-mail, blogs, forum, text chats, IM and so on.

Videoconferencing

The two forms of videoconferencing currently in use in foreign language contexts are desktop and room-based videoconferencing (O'Dowd, 2006). Desktop videoconferencing is based on one-to-one communication carried out through personal computer connections while room-based videoconferencing is generally organised on a group-to-group basis. In this case, a class sits in front of a large screen where they can view the participants at the other site as well as a smaller image of themselves. It is common in higher education institutions to use this form of the technology for distance learning programmes. In this way, students or lecturers far away from the home campus can take part in classes. A camera, a screen, a microphone, a projector, loudspeakers and an Integrated Services Digital Network (ISDN) line are standard requirements for this type of connection.

As videoconferencing is through synchronous delivery, it requires careful planning of the learning paradigm, in fact, the learners themselves can be active participants in the planning stage of the videoconferencing sequence. Many teachers and students often consider videoconferencing like a public speaking event. This means that rehearsal of the presentation (if appropriate), lighting, acoustics and staging (positions of the participants, the camera, the screen) should be included in the task or project design. Quality of audio and video can have an important impact on the final results of the videoconferencing session so any tasks included in the videoconferencing should not rely on high-quality transmission (e.g. facial cues, gestures, body language etc. may not be distinguishable). Another disadvantage of videoconferencing is the possible passivity of the learners in front of the screen. Interaction must be designed into the telecollaborative activities that use videoconferencing.

Interaction can be integrated into videoconferencing by opening up the classroom to real-world contact, for instance with experts in the subjects the learners are currently engaged in (see 'Voice chat') or it can allow students to take 'virtual trips' to museums, zoos or other organisations that provide videoconferencing links. Videoconferencing can also play an important role in telecollaboration. For instance, videoconferencing can be used with advanced language learners to promote learner-to-learner tutoring (students take turns preparing a 'lesson' to be transmitted to their online peers), to present school projects or to set up online contests between classes (e.g. spelling bees or other 'games' that the learners take turns as contestants).

Wiki

A wiki platform is basically a group of interlinked web pages, with an internal hypertext system that allows quick navigation between the links. It is a large database that can be used for storing and modifying information – information that is easily edited by all the users of the wiki. The wiki pages allow for easy creating and editing of texts as well as adding and restructuring pages – all of which can be done from any browser. The links are created by 'wiki mark-up' – a type of language code that allows links to be quickly and easily created with words serving as the 'mark' or signal for the link. There are also logs of the changes that have been made to the different pages in the system and the possibility of notifications to members of a community so they can keep track of these changes.

The wiki tool has several features that can provide interesting resources for the teacher. For instance some platforms provide a *discussion page*, which, much like the discussion board outlined above, can be used to explain the assignments associated to the wiki, to provide comments to students' contributions to the wiki, to allow a space for discussion about the construction and content of the wiki texts and so forth. The *history page*, similar to chat transcripts, can provide the teacher with information about the volume and profile of participation of the different students, the amount of collaboration for each contribution (number of authors) and the topics which have the highest volume of editing. Perhaps one of the most useful features is the *banner* – much like a bookmark or 'post-it', these banners can indicate when a topic is too short and needs more editing or as a reminder to continue on a topic along established areas.

For language learning, the wiki mode holds a lot of potential for teachers interested in shifting the focus of their students' understanding and constructing of texts from a concept of texts written by others *for them* (e.g. textbooks, newspapers, magazines and other sources) to texts co-constructed *by them for others.* It also provides a means for students to realise their own capacities to create texts with a focus that is not singularly directed by one person (the teacher in most cases) so that they can explore different genres, styles and modes of writing to find out for themselves what is most effective for communicating their ideas. This does not mean that the activities involving 'wiki writing' are not teacher-directed. Indeed, the amount of teacher direction depends on the way the activities are designed. The opening page of the wiki project – to give an example – can be set up by the teacher with very explicit instructions on *what* is to be included in the contributions and *how* it is to be included. However, it is very probable that the amount of 'branching out' into related topics will be far higher than a writing activity with one assigned topic (e.g. essay writing) simply due to the way in which the wiki mode functions. The fact that the wiki mode allows for links to be easily established connecting one word to a related topic allows for much more liberty for the students to decide what is relevant subject matter and what is not. Thus, in a collaborative wiki project with a starting topic of 'Youth in the European Union', for example, the main categories such as education, demography, geography, etc. will most probably branch into other areas of interest for the students, such as sports, hobbies, future expectations and so on.

When designing collaborative activities for the wiki mode, teachers should bear in mind that students (and teachers) are not necessarily aware of different types of writing processes apart from the more traditional idea of one text = one author. This can create tensions when texts are edited or even deleted by different contributors, as the primary author of the text may feel hurt or annoyed by the intervention of others. This means that the design of the activity should include preliminary discussion and negotiation about what it means to co-construct a text (this can include an online discussion between the distanced partners about topics dealing with authorship, plagiarism and other issues which inevitably emerge as the internet forces us to re-evaluate the origins of texts). By emphasising that the owners of the text are the students and that the final presentation is their responsibility, the students may be more inclined to collectively review and evaluate the text as a whole, not as a part (in other words, each individual contribution). Through discussion, the students can decide which texts need more information, which texts need editing and mark them with the banners, without assigning the task of editing to anyone in particular. In short, the design of the wiki writing project should aim for gradually increasing the sense of co-ownership so that the final product provides the students with a sense of community effort.

Conclusion

As Esch and Zähner (2000) have argued, learners should be seen as the key agents in the construction of new language learning environments. Just as each individual brings different styles and aptitudes to the classroom, the language learners will differ in their ability to adapt to new elements, including network-based tools. They will also differ in their understanding of what constitutes an appropriate language-learning environment – which may mean acceptance or rejection of the use of telecollaboration in the classroom. Teachers should take advantage of the opportunities that arise from internet-related tools in order to have a wide variety of interactive activities that encourage and support telecollaborative language learning (facilitated through diverse ICT modes) and help even the more reluctant students gradually move towards acceptance of ICT as an important tool for communication. Of course the teacher should bear in mind that the technology in itself will not suddenly produce a community of multiple language users. The tools can, however, act as a useful resource for teachers to motivate and engage their students in an array of telecollaborative language learning activities that appeals to different learning styles.

References

Abrahamson, C.E. (1998) Issues in interactive communication in distance education. *College Student Journal* 32 (1), 33–43.
Andrusyszyn, M.A., Moen, A., Iwasiw, I., Stovring, T., Ostbye, T., Davie, L. and Buckland-Foster, I. (2001) Evaluation of electronic collaborative international graduate nursing education: The Canada-Norway experience. *Journal of Distance Education* 15 (2), 52–70.
Bonk, C.J. and Kim, K.A. (1998) Extending sociocultural theory to adult learning. In M.C. Smith and T. Pourchot (eds) *Adult Learning and Development: Perspectives from Educational Psychology* (pp. 67–88). Mahwah, NJ: Erlbaum.
Bowers, C.A. (1988) *The Cultural Dimensions of Educational Computing: Understanding the Non-neutrality of Technology.* New York: Teachers College Press.
Brown, K.M. (1996) The role of internal and external factors in the discontinuation of off-campus students. *Distance Education* 17 (1), 44–71.
Bruner, J. (1985) Vygotsky: An historical and conceptual perspective. *Culture, Communication, and Cognition: Vygotskian Perspectives* (pp. 21–34). London: Cambridge University Press.
Cove, P.G. and Love, A.G. (1996) *Enhancing Student Learning: Intellectual, Social, and Emotional Integration.* EDO-HE-95-4. Washington, DC: ERIC Clearinghouse on Higher Education.
Cragg, B., Andrusyszyn, M.A. and Humbert, J. (1999) Experience with technology and preferences for distance education delivery methods in a Nurse Practitioner program. *Journal of Distance Education* 14 (1), 1–13.
Cragg, C.E., Andrusyszyn, M.A., Humbert, J. and Wilson, M. (1998) *Implications of Using Different Distance Delivery Methods for Learning*. (Report to the Network of Ontario Distance Education: NODE). London, Ontario.
Darke, S. (1988) Anxiety and working memory capacity. *Cognition and Emotion* 2 (2), 145–154.
Diamond, R.M. (1997) Curriculum reform needed if students are to master core skills. *Chronicle of Higher Education* 43 (Aug), B7.
Dorish, P, Belkotti, V. (1992) Awareness and co-ordination in shared workspaces. In J. Turner and R. Kraut (eds) CSCW: *Sharing Perspectives. Proceedings of the Conference of the Computer Supported Co-operative Work* (pp. 107–114). Boston: ACM Press.
Esch, E. and Zähner, C. (2000) The contribution of Information and Communication Technology (ICT) to language learning environments or the mystery of the secret agent. *ReCALL* 12, 5–18.
Fjuk, A. (1998) Computer support for distributed collaborative learning. Exploring a complex problem area. PhD Thesis, Department of Informatics, University of Oslo.

Gardiner, L.F. (1997) Producing dramatic increases in student learning: Can we do it? *National Teaching and Learning Forum* 6 (2), 8–10.

Handy, C. (1998) A proper education. *Change* 30 (5), 12–19.

Johnson, D.W. and Johnson, F. (2000). *Joining Together: Group Theory and Group Skills* (7th edn). Needham Heights, MA: Pearson Education.

Ki-hong, K. (2004) New forms of on-line communication spell end of email era in Korea. *Digital Chosunilbo (English Edition)*. November 28. On WWW at http://english.chosun.com/.

Kling, R. (1984) Value conflicts in public computing developments. *The Information Society* 3 (1), 1–38. On WWW at http://www.slis.indiana.edu/TIS.

Kohn, A. (1986) *No Contest: The Case Against Competition*. Boston: Houghton Mifflin.

Leontiev, A.N. (1983) *Virksomhed, bevissthet og personlighed*. København: Forlaget Progress.

Lund, A. and Smordal, O. (2006) Is there a space for the teacher in a WIKI? *WikiSym '06*. August 21–23. Odense, Denmark.

Papert, S. (1987) Computer criticism vs. technocentric thinking. *Educational Researcher* 17 (1), 22–30.

Rahm, D. and Reed, B.J (1998) Tangled webs in public administration: Organizational issues in distance learning. *Public Administration and Management: An Interactive Journal* 3 (1: January). On WWW at http://www.pamij.com/rahm.html.

Richards, C. (2005) The design of effective ICT-supported learning activities: Exemplary models, changing requirements, and new possibilities. *Language Learning & Technology* 9 (1).

Roueche, J.E. (1998) American Imperative-Essay, Virtual Library. On WWW at http://www.johnsonfdn.org/library/foundpub/amerimp/essayx.html. Accessed 9.11.06.

Rudd, T., Gifford, C., Morrison, J. and Facer, K. (2006) What if...? Re-imagining learning spaces. An Opening Education report from Futurelab (October 2006). On WWW at http://www.futurelab.org.uk/index.htm. Accessed 9.11.06.

Simonson, M. and Maushak, N. (2001) Instructional technology and attitude change. In D. Jonassen (ed.) *Handbook of Research for Educational Communications and Technology* (pp. 984–1016). Mahway, NJ: Lawrence Erlbaum Associates.

Simpson, B. (1985) Heading for the ha-ha. In D. Sloan (ed.) *The Computer in Education: A Critical Perspective* (pp. 84–92). New York: Teachers College Press.

Slavin, R.F. (1980) Cooperative learning. *Review of Educational Research* 50 (2), 315–342.

Thomas, K. (2001) Instant messaging: It's a teen thing. *USA Today* 06/21/2001. On WWW at http://www.usatoday.com/tech/news/2001–06-21-teens-im-main.htm. Accessed 9.11.06.

Totten, S., Sills, T., Digby, A. and Russ, P. (1991) *Cooperative Learning: A Guide to Research*. New York: Garland.

Vygotsky, L. (1978) *Mind in Society: The Development of Higher Psychological Processes*. Cambridge: Harvard University Press.

Part 4

Practical Accounts and Experiences of Online Exchange

Chapter 11
Foreword

ROBERT O'DOWD

The chapters in the first parts of this volume focussed on presenting the theoretical origins of online intercultural exchange and also identified pedagogical principles and guidelines related to various models and issues of interest. This second part takes a more practical perspective and presents various short reports from telecollaborative practitioners working in different educational contexts around the world today. For the sake of clarity and to encourage comparison of the projects, all the reports in this section follow the same organisational structure. This will enable the reader to appreciate the differences and similarities between each project's socioinstitutional context, objectives, structure and the outcomes to date. In each case, the authors conclude by looking forward and suggesting how they plan to develop their exchanges in the future.

The diversity in these reports highlights the flexibility of this activity and demonstrates clearly how telecollaboration can be put to use in different educational contexts, using a range of communication tools and with varying learning objectives. In the following pages, the reader will find accounts of online exchanges that include two and three partner classes and engage students in the use of one or two or even three different languages. Some reports, such as that reported on by Vinagre, discuss exchanges that have received the support of formal university agreements or international project funding, while others look at projects that have been organised informally by the teachers themselves and have yet to receive any official institutional support. Finally, some exchanges involve students who are studying each others' languages but others offer examples of intercultural communication using English as a lingua franca and of online mentoring between language learners and trainee foreign language teachers.

As regards the use of communication tools, the reports provide examples of good practice that involve a wide variety of tools including online discussion boards, audioconferencing (also referred to here as 'voice chat'), videoconferencing, blogs and virtual learning environments such as Moodle. Many authors in the literature have already argued for the combination of different communication tools in online learning so that learners will benefit from their different characteristics. O'Dowd (2006), for example, used e-mail and videoconferencing for the development of different aspects of intercultural competence, while Sotillo (2000) compared asynchronous and synchronous online student interaction and found that students communicating synchronously paid more attention to meaning and content than to accuracy, while those communicating asynchronously spent more time planning their answers and avoiding spelling and punctuation errors. This tendency to combine tools for different purposes appears in many of the following reports. Hauck and Lewis, for example, use blogs for student collaboration in the production of joint presentations, but they also use audioconferencing software to enable their students to socialise and interact together informally. Similarly, Chase and Alexander use videoconferencing and online discussion boards with their students in order to give them opportunities to develop spoken as well as written skills in English.

While the reports may differ significantly in many ways, many of the same key questions related to good online pedagogy appear regularly throughout the texts. These include, for example, establishing to what extent exchanges need to be integrated into the curriculum and connected with in-class training and discussion. While Hauck and Lewis found that integrating an exchange into a course does not guarantee high levels of motivation and participation, others, such as Markey, highlight the important role which the tutor still has to play in guiding students in their online interaction. Other issues that arise regularly throughout the reports include how to encourage effective learner reflection on the learning experience (through the use of diaries, questionnaires etc.) and which learning goals are particularly suited to this type of online learning.

Finally, it is worth highlighting the refreshing honesty with which the authors recount the problems, barriers and misunderstandings that characterise online student collaboration. Müller-Hartmann (2000) is rightly critical of many reports in the literature that tend to gloss over the practical problems that often characterise online interaction. In contrast, in many of the cases reported here, the authors willingly identify where their exchanges were not successful and then go on to explain how they aim to deal with these issues in the future. For example, Markey identifies the lack of chemistry between certain students as being an important cause in the failure of certain partnerships and he then describes how he has undertaken the matching of student profiles in order to avoid this problem in the second year of the exchange. Others, such as Vinagre, offer initial findings of their action research into what students felt they were learning from the exchange and what aspects of the activity need to be adapted in the future. In a complex learning activity such as online exchange, which involves many different learners and teachers working and learning together in different locations, such a reflective, action research approach (Wallace, 1998) is vital and should form an integral part of all teachers' telecollaborative methodology.

References

Müller-Hartmann, A. (2000) Wenn sich die Lehrenden nicht verstehen, wie sollen sich dann die Lernenden verstehen? Fragen nach der Rolle der Lehrenden in global vernetzten Klassenräumen. In L. Bredella, H. Christ and M.K. Legutke (eds) *Fremdverstehen zwischen Theorie und Praxis* (pp. 275–301). Tübingen: Narr.

O'Dowd, R. (2006) The use of videoconferencing and email in internet-mediated intercultural student ethnography. In J.A. Belz and S.L. Thorne (eds) *Internet-mediated Intercultural Foreign Language Education* (pp. 86–120). Boston, MA: Heinle and Heinle.

Sotillo, S.M. (2000) Discourse functions and syntactic complexity in synchronous and asynchronous communication. *Language Learning and Technology* 4 (1), 82–119. On WWW at http://llt.msu.edu/vol4num1/sotillo/.

Wallace, M.J. (1998) *Action Research for Language Teachers*. Cambridge: Cambridge University Press.

Chapter 12
Integrating Tandem Learning in Higher Education

MARGARITA VINAGRE

Introduction

The aim of this chapter is to present a summary of the findings of a year-long e-mail tandem exchange between specialist learners of English at Nebrija University in Madrid and non-specialist learners of Spanish at Trinity College Dublin during the academic year 2005–2006. While many initiatives involving e-mail exchanges as part of the foreign language learning process are set up using the International E-Mail Tandem Network, our project started with a direct agreement between the two universities. The immediate objective pursued by the parties involved was to establish a close relationship between the students of both countries, so that they could use their target language in authentic contexts and situations. We hoped this would lead to an increased awareness of what they could do with the language in the short term, which, in turn, would facilitate motivation (Vinagre, 2005; Woodin, 1997). In addition, we wanted to encourage our students to get to know and understand their counterparts' culture. The overall objective was to promote autonomy in the language learning process in order to make the students aware of the importance of being responsible for their own learning (Lewis & Walker, 2003). Given the fact that students on Spanish university courses tend to be highly dependent, we felt that encouraging and helping our students to become more autonomous was an important objective in terms of rising to the challenges which the Bologna Convergence Process entails.

Socioinstitutional Context

The approach to language learning at both universities shared certain basic features, such as emphasis on the development and use of communication skills and a focus on similar topics, which facilitated our task when it came to setting up the project. It is also worth highlighting the fact that students at both universities had access to a multimedia language learning system, which combined multimedia resources with face-to-face sessions. In addition, students were familiar with the use of new technologies, as the internet was the usual means of communicating either with their teachers (by e-mail) or with their classmates and friends (by e-mail or chat). In addition, all students at Nebrija University studied Applied Computer Science formally as part of their basic degrees.

The original group was formed by 20 Nebrija students and their Irish counterparts. The age of the learners was similar, as, with the exception of two mature students, the students were between 19 and 22 years old. Students at Nebrija majored in languages and they were required to pass a compulsory subject entitled English Language Patterns and Usage (Advanced English). This was a first year annual course and students attended lectures twice a week. In addition, work outside the class included their e-mail tandem exchange, which was considered a compulsory component of their course load and was worth 20% of their final mark.

Students at Trinity College took Spanish (intermediate) as an extra-curricular or optional subject, and they majored in Law, Engineering, Business Studies and Economics. This difference in the academic profile of the students created some problems throughout the exchange. Students at Nebrija were under pressure to work hard at their exchange and had a sense of urgency, because they wanted to perform well in order to achieve high marks. Conversely, as many as half of their partners either stopped writing when they had exams or dropped out altogether when their course load proved too stressful. This forced the author of this chapter, in her capacity as Nebrija's exchange coordinator and teacher of the subject, to look for partners in other institutions, which was not always feasible in the middle of the academic year. Furthermore, from a motivational point of view, this imbalance also had some negative effects, as students were left feeling let down and disappointed; they felt that they had put a considerable amount of effort into the exchange and that it had not paid off. What is more, they were also required to start all over again with a new partner. For all these reasons we have only included 10 students and their partners in this study, i.e. those students whose partnerships lasted throughout the entire academic year.

Objectives of the Project

As we mentioned briefly in the introduction, we had three main goals for this exchange: (a) to encourage our students to use their target language in authentic contexts and situations; (b) to encourage our students to get to know and understand their counterparts' culture; (c) to promote autonomy in the language learning process. Attaining these three objectives could be greatly facilitated by e-mail tandem language learning, as these are intrinsic aspects of this mode of learning, as we shall see below.

Tandem language learning refers to a partnership in which two people with different mother tongues work together with the purpose of learning each other's native language and learning about each other's character and culture (Little & Brammerts, 1996: 10). Thus, language learning in tandem takes place through authentic communication with a native speaker, who can support the learner in his attempts to express himself in the target language.

Moreover, tandem learning rests on two principles, the principle of reciprocity and the principle of learner autonomy (Little & Brammerts, 1996: 10). The principle of reciprocity refers to the idea of exchange and, if this exchange is to be successful, there has to be a balanced partnership in which both participants benefit equally. Thus, learners should be prepared to do as much for their partners as they expect to receive from their partners. The principle of autonomy states that tandem partners are responsible for their own learning: 'they alone [the learners] determine what they want to learn and when, and they can only expect from their partner the support that they themselves have defined and asked for' (Little & Brammerts, 1996: 11). The principle of autonomy is essential to the process of language learning, as, in order to achieve communicative efficiency in the target language, learners must have 'independence, self-reliance and self-confidence to fulfil the variety of social, psychological and discourse roles in which they are cast' (Little, 1991: 27).

Structure of the Exchange

The students at both universities were given the same general guidelines on e-mail tandem learning, which explained the importance of reciprocity and mutual help for the success of the exchange. In addition, other relevant aspects were addressed: e-mail frequency (two a week), topics to be discussed (personal and others such as customs and traditions, music, cinema and television, idioms, stereotypes, food, festivals, sports, etc) and tasks to be carried out jointly (error correction and end-of-term presentation relating to one of the tandem topics). E-mails were to be written half in English and half in Spanish and students were given specific guidelines with regard to error correction. Finally, students had to write a language learning diary in which they were to refer to their experience of the exchange, in addition to recording information about three main aspects: new vocabulary encountered, recycling of errors and cultural issues. We include the complete version of the guidelines below:

Tandem Learning by E-mail
Spanish-English
Department of Applied Languages
Dr. Margarita Vinagre

What is it?
This project consists of pairing native speakers of Spanish with native speakers of English so that they can help each other with their foreign language learning. It follows the conventions of the International E-mail Tandem Network funded by the Commission of the European Union since 1994. You can find more information about the International E-mail Tandem Network at http://www.slf.ruhr-uni-bochum.de.

Why learn a language via E-mail?
Several characteristics/aspects of e-mail make this medium ideal for language learning:

- Messages are sent and received in a matter of minutes. Communication is fast and up to date
- You have first hand access to a person who speaks the language you are studying
- Certain commands such as *Reply* or *Attach* document facilitate the exchange of corrections and other material you would like to share with your partner

Which language should you use?
It is important that both partners write in both English and Spanish. This will give you both a chance to write as well as read in the language you are learning. Reading your partner's messages in English will give you a model to follow and a feeling of how English is used by native speakers. Writing will give you a chance to put into practice what you know and discover areas in which you may have difficulties. For the same reasons your partner needs to write messages in Spanish and read your messages in Spanish too. It is therefore important that you make sure you use both languages in your e-mail exchange by taking.

What do I need for active learning?
A dictionary: Have a dictionary with you every time you write an e-mail in English. This way you will enhance your knowledge of

vocabulary by using new words/expressions different from the ones you already know.

A diary: Writing a diary about how your tandem exchange develops is essential, since it will help you evaluate how much you are learning and will allow you to make decisions regarding your own learning.

In your diary, you can write about ALL aspects concerning the exchange, but three aspects should be considered regularly and described in detail:

Vocabulary: Make note of the new words you learn, either from your partner or from the use of the dictionary.

Errors: Make note of the errors your partner corrects for you and write down a few sentences with the corrected version so that it is easier for you to avoid them in the future.

Culture: What aspects related to your partner's culture and way of life have you learned about? Compare them with your own and give your opinion briefly.

The diary must be handed in at the end of the semester since it will be used to assess your language learning progress.

What should you write about?

First, write an introductory message telling your partner about yourself and your interests. You may have common interests you want to discuss or you may want to ask your partner about several aspects of Ireland and Irish culture you would like to know more about.The following list contains activities and topics which you should note are only suggestions for what you might want to talk about with your e-mail partner.

- **Week starting October 17th**: *Getting to know each other* (2 e-mails): Where does your partner live? In what type of house? With whom? What would be a typical day in your partner's life? What does your partner usually do at weekends?
- **Weeks starting October 24th and November 1st**: *Discuss stereotypical beliefs about both countries: Spanish and Irish stereotypes* (4 e-mails). TWO e-mails to find out what the real situation is in both countries. What do you think they are like? (customs, way of life, traditions, etc.) In his/her opinion, what are Spanish people like? What does your partner think about Spanish way of life, Spanish customs and traditions, dress sense and food for example? What aspects do you have in common with your partner and in what do you differ, and to what extent is all this because of your

different nationalities and cultures? TWO e-mails to talk about one or more topics you decide to discuss together (negotiation) DON'T FORGET TO TALK ABOUT FESTIVITIES! *Halloween, El Día de Todos los Santos.*

- **Weeks starting November 7th and November 14th**: (4 e-mails). TWO e-mails at least to help your partner with *Colloquial expressions in Spanish*; he/she will do the same to help you with *English slang*. TWO e-mails to talk about one or more topics you decide to discuss together (negotiation).
- **Week starting November 21st: (2 e-mails). ONE e-mail at least:** *What do young people in Spain do when they go out?* Compare it with what they do in Ireland. ONE e-mail to talk about one or more topics you decide to discuss together (negotiation)
- **Week starting November 28th**: (2 e-mails). ONE e-mails at least to talk about *music, literature or art*. Discuss your own interests and ask about your partner's. ONE e-mail to talk about one or more topics you decide to discuss together (negotiation)
- **Weeks starting December 5th and December 12th**: (4 e-mails). TWO e-mails to talk about *Cinema. Vanilla Sky vs Abre Los Ojos* (class activities) Forum of discussion. TWO e-mails to talk about one or more topics you decide to discuss together (negotiation). DON'T FORGET TO TALK ABOUT FESTIVITIES! *El Día de la Constitución* and *La Inmaculada*. Try to find out what kind of festivities they have over there and the way they celebrate them.
- **TASK**: Discuss and prepare together the topic of your end of semester presentation. You will have to talk to the rest of class about one aspect of your choice related to Irish/British culture.
- **Week starting December 19th**: (2 e- mails). ONE e-mail to talk about *Christmas* in both countries. ONE e-mail to finish the exchange and decide whether you would like to continue writing to each other;-)

NOTE: Be polite and respectful when you express your opinion but do give your point of view and disagree when necessary. Do justify your ideas/remarks to make the exchange more interactive and productive. Be open to receive some positive criticism from your partner too! Your attitude towards the exchange should always be active; you are learning by helping someone else to learn at the same time!

Please remember to send a copy of ALL e-mails to your teacher: mvinagre@nebrija.es

How to correct your partner's writing

- Think about what you would like your partner to correct in your writing and do the same.
- Do not try to correct everything. Pick the most important mistakes (make it no more than ten), the ones that prevent understanding or sound awkward (too foreign) to you.
- Negotiate the way you are going to correct each other (using CAPITAL letters, colours, directly on the e-mails by clicking on *reply* button, etc). It is important that you come to an agreement with your partner so that you always correct each other in a manner that works for both of you.
- Write comments together with the corrections. You can ask questions or suggest other ways of expressing something.
- Remember that in order for both of you to benefit from the exchange you should both take the task of correction seriously.
- Correcting your partner's mistakes will help develop your ability to assess your own writing.
- Pay careful attention to your partner's mistakes and way of formulating things in Spanish so you can learn even more about the way English language works.
- RECYCLE ERRORS! Make sure you include some of the corrected errors in the following messages you write. If you include the errors your partner has corrected in the following e-mails you send to him/her, it is more likely that you will not make them again in the future. *This aspect is crucial for the assessment of your own learning progress.*

Taking the E-mail exchange one step further

Here are some suggestions for further work related your regular English classes once you have established contact:

- Writing essays on topics suggested above
- Discussing the topic of your oral presentation with your partner, so that you include the information you have found out
- Keep track of your own errors to ensure continued improvement
- Analyse your partner's messages in English. Review old messages

(Adapted from Appel (1999))

The role of the tutor during the exchange encompassed different aspects: She had to make sure that students wrote with the prescribed regularity, that the pre-established topics were discussed every week and that interaction between partners was at all times polite and friendly. All negotiation of meaning and solving of misunderstandings were carried out by the students themselves, except on one occasion when the tutor's intervention was required in order to explain cultural differences. In general, no action was taken regarding error correction and the tutor only intervened in order to provide assistance in the case of those students who asked for help in order to offer remediation to their partners. Finally, the content of the students' diaries and e-mails, together with some of the error corrections, were introduced into the face-to-face sessions, where they were used for further discussions on culture and grammar issues.

Outcomes of the Exchange

We administered a self-evaluation questionnaire at the beginning of the course, which was specially designed to reveal the students' knowledge and perceptions of the foreign language and culture. Some questions pertaining to their expectations regarding the exchange were also included. On the last day of class, we administered a second self-evaluation questionnaire that included open-ended questions in addition to 'yes' or 'no' type questions and was presented to the students as a tool for stimulating serious reflection and raising learner awareness. Here we include a brief sample of the data we gathered from the students' answers to some of the items in the self-evaluation questionnaires.

Students' perceived benefits of their tandem partnership included learning vocabulary (90%) and improving their writing skills (90%). They also perceived benefits in terms of increased confidence in their use of the language (100%), improvement of grammar (80%) and, to a lesser extent, oral fluency (60%). The students also mentioned that the aspects of their tandem experience that they had enjoyed and benefited from the most were 'Learning about other places, customs and cultures' (100%), 'Showing the other student my own culture and opinions' (100%) and 'The opportunity to have access to information provided by a native speaker' (100%). The item 'Learning English, especially useful vocabulary' also features prominently (90%), together with 'Helping their partner to learn' (90%) and 'Reflecting on their own mother tongue and learning process' (90%).

Besides answering these questionnaires, we asked our students to express their opinions on different aspects of the project in their diaries.

They were asked to write about those aspects they liked best, those they did not like at all, whether they thought it had been beneficial in terms of language learning and whether their perception of their partners' culture had changed. Below we include some of the students' commentaries regarding this last question:

> The truth is that Ireland was never a country that especially appealed to me, but now I see it differently. I imagine a country with very friendly people, a beautiful country with a lot of history.

> A teacher at school once told me that 'if you generalise you are always wrong', and that is what I have discovered with tandem. I have found that many of the stereotypes and preconceived ideas I had about the Irish are not true. There is more to their food than fish and chips and hamburgers, as I thought.

> I did not know any Americans before this exchange, so the only points of reference I had were films and series. Now I understand many of their forms of behaviour. Even so, I think I still need to learn more about them in order to understand them better.

> I have really changed my opinion about the Irish, because I used to think that they just went to parties, drank and had flings. They might have been at university, but they didn't study. I have realised that, in fact, we have a lot in common.

We also told students that they could suggest ways in which the e-mail exchange could be improved and comment on the how the exchange had helped them. Some students replied as follows:

> The only way I can really think to improve the enjoyment of the exchanges, is to make the guidelines a little less strict. If you were to stick with demanding two per week, make only one of them about a mandatory topic. I think this might make the exchanges a bit more personal, and create a bit more motivation to complete them.

> I think it was very effective in cultivating conversation style, and new vocabulary. We had a lot of things to talk about and write about

> I feel like I increased my confidence in writing and speaking as the semester went by. [...] It forced me to be creative to express what I feel and think of the topics we talked about.

It helped me to learn a lot more about Spanish people and their cultura, and it was nice to know that I was helping someone else to expand their horizons as well.

The students' perceptions as to whether they had achieved objectives (a) and (b) of the exchange were overwhelmingly positive. They clearly felt that they had used their target language authentically and that they had learned about their partners' culture. With regard to objective (c), we felt that the development of learner autonomy pervaded the entire learning process and, therefore, it greatly facilitated the attainment of the previous two objectives. The students' perceptions were actually quite accurate, as the final marks of those students taking part in the project showed a clear improvement in the development of their writing skills, higher confidence in their use of the foreign language and a greater knowledge of the foreign culture.

Plans for the Future

In addition to continuing with the e-mail exchange already established with Trinity College Dublin, we expect to open up two more exchanges with institutions abroad that will allow a higher number of under-graduate students to take part in telecollaborative projects. Furthermore, postgraduate students who specialise as teachers of Spanish as a foreign language at Nebrija University will be trained to incorporate collabora-tive learning via the internet into their teaching approaches and methodologies. Finally, in addition to e-mail, we intend to introduce the use of Moodle and Wikies as other alternatives to learning languages on the web.

References

Lewis, T. and Walker, L. (eds) (2003) *Autonomous Language Learning in Tandem*. Sheffield: Academy Electronic Publications.

Little, D. (1991) *Learner Autonomy 1: Definitions, Issues and Problems*. Dublin: Authentik.

Little, D. and Brammerts, H. (eds) (1996) *A Guide to Language Learning in Tandem via the Internet*. CLCS Occasional Paper No. 46. Dublin: Trinity College, Centre for Language and Communication Studies.

Vinagre, M. (2005) Fostering language learning via e-mail: An English–Spanish exchange. *Computer Assisted Language Learning* 18 (5), 369–388.

Woodin, J. (1997) Email tandem learning and the communicative curriculum. *ReCALL* 9, 22–33.

Chapter 13
The Tridem Project

MIRJAM HAUCK and TIM LEWIS

Introduction

Telecollaboration takes many forms. This account of work in progress describes a project that has a number of particular features, one of which is identified in its name. It links learners from *three* different parts of the world in a so-called *Tridem*. It was inspired by a number of earlier collaborations. One of us was a founder member of the EU-funded International Email Tandem Network, co-ordinated throughout the 1990s by Helmut Brammerts, of *Ruhr-Universität Bochum*, who was a regular practitioner of such three-way exchanges (see Brammerts, 2003). The other took part in a more recent tripartite telecollaborative project, involving students of German from the UK and Australia and mother tongue informants from *Friedrich Schiller Universität Jena*, which yielded important insights into the factors that influence the success of synchronous online language learning (see Hampel *et al.*, 2005).

Another quite singular aspect of the Tridem project was its use of *Lyceum*, a piece of synchronous audiographic conferencing software developed in house by the Open University's Knowledge Media Institute, which is now a standard means of delivering language courses in our institution. In the Tridem project students of French in the UK and the US worked online with native speakers in France synchronously in *Lyceum* and asynchronously in weblogs to complete several collaborative tasks. Meetings covered a period of over 10 weeks in autumn 2005. In addition to the oral, written and graphic output produced in *Lyceum*, project outcomes took the form of several collaborative blogs.

Socioinstitutional Context

The project brought together 5 adult learners of French from the Open University (UK), 10 campus-based students of French from Carnegie Mellon University (USA) and 10 French native speakers enrolled on a Masters' programme in Open and Distance Learning (Master FOAD) at the *Université de Franche Comté* (Besançon, France). While, for the second and third groups of learners, participation in the Tridem project was closely linked to course work and assessment, Open University learners took part voluntarily. The project team comprised seven academics – six of which took part as tutors and researchers, and one as a researcher only – from all three institutions.

Although the French and American students had to be trained in the use of *Lyceum*, all participants could be described as ICT-literate and access to the internet was not an issue. The majority, however, had never before contributed to a blog – and certainly not for language learning purposes. Most took part both in the formal and informal synchronous online sessions and posted contributions to their blogs from the comfort of their own home or student accommodation. The Carnegie-Mellon students, whose formal *Lyceum*-based sessions were scheduled alongside their language classes, also had access to a computer lab. A lab was available too at the *Université de Franche Comté*, though normal practice at Besançon is to encourage learners to work at a distance both from their tutor and one another. Open University participants invariably took part from home.

In several other respects, however, including age, ethnicity and life experience, the mix of project participants was extremely varied. Those at Carnegie-Mellon University were first-year students from a range of ethnic backgrounds, studying French at beginners' level and with relatively little experience of travel outside the USA. Their youth and relatively low level of proficiency in spoken French placed them at a distinct disadvantage in Lyceum sessions, where they often struggled to express themselves in their second language. The Besançon students, all graduates with a professional interest in the use of ICT for educational purposes, were most at home in online environments, confident and ready users of both *Lyceum* and blogger.com. They were also largely fluent in English. The Open University learners, while not all practised *Lyceum* users (some had to be sent the software), were – as volunteers – uniformly well motivated. Older than both their French and American counterparts, and largely familiar with France and the French way of life, they put their life experience to good use. In particular, they were a good deal more autonomous than their American partners and seemed to be prepared to relax and enjoy the project, of which their evaluations were unanimously positive. Our experience suggests that it is in fact possible, though not unproblematic, to bring together learners with different aims and motivations in a successful shared experience. More difficult to accommodate than disparities of age or motivation are learners who lack any grounding in autonomy or self-management.

Objectives of the Project

Pedagogically, the aim of the project was to break away from the standard pattern of bipartite intercultural exchange, which risks becoming a kind of confrontation between two groups of participants, with a consequent hardening of stereotypes. With a more complex mix of participants we wanted to attempt a more dynamic, comparative approach to intercultural encounter. Adopting the precept enunciated by J.G. Christensen, that all intercultural encounters are initially interpersonal, the participants' learning goals were framed as follows. As well as interpersonal and intercultural objectives, they included linguistic and reflective ones.

- Get to know your partners and their immediate and wider environment.
- Think about points of comparison between their cultures and your own.
- Use your foreign language (French or English).
- Help both your partners to practise their foreign language (correct their errors, suggest words and phrases).
- Create a final project that reflects the work done during the exchange.

In research terms, partners had a number of objectives, as one would expect of such a large team. Broadly speaking, however, our aim was to study the relationship between the affordances of synchronous and asynchronous multimodal environments and their impact on:

- learner interaction,
- the development of intercultural competence and
- learner experience and self-management strategies.

Our research design was corpus-based and non-intrusive combining both quantitative and qualitative methods of analysis. We operated to a research protocol jointly agreed among all three partner institutions. Our prime aim was to assemble a comprehensive body of recorded data through:

- pre- and post-treatment questionnaires,
- post-treatment semi-structured interviews,
- screen data capture (using CAMTASIA),
- audio recordings (*Lyceum*),

- log files (*Lyceum*) and
- student production (in blogs and *Lyceum*).

Methodological Approach and Learning Environments

The project adopted the principle established in Tandem learning, of encouraging dual language use (50% English/50% French) and the reciprocal correction of errors. The syllabus devised for the exchange was broadly task-based. First of all learners were given instructions on how to prepare for *Lyceum* sessions. Below are the preparatory instructions for *Lyceum* session 1, which was essentially an icebreaking activity.

Session 1

Task 1 (Preparing for the session)

Before we meet in *Lyceum* think about how you will present yourself to your new partners. What do you want them to know about you? For example, consider these possibilities:

- what you like to do in your free time
- what you study and why
- where you study
- where you work
- something about your family
- what is important to you.

Secondly, because time in the synchronous *Lyceum* environment was both limited and precious, learners were advised in advance about what they would be expected to do during the session:

Task 2 (During the session)

Bring with you to the session something that shows who you are, for example:

- a picture of your favourite place
- a picture of your favourite person
- a quote that means a lot to you
- a symbol of what or where you want to be in the future
- if you met your exchange partners by accident on the street, how would they recognize you?

Thirdly, the variable language level of the different groups of participants made it advisable to offer some advice about the language they might need to use in specific sessions. These instructions again relate to Session 1:

Ask your partners questions, for example:

- Where are you from?/*D'où tu viens?*
- What do you do for fun?/*Qu'est-ce que tu fais pour t'amuser?*
- What do you study?/*Tu étudies quelle matière?*
- Where do you study?/*Où tu étudies?*
- Do you work?/*Tu travailles?*
- What do you do?/*Qu'est-ce que tu fais comme travail?*

In addition to its intercultural and linguistic aspects, the project was also aimed at familiarising learners with different online environments. As researchers we were particularly curious to see how well our learners would use these and how they would interact in them. To test this, at least one task was set per session which required them to make use of the specific affordances of either *Lyceum* or their blog. For example, their instructions for Session 2 were as follows.

Session 2

Describe to your partners where you live. Pick your favourite room where you live. Can you take a digital picture of this room to upload onto the blog and eventually into *Lyceum*?

Another aspect of the project – as indeed of Tandem learning – was its emphasis on collaboration and negotiation. While the former has its roots in Vygotskian ideas on socially constructed learning, the latter owes more to interactionist SLA theory, in particular as articulated by Gass, Varonis and Long (see, for example, Gass, 2003, Gass & Varonis, 1994, Long, 1996). One example of the impact this had on task design may be discerned in the following set of instructions.

Final Writing Task

1) Discuss and **agree** with your partners what are:

- the three things you liked the most about working in Tridem
- the three things you found most difficult about working in Tridem

Post a short **joint** account of them in the Blog.

Lastly, there is a tradition at the OU of encouraging reflection by online learners as a means of making the learning process more effective (see, for example, Lamy & Goodfellow, 1999). This is embodied in the following task instructions:

Final Writing Task
2) Also in the Blog, write your own personal evaluation of the different ways of working (synchronous/asynchronous; oral/written; mother tongue/foreign language; *Lyceum* Tridem; *Lyceum* plenary; Blog)

Structure of the Exchange

During a two-week 'warm-up period' the Tridems – made up of groups of three or four learners – were established, the blogs for each Tridem were created and invitations to join the blogs sent to the members of each group. Everybody was encouraged to use the basic blog functionalities (simple written entries, written entries inviting feedback in the form of entry-specific comments, pictures with text or captions) in order to get to know each other. Concurrently, two initial tutor-led online meetings took place at each of the participating institutions focusing on technical training in order to give the learners the opportunity to 'play' with the various tools in *Lyceum* and to get a 'feel' for their affordances.

In Weeks 3–9 all participants engaged in a series of collaborative tasks using their blogs to produce a presentation on their immediate (e.g. student accommodation, family home, etc.) and wider environment (e.g. facilities used during leisure time activities) and its distinctive features. During this period they also used *Lyceum*, in five timetabled tutor-led sessions to monitor progress, and in a few smaller, informal meetings to negotiate their blog activities and/or to simply socialise. The task design moved from closed to open subtasks incorporating further familiarisation with the affordances of two very different multimodal online learning contexts. As we have seen, in Week 10 the students were asked to complete their work by posting brief individual and collective evaluations of the project in the blog.

Outcomes

Analysis of the copious data generated by the exchange is in progress. It will be some time before rigorous conclusions can be published. But there is broad consensus about some of the lessons learnt. Firstly, while synchronous computer-mediated communication tools (e.g. chat, audio-, audiographic- and videoconferencing) enable students to establish direct real-time contact with native-speaker learning partners, asynchronous virtual spaces (e.g. blogs and wikis) also have significant advantages. They are both pedagogical and practical:

- they offer learners more time for reflective activities based on co-publishing;
- they give learners freedom to work in their own time, which is especially important if there is a significant time difference between participating locations;
- by allowing learners to work offline and at their own pace, they can accommodate different levels of second language proficiency; and
- once set up, they require no timetabling by the project organisers.

Thus the blogs enjoyed overall greater popularity among the participants. The UK participants emerged as the most active members in the asynchronous environment with three out of five posting not only to their own Tridem partners but also to other project blogs. This was unexpected as they had originally been closer to *Lyceum* than their counterparts – their 'natural' tuition environment at the British Open University. Figure 13.1 shows the number of messages sent by UK students overall.

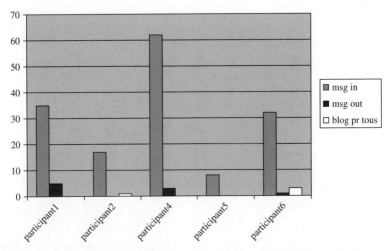

Figure 13.1 Number of messages posted to own blog (blue) and other blogs (purple) by Open University students (Audras & Chanier, 2006)
Note: Initially 6 OU students took part in the exchange. Participant 3 dropped out two weeks into the project.

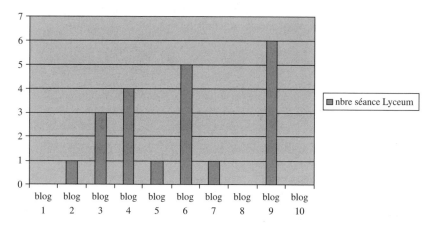

Figure 13.2 Number of informal *Lyceum* sessions per blog (Audras & Chanier, 2006)

Participants mentioned lack of time as the main reason for having failed to organise and/or to participate regularly in informal synchronous gatherings:

> I didn't have as much time to put towards the meetings as some of the other members did because of my other classes. Since some of them were in their 50's and had a good amount of time to spend I always felt like I wasn't doing enough. I think if we had had more meetings I would have felt more like part of a group. (US participant)

Figure 13.2 shows that only a few blog partners took the opportunity to use the audiographic conferencing system for informal 'coffee house' or 'virtual pub' type of meetings.

Preliminary findings from our study also indicate that embedding a telecollaborative project in an existing university course does not necessarily guarantee a high level of student participation and may even have an adverse effect on learner motivation. Our American learners, who undertook the project in class time, as part of an accredited course of study, were least assiduous both in attending *Lyceum* sessions and making posts to blogs.

Future Plans

We have now been fortunate enough to receive British Academy funding to reiterate the Tridem project, with a fourth partner, the

Université de Genève. In the light of the experience reported above, the following modifications have been made:

- the asynchronous environment (three- and four-person collaborative blogs) has become central to the project, with synchronous audiographic conferencing being used for three plenary sessions, for sharing of experiences more widely;
- synchronous sessions are no longer timetabled in class time;
- each Tridem blog has an individual tutor/moderator;
- a process-based syllabus, using Byram's five intercultural savoirs has replaced last year's task-based syllabus;
- course documents are available online, in a modified version of the *Dokeos* virtual learning environment; and
- this year's learners have been selected to ensure a more homogeneous level of second language proficiency

References

Audras, I. and Chanier, T. (2006) Tridem et interaction à l'oral et à l'écrit dans une formation à distance en langue. 'Technologies de l'Information et de la Communication pour l'Enseignement supérieur et l'Entreprise 2006'. Toulouse. On WWW at http://archive-edutice.ccsd.cnrs.fr/edutice-00087737. Accessed 3.11.06.

Brammerts, H. (2003) Autonomous language learning in tandem: the development of a concept. In T. Lewis and L. Walker (eds) *Autonomous Language Learning in Tandem* (pp. 27–36). Sheffield, UK: Academy Electronic Press.

Byram, M. (1997) *Teaching and Assessing Intercultural Communicative Competence*. Clevedon: Multilingual Matters.

Gass, S.M. (2003) Input and interaction. In C. Doughty and M. Long (eds) *The Handbook of Second Language Acquisition* (pp. 239–240). Oxford: Blackwell.

Gass, S.M. and Varonis, E.M. (1994) Input, interaction, and second language production. *Studies in Second Language Acquisition* 16, 283–302.

Hampel, R., Felix, U., Hauck, M. and Coleman, J. (2005) Complexities of learning and teaching languages in a real-time audiographic environment. *GFL-German as a foreign language* 3, 1–30. On WWW at http://www.gfl-journal.de/3-2005/hampel_felix_hauck_coleman.html.

Lamy, M.-N. and Goodfellow, R. (1999) Reflective conversation in the virtual language classroom. *Language Learning & Technology* 2 (2), 43–61. On WWW at http://llt.msu.edu/vol2num2/article2/.

Long, M.H. (1996) The role of the linguistic environment in second language acquisition. In W.C. Ritchie and T.K. Bhatia (eds) *Handbook of Second Language Acquisition* (pp. 413–468). London & San Diego: Academic Press.

Chapter 14

The Japan–Korea Culture Exchange Project

CHRISTOPHER CHASE and PAUL ALEXANDER

Introduction

Initiated in the autumn of 2004, the JKCE Project is an ongoing English language programme that has been using computer-mediated communication (CMC) technologies to connect university students from Korea and Japan. Although their countries are next-door neighbours, there has been very little communication going on between citizens of the two nations, until very recently. Now, with growing interest in cross-cultural ties between Japan and Korea (i.e. movies, music, travel, food, etc.), we believe the timing is right for educators to promote greater cultural awareness and understanding through online student interactions, using English as a medium for communication.

Socioinstitutional Context

Most young people studying English as a foreign language in Eastern Asia lack real opportunities to actually use the language for cross-cultural communication, unless they travel or study abroad. With highly competitive college entrance exams as the primary focus of their studies, there is very little emphasis on developing students' English communication skills. After graduating from high school, most students feel that English is something academic and abstract, impossible to master or incredibly boring. Accordingly, most university students feel uncomfortable with English, especially when using the language to communicate.

Fortunately, online social networks are now becoming extremely popular with young people in both Korea and Japan (Cashmore, 2006), thereby allowing them to become quite familiar and comfortable with CMC technologies. While videoconferencing is something new for them, most of our project participants have computers in their homes, and have already used chat rooms, e-mail and message boards to communicate in their native language, online.

Objectives of the Project

Keeping the background of our students in mind, we decided (Chase & Alexander, 2006) to focus on creating communication opportunities that they could enjoy, that would allow them to use English to converse informally, to build friendships if possible and learn more about one another's cultural background and interests. Taking an approach consistent with the principles of communicative language teaching (Brown, 2001), we attempted to create opportunities for cross-cultural social interaction that would be authentic, meaningful, collaborative, learner-centred, as well as content- and task-based. For many of our students this would be their first opportunity to actually get to know something about the lives of their closest neighbours, to make attempts to communicate with real people from across the sea.

We wanted to use the simplest and most user-friendly technologies possible, so that our programme would be inexpensive, and if successful, easily replicated. From the start we decided that we would try a 'dual mode' approach, providing both videoconferencing and text-based communication opportunities for students. It was important for us to provide them with chances to use all 4 language skills – reading, writing, speaking and listening – so that their experiences would have a pedagogical purpose, and utility.

Furthermore, as our students were coming from two cultures that had a history of animosity in the past century, we did not feel that it was appropriate for us to probe too deeply into sensitive areas of culture or history during our initial exchanges. Helping students to develop feelings of friendship, closeness and trust were our top priorities.

Structure of the Exchange

We began the project in the autumn of 2004, with a small group of volunteers, four from each side. We each equipped our Windows-based laptops with Logitech web cameras and installed MSN Messenger, an instant messaging programme. We conducted all our weekly videoconferencing sessions during lunch hours, from multimedia classrooms at our schools. We also set up an online discussion forum, using Moodle's course management system, where the Japanese and Korean students were able to meet after school, to discuss topics that interested them. Hence, students would be provided with both live (synchronous) videoconferencing and delayed in time (asynchronous) text-based communications opportunities.

We experienced a mixture of success and challenges during the first semester. The students thoroughly enjoyed using the text-based discussion forums to communicate in English and learn about one another. Our initial efforts were not as successful, however, in terms of live videoconferencing. The MSN messaging program did not always work well, especially for audio. This meant that while we were able to see each other we could not hear our partners on the other side. We frequently had to write messages back and forth, using the Instant Messaging software. While students actually enjoyed the experience, it was a bit tiring for the teachers, who were doing the typing!

In March of 2005, we decided to experiment with MacIntosh computers (using iSight cameras and the iChat application) to conduct videoconference sessions. The improvement in terms of quality and reliability was substantial. With the MacIntosh computers the video images moved faster and the sound was crisp and clear. As teachers, we found ourselves using the technology frequently, from our homes and offices, to collaborate and plan new lessons.

We moved the student videoconferences into our offices, making them easier to set up and schedule. Each week we provided participants with a topic or theme to discuss both during the videoconferences and in the forum. For our final videoconference session, gift boxes were exchanged between the two groups, and opened simultaneously. The students reported that they greatly enjoyed sharing this experience together, discovering foreign snacks, soft drinks, photos, CDs and small cultural items such as fans and statues, sent to them by their international neighbours. While such experiences may not seem important from an educational viewpoint, for members of high context cultures like the Japanese and Koreans (Hall, 1976), these kinds of informal small group gatherings and gift exchanges may be essential for developing feelings of closeness and trust.

Since the spring of 2006 we have gradually expanded the number of participants and the scope of our video chats, in what O'Dowd (2006) would refer to as a shift from desktop (intimate one-on-one or small group exchanges) to classroom-based (much larger group-to-group) videoconferencing. In unison with these videoconferences, the use of online message boards is proving to be essential, with student-initiated threads allowing for a much more sophisticated and intimate level of communication outside of the classroom.

With a total of about 50 students we have numerous text-based conversations going throughout the week (asynchronously), all of them in English. Students are communicating about life in their cities, posting links to Korean, Japanese and Western music at YouTube, writing about sports, sharing photos of favourite foods, movie actors and other topics that interest them.

While the main exchanges in English are occurring through writing, our students are using the kinds of vocabulary and phrases that they would need to use if speaking with each other. Again, most of them report that they are very pleased to have this opportunity to communicate with their closest international neighbours, as well as experience English as something enjoyable and useful.

Outcomes of the Exchange

While we began with the intention of using a 'dual mode' approach, over time we have expanded this goal to utilise as many different communication modes, methods and technologies as we could, to find what worked best, and what the students would be most comfortable with. We feel our newfound approach is reflective of recent conclusions of Al-Jarf (2006), who has examined various studies and believes that the integration of different forms of technology (such as e-mail, audio- and videoconferencing, webpage design, culture portfolios, online newspapers and chat rooms) in the teaching of a target culture to EFL college students can result in significant gains in learners' cultural knowledge and positive attitudes toward that culture. In our case, although English is the language and culture we are teaching to our students, this project is giving our students the opportunity to use the language to learn about a non-English culture as well.

In terms of technology, we believe that a 'multimodal' approach to communication is optimal, allowing for a mix of synchronous and asynchronous situations, hi and lo technologies, written, visual and oral forms of communication. While our message board provides the heart of communications, this semester we are experimenting more with our Moodle chat rooms, and have initiated a special chat time in the evenings, and on the weekends. Many students seem to enjoy the live and informal nature of synchronous 'chat', so we hope to make further creative use of that in the future.

It should also be mentioned that we ourselves participated in most of the videoconferences and quite a few of the online discussions. The extra time we spent communicating with our students outside of class allowed us to get to know them better. This in turn had an impact on our classroom interactions, leading to more frequent and informal conversations than we would normally have with students. The collaborative nature of the project created a special bond or 'community of practice' of sorts, connecting all of us, in a way that is hard to put into words.

Plans for the Future

We each hope to get at least 20 of the computers in our computer rooms equipped with web cameras and headsets, so that we can try to replicate our successful office videoconferencing exchanges, with larger groups, during class time. Having individual computers equipped this way will allow students to do videoconferencing and/or live chat (text-based) with one another, individually or in 'pairs of pairs', which is what we found to be the optimal situation for synchronous communication. We also have plans to create an 'alumni' forum, where students may continue their cross-cultural interactions after their semester has finished.

One caveat worth noting: ideally we would like to set up future video communications among the students themselves with MacIntosh's iChat application, but that may not be financially possible at the present time. Hence, we may have to experiment again with free audio–video applications such as MSN Messenger, Yahoo, Skye, Red5, or perhaps even attempt communication with another proprietary system, such as Flash Media Server.

Finally, we are also looking around for a third (and perhaps even fourth) partner, in a neighbouring nation. Fifty students in a forum is working rather nicely; what would happen if we expanded that to 75 or 100, inviting a class of Chinese, Russians, Indonesians or Australians to join us? We intend to keep experimenting, until we discover what works best, which we would define as cross-cultural communication experiences that are not too difficult for teachers to implement, pedagogically grounded, challenging and satisfying to our students.

References

Al-Jarf, R. (2006) Cross-cultural communication: Saudi, Ukraine, and Russian Students On-line. *The Asian EFL Journal Quarterly* 8 (2), 7–32.

Brown, H.D. (2001) *Teaching by Principles: An Interactive Approach to Language Pedagogy*. Upper White Plains, NY: Pearson Education.

Cashmore, P. (2006) Mixi, Japan's Biggest Social Network. On WWW at http://mashable.com/2006/07/08/mixi-japans-biggest-social-network/. Accessed 5.11.06.

Chase, C. and Alexander, P. (2006) *Using the Internet to Connect Students Globally*. Presentation made at the 33rd annual meeting of the Japanese Association of Language Teachers. 4 November 2006, Kitakyushu, Japan.

Hall, E. (1976) *Beyond Culture*. New York: Anchor Books.

O'Dowd, R. (2006) The use of videoconferencing and email in internet-mediated intercultural student ethnography. In J.A. Belz and S.L. Thorne (eds) *Internet-mediated Intercultural Foreign Language Education* (pp. 86–120). Boston, MA: Heinle and Heinle.

Chapter 15

Using the Moodle Platform in Online Exchanges

ALFRED MARKEY

Introduction

Since the academic year 2004–2005 the Department of Filología Moderna at the University of León has been using the Moodle virtual learning environment (VLE) as a key component of its courses, with the platform permitting the storage of online course elements and easy student access to this material. The strengths of Moodle are particularly that it is open source, it is very adaptable to the necessities of both learners and teachers, as well as being both free to install and easy to use. Based on a series of 'learning blocks' containing activities and resources, tutors may add weblinks, Office documents, Hot Potatoes activities, sound files or pictures. Also, it is especially adaptable for the needs of online student exchanges, facilitating discussion forums, chats and wikis. Tutors can closely monitor all of these, set assignment deadlines, check out students' complete log-in history and even avail of a grading facility.

The adoption of the VLE Moodle by the department of Modern Philology at the University of León formed part of the department's increasing development of research in the area of CALL, leading in turn to the research project 'Telecollaboration in the Teaching of Foreign Languages', financed since 2005 by the regional authority the 'Junta de Castilla y León'. This present study forms part of the aforementioned project and is a continuation of the Moodle platform exchange established in the academic year 2004/2005 by Robert O'Dowd and Martha Blumberg of Barnard College, New York.

Socioinstitutional Context

The University of León is a multidiscipline, public university, which draws its student base from the local area, whereas Barnard College is a private, liberal arts institution affiliated to the Ivy-League Columbia University. Barnard has a mainly female student body drawn from all

264

over the USA, and in some cases from abroad, with the result that ethnically and geographically the participating group was notably more heterogeneous than its partner group at León, although both were broadly similar in terms of age and life experience. Students from both centres were in their first year and had some limited previous experience of Moodle, those from León having already familiarised themselves with the basic functioning of the platform in other first-year courses. All students were ICT-literate and internet access was mostly unproblematic. In each case the exchange formed an integral part of course work.

The Spanish course was just one of a broad range of subjects being undertaken by the American students at Barnard while, for those at León, the English language course was the core element of their degree. Additionally, the latter group's level of English was upper-intermediate, students having, in most cases, studied it for several years, whereas their counterparts had acquired a lower-intermediate standard of Spanish over a much shorter period. In most cases this difference in level proved unimportant as both the high degree of motivation of the Barnard group and a dual language approach ensured the imbalance was compensated for, with relatively effective communication being achieved.

Objectives of the Project

The primary objective of the project was to permit direct, sustained and structured interaction with native speakers of the students' target language. The exchange would thus facilitate an authentic context in which students could develop their language skills as well as providing a framework within which the potential benefits of autonomous learning habits could be readily appreciated. Further to this, students could benefit particularly through the reciprocal correction of errors, as well as being given the opportunity to deepen their knowledge of the target culture.

Emphasis was placed on the need to respect the principle of reciprocity. In other words, students were to take particular care to address the needs of their partners as well as using the exchange for their own benefit. Both dual language use and the reciprocal correction of errors were emphasised as fundamentally important in this respect, but so too was the need to develop a personal rapport with the chosen partner. It was stressed that where set tasks were established it was important for students to duly complete the tasks within the parameters outlined, particularly as their partners' intervention would often be dependent on their prior participation. Sensitivity to sociolinguistic factors such as attentiveness and politeness was highlighted, with students being made aware that the exchange was far more likely to be successful, and the benefit accruing considerably greater, if their partner was made to feel respected and his or her needs attended to.

Structure of the Exchange

Students were instructed to use both English and Spanish with a recommended target of 200 words in each language suggested per post. A set task was to be completed although further initiative could freely be taken. A limited selection of each partner's errors was to be corrected but students were encouraged not to be over rigorous in this area. It was emphasised that the key focus was to be on fluency and on effective interaction with partners, and it was also established that in the case of the students at León, participation, but not content, would go towards end-of-year evaluation.

The chief themes around which the interchange would be based were first a personal introduction followed by subsequent posts on St. Valentine's Day customs, the Oscars ceremony, each student's home-town and stereotypes, particularly of the nations of the participants – the fact that some of the students were neither Spanish nor American led to some fruitful exchanges of opinion in this area.

The exchange was initiated on February 15 and ended in early May. A total of 57 students took part, 19 from León and 38 from Barnard College, which meant that on average each student from León had two partners. Initially the planned number of posts per student was 8, but this was subsequently reduced to 6 for reasons that are outlined below.

Outcomes of the Exchange

The first online session brought some difficulties due to micro-level environmental factors. For example, lack of awareness of the time-limit function on the Moodle discussion forums meant that some students lost their initial compositions, leading to evident frustration. In addition, not all of the students had access to an individual computer unit, with the result that where more than one student worked together each did not have time to complete a full message and consequently the initial posts were in some cases joint-authored, leading to some complication later as the recipient replied to the two students together rather than to the designated partner. This delayed somewhat the development of a working relationship with the chosen partner and, given the exchange was so short, meant that in some cases the relationship never developed to a fruitful level. Also some of the students who participated in the first online session were less motivated students who had previously failed the subject and who after the initial contact failed to continue the exchange, so requiring a restructuring of the partnerships. As well as these first-day difficulties, a further problem arose with regards to the coordination of posts in relation to the Barnard students' Spring Break and León's Easter Week. We had factored these in but found that it was not enough to take into account the days of actual holidays alone as there was a period of inactivity both before and after these, with the result that we were forced to revise our initial target of 8 posts per student.

As for the degree of participation, we found that of the partnerships established approximately 40% of the students posted 5, 6 or more times to each partner, 40% approximately posted 3 or 4 times, with the remaining 20% making two or fewer posts. On examining the reasons for this considerable variation, we have found that in the latter category the evident failures occurred where the basic parameters of the exchange were not respected, such as the need to use both languages evenly, post punctually and carry out the set tasks. It was clear that students were unwilling to put the effort in when it became evident that this wasn't being corresponded, particularly when they realised they could invest their efforts more profitably in other more accommodating partners. Another striking conclusion was that the degree of compatibility with regards to personal character and interests was a major determinant of success. In one notable case a participant who plainly failed to follow the basic criteria managed to 'lose' two exchange partners as a result, but successfully sought out another with whom the degree of compatibility was so great that the partner was willing to overlook the cavalier attitude to the exchange guidelines. Elsewhere, there were others who struggled with unsympathetic partners and good practice was clearly not enough to make the exchange really effective, to give it a dynamic of its own.

As for the more successful cases, it seems that off-task initiative greatly enhances and solidifies the partnerships, and above all it becomes apparent that sensitivity to sociolinguistic variables such as attentiveness, politeness and the use of compliments is paramount. Where positive face needs are duly attended to, the exchange will likely succeed, whereas loss of positive face, it would appear, means loss of a profitable exchange.

Plans for the Future

Evidently some of the problems were due to lack of experience on my own part and for this current academic year – 2006–2007 – a similar

Moodle exchange has been set up, again involving first-year students at León and Barnard, but in this case I have taken a number of initiatives designed to counteract some of the problems outlined above. Of particular interest has been the attempt to avoid the sort of character clash we found hampered the development of some of the partnerships. To this end, participating students were requested to submit a brief personal profile indicating key interests, and partnerships were established according to compatibility in this respect. Initial indications are that this has been a notable success although, evidently, any conclusions are as of yet premature. In addition, the first contact session with the León students consisted of initial familiarisation with the platform and a relatively thorough 'coaching session' designed to highlight some of the pitfalls referred to above and to promote the effective practices evident in the more successful partnerships (see O'Dowd, 2005 for more on training student in online interaction skills). Students only posted for the first time after this session, at their convenience, so avoiding the problems that arose before due to doubling up on the facilities. As well as these first steps, both tutors have established that a more hands-on approach is appropriate, so the intention is to monitor closely the evolution of the exchange and to intervene more actively where difficulties become apparent. Progress will be gauged through group feedback, individual interviews and periodic questionnaires. Outcomes will be reflected in a researcher's reflexive journal and it is hoped that the modest success of this first exchange can be built on.

References

Franklin, S. and Peat, M. (2001) Managing change: The use of mixed delivery modes to increase learning opportunities. *Australian Journal of Educational Technology* 17 (1). On WWW at http://www.ascilite.org.au/ajet/ajet17/franklin.html.

O'Dowd, R. (2005) Telecollaboration: What teachers and students need to know. *IATEFL CALL Review* November, 32–35.

Chapter 16

Voice Chats in the Intercultural Classroom: The ABC's Online Project

EVA WILDEN

Introduction

This chapter reports on the *ABC's Online* project, a bilingual intercultural online exchange that was carried out with foreign language teachers from September to December 2004. Although the participants in this project were language teachers, the basic structure of the exchange could easily be adapted to other educational settings, e.g. secondary or tertiary foreign language courses. The project adapts the model of the *ABC's of Cultural Understanding and Communication* (Schmidt, 1998; Schmidt & Finkbeiner, 2006) – a successful model for intercultural learning and teaching, which so far has been used almost exclusively in face-to-face settings – to the demands of telecollaboration. The implementation of voice chat technology to the intercultural setting is a further innovative aspect of the *ABC's Online* project since voice chats have so far mainly been used for distance foreign language teaching (Hampel & Hauck, 2004). In the following the background and structure of the *ABC's Online* exchange will be sketched out, as well as preliminary outcomes of the project.

The Socioinstitutional Context of the *ABC's Online* Project

The participants in this project were 13 foreign language teachers in Germany and Great Britain. Most of them were secondary school teachers who joined the project as part of their in-service teacher training. However, some of them were – at the time of the *ABC's Online* exchange – in the process of doing their initial teacher training in a Post Graduate Certificate in Education (PGCE) programme at an English university. The participants were aged between 22 and 51 years.

The participants' prior knowledge about computers and their experience in using online communication tools were very diverse. All of them owned a personal computer, however two did not have internet access at home. Some of the teacher trainees in England used their university's computer labs to participate in the project. The participants had 2–24 years' experience of using computers. In a questionnaire completed prior to the *ABC's Online* project, the statement 'I know a lot about computers' was rated as follows: One teacher fully disagreed, four somewhat disagreed, two teachers somewhat agreed and four teachers fully agreed. Except for one teacher, none of the participants had ever used voice chats before. Five of them had used text chats before the project and seven had experience using online forums.

Objectives of the *ABC's Online* Project

The objectives of the project were (a) to familiarise the teachers with the *ABC's* model (Schmidt, 1998; Schmidt & Finkbeiner, 2006), (b) to promote their professional and personal development with regard to their intercultural competence and (c) to further their computer literacy.

The *ABC's* model is a successful method for intercultural learning and teaching. It is based on the guiding principle 'Know thyself and understand others' and thus takes up the idea that learning about other cultures always implies becoming aware of one's own cultural background. The basic structure of the *ABC's* model is very simple: (1) Participants first write an autobiography about key life events and important experiences they have had. This first step fosters an awareness of one's own cultural identity, of personal beliefs and attitudes that underlie one's behaviour and customs. (2) The second step consists of several interviews in which participants question a person with a different cultural background about his or her life. On the basis of these interviews, they write a biography about their interview partner. (3) Finally, in the third step the participants study their own autobiography and the biography about their partner, charting a list of cross-cultural similarities and differences. Furthermore, they write an analysis of the cultural differences and similarities they found and critically reflect upon the exchange with their interview partner. This final step of the *ABC's* model is the most important one as it encourages reflection and appreciation of cultural differences and ideally helps participants to develop a new perspective.

In the *ABC's Online* project this model was adapted to the demands of telecollaboration. A more detailed description of this adaptation can be found in Wilden (2006). The two most important changes will be presented as follows: (1) The participants completed an introductory phase before the actual start of the *ABC's* exchange. In this step they familiarised themselves with the online communication tools available in the project (see below). Also, they got in touch with each other and introduced themselves without talking (or writing) about the very personal topics of the *ABC's* right from the start. In any online exchange project this phase is of crucial importance due to the lack of face-to-face interaction. It facilitates the development of confidence and a sense of community. Moreover, it is advisable to have participants acquaint themselves with the online communication tools in order to eliminate any inhibitions or insecurities that might arise when someone has no prior experience with them. (2) Communication and collaboration in the *ABC's Online* project were done exclusively online. The most important online communication tool in the project was the voice chat (see below) where participants 'met up' to talk about their respective life stories. Besides, they composed their *ABC's* texts (autobiography, biography and comparison) in a word processor in order to exchange all except the autobiography with their *ABC's* partner in the online forum. (According to Schmidt & Finkbeiner (2006), it is a central characteristic of the *ABC's* model that the participants' autobiographies remain private – they are not shared with the *ABC's* partner.)

Structure of the *ABC's Online* Exchange

The *ABC's Online* exchange was carried out over a time span of 10 weeks (for a detailed schedule of the project see Wilden, 2006). In the first two weeks the participants got in touch with their *ABC's* partners and wrote their autobiographies. In Weeks 3–5 the participants met up for at least two reciprocal interviews in the voice chat and composed their biographies on the basis of these interviews. Also, they exchanged their biographies in the online forum. In Weeks 6–8 the participants once again met in the voice chat to validate the biographies. Following that they composed their cross-cultural analyses and exchanged them in the online forum. In the last two weeks the participants met for the last time in the voice chat (optional) to conclude the exchange and to plan further co-operation. All in all, the schedule of the exchange was rather flexible so as to accommodate to the participants' needs and overall workload.

The online communication tools used in the project were voice chat, online forums and a Moodle-based exchange website. However, asynchronous written communication in the online forums was mainly used to arrange voice chat meetings and to disseminate information. The voice chat was the most important tool for online communication. Voice chats (also called audio-graphic-conferencing; Hampel & Hauck, 2004) allow participants to talk to each other via the internet. Technically, only a standard PC, a headset and voice chatting software are needed. For the *ABC's Online* project synchronous communication in the voice chat was instrumental in creating a confidential atmosphere. A good atmosphere is of vital importance for any *ABC's* exchange. The voice chat used in the *ABC's Online* project was Centra. However, there are a number of free voice chatting tools sufficient for most educational purposes, e.g. Skype, MSN Messenger or Yahoo! Messenger.

The following example is a passage from one of the earlier voice chats in the *ABC's Online* project between teacher A and B (all voice chats have been transcribed). It was chosen to illustrate the interactional aspects of spoken exchange through the internet.

A: Hello [B]. Can you hear me?

B: Yes I can hear you [A].

A: Well anyway welcome to the voice chat. I am really worried about writing a biography. (laughs) Because I do not think I have enough material for six pages. So I am really glad this is working so I can ask you.

B: I totally agree. It is oh my God. I can write I can write about myself but ooh. (laughs)

A: Yes it is exactly the thing with me too. And it is very wicked that [moderator] has our autobiographies. So (laughs) we have to eh we have to eh guess a lot of guessing and all that.

B: (clicks on smiley icon)

A: Have you ever done this kind of voice chat before? (laughs) I think it is kind of odd not being able to hear the other person.

B: I agree because I am trying to (-) I am laughing and you cannot hear me laugh. So everybody around me can. There are about oh forty people in the room. And they are all doing their own work. And I am just sitting here with a headset on. Really really strange. (laughs)

This short passage exemplifies some of the typical features of voice chat interaction. Due to the technical nature of the voice chat used in this project only one person could speak at a time and while speaking could not hear his or her exchange partner. In this aspect voice chat interaction is different from telephone communication. Both teachers comment on the fact that this is unfamiliar to them as they cannot hear their partners' reactions when speaking themselves. However, both teachers quickly adapt to the voice chat environment by using the following communicative strategies: (1) They use visual icons provided in the voice chatting software (e.g. smiley, sad face, buttons for 'yes' and 'no') to give immediate feedback. (2) They describe their immediate surroundings in order to contextualise the voice chat.

Outcomes of the *ABC's Online* Exchange

Data analysis of the *ABC's Online* project is still in progress. However, a few preliminary outcomes will be sketched out in the following. One objective of the project was to familiarise the participants with the *ABC's* model as a new teaching method and at the same time have them experience the *ABC's Online* in action (*loop input*). In an interview after the exchange one teacher explicitly highlighted that this procedure had been very fruitful and valuable for her. She especially considered it an important experience having had to change roles by 'being a student [=participant in the *ABC's Online* exchange] again and having to do homework'.

Another goal of the project was to further the teachers' computer literacy. Some of the teachers in the project were very experienced computer and internet users. However, one teacher was particularly self-conscious and insecure at the beginning. Over the course of the project she seemed increasingly motivated and enthusiastic about telecollaboration. At the end of the project she said that she had been positively surprised about the personal and informal nature of the exchange with her *ABC's Online* partner. Prior to the exchange she had expected a rather professional and formal atmosphere because of the technical dimension of the project.

The third objective of the *ABC's Online* exchange was to promote the teachers' professional and personal development. As all participants were teachers, part of their exchange was about their professional lives. Thus, they learned about their roles as teachers in their respective countries and shared experiences from their everyday professional lives on topics such as teacher education, school trips, teaching methods or disciplinary problems. With regard to intercultural communication, the personal aspect of the exchange was especially meaningful. The *ABC's* exchange focuses on individual lifestories that have strong links to the cultural background of a person (Finkbeiner & Koplin, 2002; Schmidt & Finkbeiner, 2006). By having participants critically compare and analyse their own experiences with those of their partners, the *ABC's* exchange allows for a change of perspectives, which is a central concern of intercultural education. One teacher's comment in her comparison emphasises her experience in the *ABC's Online* project with regard to this goal: 'Never would I have considered sitting down and writing about my life. Reading my life through the words of another person makes me appreciate my curriculum vitae in a different perspective that I have [sic] before'.

Plans for the Future

The *ABC's Online* project proved a valuable experience for everyone involved. A thorough analysis of the exchange data and interviews with the participants will result in further suggestions on how to implement the *ABC's Online* in teacher education and foreign language teaching in general. However, other adaptations of the *ABC's Online* to foreign language classrooms on secondary or tertiary level have already been put into practice (Schmidt & Finkbeiner, 2006) and further implementations are planned. Especially in the secondary language classroom the following two modifications ought to be considered: (1) The exchange should evolve over a longer time span – preferably one school year – in order to allow for an in-depth exchange. (2) Depending on the foreign language competence of the students an emphasis on asynchronous written and oral communication may be beneficial. As synchronous oral communication in the voice chat can easily overtax foreign language students on the intermediate level, they might prefer asynchronous written (e-mail) or oral (voice mail, voice board or video mail) exchanges. Thus, students have greater freedom to plan, produce and revise their messages. Especially the integration of video into the *ABC's* exchange may prove successful as it allows for a more holistic interaction: participants see each other in motion and in their everyday surroundings. One of the teachers in the *ABC's Online* project explicitly stated that she had missed having a visual impression of her partner.

The *ABC's* model itself is very adaptive and has been used with various age groups from elementary to university level and in numerous educational settings, e.g. in literacy education, foreign language learning, business education or teacher training. Therefore, adaptations of the model to other disciplines may prove to be equally successful. Also, further adaptations and modifications in the field of foreign language teaching are conceivable as long as the core elements of the model (autobiography, biography and comparison) are maintained.

References

Finkbeiner, C. and Koplin, C. (2002) A cooperative approach for facilitating intercultural education. *Reading On-line* 6 (3). On WWW at http://www.readingon-line.org/newliteracies/lit_index.asp?HREF=/newliteracies/finkbeiner.

Hampel, R. and Hauck, M. (2004) Towards an effective use of audio conferencing in distance language courses. *Language Learning & Technology* 8 (1), 66–82. On WWW at http://llt.msu.edu/vol8num1/pdf/hampel.pdf.

Schmidt, P.R. (1998) The ABC's of cultural understanding and communication. *Equity and Excellence* 31 (2), 28–38.

Schmidt, P.R. and Finkbeiner, C. (eds) (2006) *The ABC's of Cultural Understanding and Communication. National and International Adaptations*. Greenwich, CT: Information Age Publishing.

Wilden, E. (2006) The ABC's On-line. Using voice chats in a transnational foreign language teacher exchange. In P.R. Schmidt and C. Finkbeiner (eds) *The ABC's of Cultural Understanding and Communication. National and International Adaptations* (pp. 189–212). Greenwich, CT: Information Age Publishing.

Chapter 17

Learning to Teach Online: 'Le français en (première) ligne' Project

CHRISTINE DEVELOTTE, FRANÇOIS MANGENOT and
KATERINA ZOUROU

Introduction

Most telecollaborative projects are designed to link students who are studying each other's language, permitting them to communicate on an equal basis. By contrast, 'Le français en (première) ligne' brings two different types of students into contact: those studying a Masters in teaching French as a Foreign Language ('student-teachers') and those learning French as a foreign language ('student-learners'). While the main goal of the former is to develop the use of technology in foreign language education, the latter aim to communicate with members of the target language and culture, rendering their learning experience more authentic and intercultural.

The theoretical background of the project is mainly based on the *situated cognition* and *situated learning* paradigm, which can be roughly defined as a process that occurs in a context reflecting real-life conditions. The emphasis is put on context, 'enculturation' into communities of practice, authentic tasks and 'cognitive apprenticeship' (Brown *et al.*, 1989, Lave & Wenger, 1991). The project corresponds to this paradigm in so far as it allows the student-teachers to have 'real' learners as addressees for their multimedia tasks, and the student-learners to interact with authentic conversational partners, thus taking into account the social and cultural dimensions of language (Develotte *et al.*, 2005).

Socioinstitutional Context

Thus far, only student-teachers from French universities have participated (Besançon 2002–2004, Grenoble from 2004 onwards), whereas learner-students have included students from Australia (Sydney and

276

Monash Universities), the USA (North Virginia Community College 2005–2006 and Berkeley from 2006 onwards), Spain (University of León from 2005 onwards) and Japan (Sophia University from 2006 on). The learner-students' level of French ranged from near beginner to advanced. All student-learners were undergraduates, French being one of several degree subjects.

The number of teaching hours per week had a significant influence on the success of the project. When only a short period of time was devoted to the project per week (for instance, 90 min in North Virginia), student-learners lacked commitment. When a longer period was spent on the project (such as two to three hours per week) student-learners felt more involved and achieved more as a result. For this reason, we would argue that the project should be carefully integrated into both the student-teachers' and the student-learners' courses. For the student-teachers, designing multimedia materials, tutoring foreign students and reflecting on these processes was in itself intended to form a 25- or 50-h course. For student-learners, participation in the project formed part of their overall grade, to a greater or lesser degree.

A task-based approach was chosen in order to foster online communication. Student-teachers were required to design their tasks broadly following student-learners' course contents, but at the same time combining their own information and point of view about (inter)cultural topics.

The student-teachers were assigned a computer lab for a minimum of 10 h per week including two hours during normal class time when they benefited from their own teacher's assistance. In addition, students of Besançon University (2002–2004) had the help of an assistant several hours per week while students of Grenoble University were given a 50-h course on the use of technology in language education the year before they joined the project.

The student-learners did not always have adequate internet access. For instance, it was mistakenly assumed that Australian students would all have internet access at home. Student-learners showed greatest commitment to the project when they were given internet access in a computer lab once or twice a week, under their French teacher's supervision.

For student-teachers, the internet provided an opportunity to teach real students, as opposed to simply following more or less theoretical courses about the methodology of language teaching. Moreover, it enabled them to become even more aware than they were before of the importance of integrating the use of technology into their teaching. As a result, the commitment showed by this group was consistently high, student-teachers spending around four to five hours per week designing tasks and tutoring the distance learners (in addition to normal class time).

For student-learners, while they may have appreciated the opportunity presented by the internet to engage in authentic communication with native speakers, they often found the project time-consuming. Only motivated and advanced-level student-learners showed the degree of autonomy necessary to carry out the tasks and communicate with the French tutors outside the institutional framework. Low-level student-learners required a greater degree of integration in their course and strong support from their regular teacher.

Structure of the Exchange

As mentioned above, online interaction was based on specific learning tasks designed by the student-teachers (see project website). During the first three years of the project (2002–2005), task design was conducted during the first semester (October–January), while online tutoring took place in the second semester (February–May). This was mainly due to the different academic calendars in France and Australia. From 2005, task design and tutoring occurred more or less simultaneously, which meant that the student-teachers had less time to design the tasks, but were better able to adapt them to the student-learners' needs.

Communication took place through Learning Management Systems (LMS) or Groupware such as WebCT, Quickplace, Dokeos, Moodle or Webboard. With the exception of a few chat sessions, the students generally used tools such as discussion boards (forums). The main reason for this choice was the greater flexibility provided by asynchronous communication. All the above LMS allow files to be attached to messages, a feature which was frequently used for sending pictures, sound files and a few videos. In 2005–2006 and 2006–2007, Spanish and Japanese student-learners appreciated the regular exchange of sound and video files: for instance, after having watched a video (made by their tutors) about some French traditions, Japanese students recorded sound documents and sent pictures about some of their shintoist observances and about the way they celebrate New Year. Some tutors even proposed a correction of phonetic errors by inserting their voice into the sound file submitted by student-learners (see Mangenot & Zourou, in press), using the Audacity freeware, which allows insertion of a sound into an existing mp3 file.

Group size has been an ongoing concern throughout the project. While the number of student-teachers has remained stable (between 13 and 18), the number of student-learners has fluctuated between 21 and 83. The basic principle is to form small groups in order to stimulate a more personal interaction. But what is an ideal group size? For the student-teachers, designing tasks in pairs proved to be the best solution; tutoring took place in pairs as well, but sometimes also singly. For student-learners, groups of two or three turned out to be too small, especially where one group member was less active than the others. Groups of eight worked well with intermediate and advanced learners (2004–2005, 2006–2007 with Japan), but would probably be too demanding for the tutors in the case of near beginners. Where the latter were concerned, groups of four were formed. In all cases, participants were able to view the contributions of all students.

Outcomes of the Exchange So Far

One recurrent opinion expressed by student-teachers is the importance of having real learners to teach. For example, one student-teacher who participated in the first year of the project stated: 'For once, we weren't pretending or imagining an audience that we were going to talk to, for the first time it was concrete stuff'. Through the use of technology the project therefore offers a meaningful way to train student-teachers, which is highly relevant to the situated learning paradigm.

From the student-learners' point of view, the exchange is all the more appreciated as they feel the project is well integrated into their programme. The lower-level student-learners appreciate tasks based on live materials and having their errors thoroughly corrected, while the more advanced learners seem to favour discussions or role play, with less focus on form.

As far as the cultural aspects of the project are concerned, Develotte et al. (2005) report that multimedia materials created by student-teachers tend to underline aspects of French culture different to those outlined in traditional French textbooks. Student-teachers were able to project a personal depiction of France today, taking into account the presumed interests of the young foreign students in order to boost their level of motivation. This approach is likely to help learners access a multifaceted view of French culture. As for its leaders, the project requires a strong and consistent commitment, however the reward lies in the level of student satisfaction and the discovery of novel methods of teaching and communicating via the internet.

References

Brown, J.S., Collins A. and Duguid, P. (1989) Situated learning and the culture of learning. *Education Researcher* 18 (1), 32–42.

Develotte, C., Mangenot, F. and Zourou, K. (2005) Situated creation of multimedia activities for distance learners: Motivational and cultural issues. *ReCALL* 17 (2), 229–244.

Lave, J. and Wenger, E. (1991) *Situated Learning: Legitimate Peripheral Participation*. Cambridge: Cambridge University Press.

Mangenot, F. and Zourou, K. (in press) Pratiques tutorales correctives *via* Internet: le cas du français en première ligne. *Apprentissage des langues et systèmes d'information et de communication (ALSIC)*, Vol. 10 http://www.alsic.org

Project website: http://w3.u-grenoble3.fr/fle-1-ligne

Chapter 18

One-to-one Desktop Videoconferencing for Developing Oral Skills: Prospects in Perspective

LINA LEE

Introduction

Desktop videoconferencing (DVC), a two-way transmission of audio and video from a personal computer equipped with a fast internet connection, a microphone and a video camera, supports ever closer authentic interaction in real time. Given the limited time that L2 learners have for oral practice in the classroom, DVC exposes students to genuine human-to-human interaction in which they negotiate for meaning within a socially and culturally rich context. Despite the fact that this DVC project was not a class-to-class telecollaboration, it was designed to foster one-to-one collaborative interaction between the students of Spanish and expert speakers on campus. It is hoped that this project provides an insightful perspective of the practicalities and advantages of integrating one-to-one DVC into pedagogical practice.

Socioinstitutional Context

The Department of Languages, Literatures and Cultures at the University of New Hampshire offers 10 different language programmes to prepare our students for their specialisations, professional needs and interests. Our pedagogical principles focus on the development of students' communicative language skills, as well as their understanding and awareness of the Spanish-speaking world. In general, students do not have the opportunity to use the target language to interact with others outside of class as they live in small New England towns and cities where English is the only language used for daily communication. For this reason, I have been using internet technologies to extend students' communicative experience beyond the spatial and temporal limitations of the classroom.

This DVC project was carried out in the spring of 2005 through a Faculty Innovation Grant for Instructional Technology funded by the author's institution. The majority of the students were undergraduate Spanish majors and minors. Most of these students had an intermediate level of language proficiency and had not yet studied aboard in a Spanish-speaking country. They were enrolled in a third-year advanced Spanish course and were required to use Blackboard as part of their course requirement but had no experience with DVC. The expert speakers were native speakers of Spanish recruited from the ESL programme and the local community, as well as instructors from the Spanish programme. In terms of computer access and literacy, many participants owned a computer or a laptop. They were comfortable with internet technologies including e-mail and text-chat.

Objectives of the Project

According to constructivist learning theory, learning is no longer a matter of the transmission of knowledge from the external world; rather, it is an active, social and collaborative process whereby learners use a system of symbols (e.g. language) or a material tool (e.g. computer) to co-construct knowledge with others. Language then is viewed as a cognitive tool to enable learners to express and develop ideas through collaborative scaffolding by which the expert (e.g. native speaker or teacher) assists the novice (e.g. learner) in problem-solving situations. Using a social constructivist paradigm of language learning as a theoretical framework, the project set two main objectives: (1) to create a collaborative and nonthreatening learning environment where the students co-construct meaning with the expert speakers using task-based activities; and (2) to build students' communicative language skills through audio and visual interactions in real time.

Structure of the Exchange

As Lee (2005) points out, effective pedagogical principles including specific instructional goals and procedures, as well as technological tools, must be thoughtfully taken into account at the stage of implementation in order to ensure maximum learning outcomes. The DVC project was built in as a part of the course work. These online task-based activities were scheduled in their course syllabus. DVC activities were worth 20% of their final grade.

For this project, task-based activities were chosen because they not only ensured a primary focus on meaning but also allowed for incidental attention to form (Ellis, 2003). The information-gap task 'jigsaw' and the problem-solving 'how to budget for a one-week trip to Spain' were used for two-way exchanges. For instance, one of the jigsaw tasks is a set of drawings numbered one through ten that represent a story of 'Community Service' and each half of the drawings was distributed to one partner of the pair (one received odd numbers and one received even numbers). Each pair was asked to work closely to produce the story to meet the common goal.

Successful videoconferencing relies on a sophisticated quality of audio and visual cues as well as high-speed broadband connectivity. Due to the low budget allowed for this project, we resorted to using a local area network (LAN) on campus. Several cost-effective technological tools – the free software program iChat provided by AOL in conjunction with Apple's iSight (high-quality audio and video camera) – were chosen for carrying out two-way exchanges. The desktop video capturing software Snaps Pro X was purchased to create QuickTime movie files. In addition, we provided high-quality headsets and microphones to maximise the quality of audio and oral transmissions. For technical support, a graduate teaching assistant (TA) was hired to assist with the equipment set-up and troubleshooting. A training session was scheduled to familiarise the participants with the tools in conjunction with a trial session to field-test the DVC.

Before the DVC took place, each student was paired with an expert-speaker partner and was asked to initiate the contact with the partner via e-mail or telephone calls. If after several attempts the student failed to make initial contact with the partner, the teacher would find a replacement for the student. The students first became acquainted with their assigned partners via text chats using the Group Pages of the Communication in Blackboard. One of the challenges of using CMC is to find a common time to meet online. At the beginning of the semester, students were advised to arrange mutually agreed upon times to work with their partners. The TA assisted in the coordination of scheduling. E-mails were sent out to remind the participants of each assignment and meeting time.

Upon arriving at the lab, each student was assigned a different room and received a manila envelope containing instructions for carrying out the task. Students were allowed 5–7 min to read the instructions and view the materials. The use of a dictionary or notes was not allowed during the recording. The instructions merely reminded the participants to speak as clearly as possible and allow each other to express ideas freely without interrupting the partner. Each session lasted approximately 40 min. During the recordings, the TA was present to solve any technical problems. The participants wrote a brief reflection log to report their observations one week after each recording. All reflections were sent to the instructor through Digital Drop Box in Blackboard. In addition, the instructor conducted an interview with the participants at the end of the semester. They were asked to comment on the most valuable and difficult aspects of their experiences with DVC, as well as make suggestions for future improvements.

Outcomes of the Exchange

Although the short duration of one-to-one DVC interaction did not directly transfer to the improvement of students' oral skills, students' feedback was encouraging. The majority of the students enjoyed the experience and they were thrilled with the real time oral and visual interaction with the expert speakers. Students repeatedly commented that DVC pushed them to speak and respond to their experts spontaneously and quickly in a way that text-based CMC cannot do (O'Dowd, 2000). Importantly, DVC engendered negotiation of meaning and corrective feedback on both the learners' linguistic and pragmatic shortcomings through expert scaffolding as this student remarks in his final reflective log: 'DVC is awesome. It allowed me to use my Spanish in a real time with a real person in a meaningful way. It was a very positive experience for me.'

However, some negative aspects to the technology also emerged. Some of the participants maintained that because communication via DVC did not allow one to actually see all of one's partner, the communication did not feel as truly personal as face-to-face conversations. Students with lower language skills also felt discomfort speaking over the air in front of the expert speakers. Furthermore, the results revealed that students with less sophisticated listening skills experienced difficulties comprehending the experts' utterances. One of the students made the following comments during the final interview: 'My listening skills are not very good. I had a hard time to understand my partner's accent. I felt bad that I had to ask him to repeat what he has said many times. He could have spoken more clearly and louder.'

Consequently, this student found it quite difficult to collaborate in DVC as she struggled in comprehending the Puerto Rican accent. In addition, the students were challenged by linguistic variations including unfamiliar accents and lexical varieties. They experienced difficulty understanding Mexican lexical items, such as 'chamba' for 'job' and 'chamaco' for 'small child'. Pragmatically, the students were not aware of social appropriateness in their use of '*tú*' (informal you) instead of '*usted*' (formal you).

The high quality of audio and visual tools does not guarantee the most effective use of these resources. Despite the training received prior to the use of DVC, some of the participants did not project their voices as clearly as was possible; they ended up repeating themselves to their partners. In particular, the students did not take advantage of available voice and visual channels as they did not use body gestures (e.g. nodding the head) or voice (pitch or volume) to compensate for their linguistic breakdowns.

Plans for the Future

Although DVC opened up a unique opportunity for students to develop their oral skills, it presented certain limitations for the one-to-one online exchanges at a distance. The Horizon Wimba software in conjunction with Blackboard will be used for future projects. Horizon Wimba consists of 3 products: Live Classroom, Pronto and Wimba Voice Tools, each of which allows the user to add collaborative and interactive elements to current online courses as well course management systems such as Blackboard and WebCT.

A pilot study will be field-tested involving native speakers from other parts of the Spanish-speaking world during the year 2007–2008. Based on both the instructor's observations and students' feedback, several practical pedagogical issues will be considered and implemented with DVC projects. First, desktop recorders in conjunction with sound (WAV) files will be used to record and listen to native speakers' speech on a regular basis in order to improve the listening skills of students with regional accents and lexicon. Second, students will be taught online communication strategies including nonverbal skills such as the use of body language and facial expressions in order to optimise the effective use of DVC. Third, after the DVC, the instructor will review the video recordings to discuss pragmatic errors with the students. Finally, group members should get acquainted with each other via e-mail to build up trust and establish good rapport between two parties to raise the comfort level and self-confidence before they execute the assignments.

In closing, the implementation of multichannel-mediated communication offers new and stimulating prospects in the world of language learning. Feedback that reflects the perspectives of both expert speakers and learners will help maximise the prospect of communication offered by DVC.

References

Ellis, R. (2003) *Task-based Language Learning and Teaching*. Oxford: Oxford University Press.

Lee, L. (2005) Using web-based instruction to promote active learning: Learners' perspectives. *CALICO Journal* 23 (1), 139–156.

O'Dowd, R. (2000) Intercultural learning via videoconferencing: A pilot exchange project. *ReCALL* 12 (1), 49–63.